The Pioneer Gift

Edited by
Jonny Baker and Cathy Ross

CANTERBURY
PRESS

Norwich

© The Contributors 2014

First published in 2014 by the Canterbury Press Norwich
Editorial office
3rd Floor, Invicta House,
108–114 Golden Lane,
London EC1Y 0TG

Canterbury Press is an imprint of Hymns Ancient & Modern Ltd
(a registered charity)
13A Hellesdon Park Road, Norwich,
Norfolk, NR6 5DR, UK

www.canterburypress.co.uk

British Library Cataloguing in Publication data

A catalogue record for this book is available
from the British Library

978 1 84825 651 4

Typeset by Regent Typesetting
Printed and bound in Great Britain by
Ashford Colour Press, Gosport, Hampshire

Contents

v

Contributor Biographies

Karlie Allaway is a student on the CMS Pioneer Leadership course. Catholic for almost three years, she is Community Missioner for Eastbourne Ordinariate, exploring mission rooted in sacramental and contemplative spirituality. She is also part of a creative ecumenical team who form a respectful presence at pagan festivals and gatherings attracting spiritual seekers uncomfortable with approaching church.

Gerald A. Arbuckle sm is Co-Director of Refounding and Pastoral Development Unit, a research ministry, in Sydney, Australia. A graduate in social anthropology from Cambridge University, he is well known for his expertise in helping church leaders minister effectively in a postmodern world.

Jonny Baker is the Director for Mission Education for the Church Mission Society. He founded and leads the CMS Pioneer Mission Leadership Training, which began in 2010. He is a member of Grace, an alternative worship community in London.

Jim Barker is currently the Director of Fundraising for Mission at the Church Mission Society. In the past he worked as an independent consultant, facilitator and trainer, and at Friends of the Earth and Oxfam.

Andrea Campanale lives in Kingston-upon-Thames and was one of the first students on the CMS pioneer course. She is a CMS mission partner and leads outreach to spiritual seekers at

YMCA London South West, Kingston University and through her missional community. She now trains teams nationally to engage with spiritual seekers and is in the process of setting up a town centre chaplaincy.

Doug Gay is Lecturer in Practical Theology at the University of Glasgow and an ordained minister in the Church of Scotland. He was formerly part of the Late, Late Service in Glasgow and the Host congregation in Hackney, East London.

Kim Hartshorne leads a small missional community (in a small market town) that she and several women founded six years ago. They serve a marginalized group who would not be likely to attend traditional church. Before becoming involved in the missional community she worked as a community activist and before that had a career as an engineer in the aerospace industry.

Beth Keith is a doctoral student at Durham University researching mission vocation while undertaking ordination training at Cranmer Hall. She was previously part of the Fresh Expressions Team and a member of the Church Army research unit.

Emma Nash is an evangelist accredited by the Baptist Union of Great Britain. She is currently working as mission development minister for her church's coffee shop, exploring appropriate ways to share faith on the high street.

Cathy Ross co-ordinates the MA for the CMS Pioneer Mission Leadership Training. She is also Tutor in Contextual Theology at Ripon College Cuddesdon and Lecturer in Mission at Regent's Park College, Oxford. She has worked in East Africa as a mission partner with NZCMS.

Anna Ruddick is Associate Director for the Eden Network having been involved with urban ministry for the last eight years. She is currently researching perceptions of transformation in urban communities for a doctorate in practical theology at the University of

Chester and is on the Council of the William Temple Foundation, a research body concerned with faith and public policy.

Simon Sutcliffe is an ordained presbyter in the Methodist Church. He works part time with Venture FX (the Methodist pioneering scheme), where he has helped to form a missional collective called Immerse in Kidsgrove, North Staffs. He also works as Tutor for Evangelism and Pioneering Ministries at The Queen's Foundation, Birmingham.

Foreword

BY CHRISTOPHER COCKSWORTH

Whenever I sit at my desk in my study I look onto Lindisfarne's magnificent statue of St Aidan. I hasten to add that I do not (unfortunately) actually live on Holy Island itself and that I have to content myself with a photo of this remarkable seventh-century missionary bishop. Aidan was a pioneer. At the invitation of Oswald, the godly Northumbrian king, the monks of Iona sent Aidan to evangelize the massive swathe of northern England that lay in Oswald's kingdom and which had proved very resistant to the gospel. Aidan's missional strategy was simple – it was to walk. Bede tells us that 'whether in town or country, he always travelled on foot unless compelled by necessity to ride; and whatever people he met on his walks, whether high or low, he stopped and spoke to them' (Bede, 1990, p. 150). Walking led to talking; and Aidan talked about Jesus, though always apparently beginning with a question. Tradition tells us that he would ask, 'Do you know about Jesus?' If the reply was, 'no', he would say, 'Then let me tell you about the love of God in Jesus.' If it was, 'yes' (for some of those he met were already Christians, at least by background), he would say, 'Then let me show you how to love him more.'

Aidan was by no means a solitary missionary, though. Before he began to walk he first established a base on Lindisfarne from which he could pray, gather others into a common life and then return to renew his spiritual energies. During his journeys to share the gospel with the people of Northumbria, Aidan was sometimes accompanied by Oswald, especially in the early days when he was still learning the language. As time went on, he gathered people who, as Bede says, 'walked with him', requiring them only 'to read the scriptures or learn the psalms'.

Daniel Hardy, one of the most serious thinkers about the life of the Church that Anglicanism has generated for decades, said, 'Ecclesiology is embodied: in Jesus' walking' (Hardy, 2010, p. 83). He wrote those words sometime after returning from a pilgrimage to the Holy Land during which he had been deeply affected by the simple thought of Jesus walking from place to place, encountering people and making the kingdom of God known to them in his teaching and healing. That is how Peter summed up Jesus' ministry to Cornelius – how, after 'God anointed Jesus with the Holy Spirit and with power ... he went about doing good and healing all who were oppressed by the devil, for God was with him' (Acts 10.38). Jesus, walking with God, meeting people along the way, drawing them into the way and truth and life of God, gathering them into a new sort of community that could reshape the world: that is the archetypal mission revealed in Jesus that we see prototyped in the early life of the Church. It has been the pattern of missionary movements in the succeeding generations of the Church. It is what we are seeing in the pioneer movement of our own day, and there is plenty of evidence for it in this attractive book.

The contributors to *The Pioneer Gift* are committed to walking with Jesus into the situations where Christ had led them so that, like Aidan, they may encounter people in their present conditions of life, in their places and on their levels, engaging them in the new possibilities of God's future for the world in Christ – the new realities of God's *just love*. In walking with Jesus, these pioneers are determined to walk with those who also walk with Christ and whom we call the Church. They do not want to walk alone, but alongside others who will work with them, support them and with whom they can pray and, in some situations described in the book, live a form of common life. Walking with the Church is not always an easy journey as pioneers in different stages of the Church's history have known. But the pages that follow show a real desire to live within both the present life and structures of the Church and its long tradition of walking and learning.

Walking, by definition, is not the same as arriving. So, as you set out on the journey into which this book invites you – a journey accompanying twelve people passionate to share the good news of Jesus Christ to those who have not heard or seen it – do not expect to find the finished product. These are missionaries on the move, thinking, praying and working hard to discern the way of Christ and to walk in it. Like Paul, they have been ready to share their 'own selves' with us (1 Thessalonians 2.8) as they not only tell some of the moving stories of their present ministries but also share some of the formative influences of their past. Their journey into scripture and into the theological traditions and missionary practices that have shaped many of us deserve real discussion, so that together we can reconfigure the life of the Church for the present missionary task and recalibrate the way we live and communicate the gospel.

The contributors to *The Pioneer Gift* are themselves gifts to the life of the Church. Without complaining, they share some of the frustrations of pioneer ministry and plead for the right sort of permission giving and support from those who have the powerful privilege to give it. My hope is that those of us who in some way oversee – *see over* – the Church's life and witness will look to the example of Oswald and find inspiration in the way he saw the need to reach out to his culture in new ways, discerned someone who, with others, could help that to happen and then provided material and spiritual support showing, at the same time, a readiness to learn not only from what God was doing through Aidan but how God was doing it.

+Christopher Cocksworth
Episcopal Visitor to CMS

References

Bede, *Ecclesiastical History of the English People*, 1990, London: Penguin.
Hardy, D. W., Ford, D. H., Ochs, P. and Ford, D. F., *Wording a Radiance: Parting Conversations on God and the Church*, 2010, London: SCM.

I

The Pioneer Gift

JONNY BAKER

An extraordinary gift

People who are pioneers bring an amazing gift. One of the ways I
have come to think of it is as the gift of not fitting in. This is not to
suggest for a moment that pioneers are the awkward squad. It is
that they see and imagine different possibilities to the way things
are now, to business as usual. They are then able to build a pathway to make real what they see or imagine. I think the simplest
description I have come across is from Beth Keith, who puts it
this way: 'A pioneer is someone who sees future possibilities and
works to bring them to reality' (Goodhew et al., 2012, p. 137).
Not only do they dream up new strategies, they implement them –
they are 'dreamers who do' (Arbuckle, 1993, p. 7). Every culture
or organization or church needs this if it is to have a future and
not get stuck. And every church needs this if it is to be missional
and move out of its comfort zone.

It is not a new gift. Many of the heroes of our faith, such as
Abraham, who set off by faith in obedience to God's call without knowing where he was going (Heb. 11.8), were pioneers who
took great risks in leaving the safety of their known world to
journey towards something new, crossing borders and boundaries to do so. Jesus is described as the pioneer of our faith (Heb.
12.2). It is an interesting exercise to go through the list of saints
commemorated by the Church as inspirational for our faith. The
vast majority of them were pioneers, though once their pioneering endeavours become accepted we forget the initial prophetic

challenge and difficulty of what they brought. The word has come to the fore in the Church in the UK over the last few years off the back of *Mission-Shaped Church*.[1] The report recommended that the Church needed to identify, select and train 'pioneers and mission entrepreneurs' (Cray, 2004, p. 147). Subsequently the Church of England recognized a new designation that joined the word 'pioneer' together with 'ministry', calling this vocation pioneer ministry, which was a descriptor for people (pioneer ministers) who could church plant and develop fresh expressions of church with those beyond the reach of existing churches. It has been part of the discourse since in the Church of England and Methodist Church but also more widely across other denominations and networks. The Fresh Expressions website has this description:

> A pioneer minister is someone who has the necessary vision and gifts to be a missionary entrepreneur: with the capacity to form and lead fresh expressions and new forms of church appropriate to a particular culture. Pioneer ministers may be ordained or lay (not ordained) and different denominations and streams have ways of training and authorising pioneer ministers.[2]

Of course, pioneers existed before this resurgence of the word but it just named it in a particular way.

The word pioneer is a metaphor and therefore laced with possibility and ambiguity. Depending on the mental images it conjures up, it might be a rich word that opens up vistas or one that is an immediate turn-off. Even if it plays out well in one context, it might be heard very differently in another. This is often the way with language. To further complicate matters for those who like to be on the front edge of change, language that was once used at the edge and is now used in the centre can become uncomfortable or shift its meaning over time. So it is already an interesting question whether the word pioneer is one that will stick or not. Is it the right word? As soon as you come up with another, such as entrepreneur or missionary, they turn out to be just as problematic. Language makes and remakes the world, so this is not surprising

– finding language is a huge part of the journey to the new. I personally hope that we are able to work with the metaphor of pioneer for a good season and in doing so keep its ambiguity open rather than pin it down too quickly. Not all pioneers are pioneer ministers (an equally difficult and rich word). The Fresh Expressions definition understandably pulls it into pioneering church communities, which is much needed, but there are many pioneers in mission who see and build other possibilities that equally join in with God's mission in the world. I am in danger of weaving a complex web already, but the point I am trying to make is that the pioneer gift is not straightforward. It has elusive qualities and can be opened up and unfolded in multiple directions, many of which we are yet to discover. While for some this might be frustrating, I want to suggest that this is a good thing. There is something intriguing and wonderful about the mystery of it.

Church Mission Society (CMS) was first involved in missiological education by training leaders in 1807 in a space that was different to the then existing colleges, presumably recognizing that a different formation and curriculum was needed for cross-cultural mission to what was currently in existence for training for church ministry.[3] I have worked for the CMS for over a decade in several roles, all focused on mission in the UK especially in relation to the emerging culture. The most recent has been setting up the CMS Pioneer Mission Leadership Training as a pathway for equipping both lay and ordained pioneers.[4] We stand in a line of a long and good tradition in CMS. We had our first intake of pioneers in 2010, and now run a Diploma and Masters programme as well as having pioneers who audit modules with us. Like any start-up, it has been quite an adventure, with a steep learning curve and a lot of hard work, but has been one of the most exciting ventures I have ever been involved in. The thing that has made it so exciting is the pioneers themselves and the gifts they offer through who they are and what they then bring to birth.

We are reflecting together, learning all the time. It never seems to stay still. We have discovered that the gift is multifaceted and each pioneer has a unique shape and calling. There is a wide spectrum of the pioneer gift.[5] Things go best when they develop self-awareness and pioneer out of who they are rather than some-one else's expectation of what a pioneer might be. It is not age or gender or culture specific, exclusively lay or ordained. It is not the preserve of any one denomination. It is a gift that is best carried in or with a team, and it is definitely not a word or gift reserved for the most extreme pioneers. I have had many conversations with people who are wondering about their own gift and pioneering because they are comparing themselves to the most entrepreneur-ial and innovative pioneers on the course or that they have come across, when their vocation is to be who they are called to be and not someone else. Mike Moynagh helpfully recognizes that a presumed set of characteristics can be a problem that puts people off and suggests we should look for qualities that can be unfolded in various ways that fit the person's capabilities and their context (Moynagh, 2012, p. 231). I had a conversation with one student who thanked me for a module she had found extremely helpful because it had enabled her to reflect on her sense of call and gift. She said that she was now leaving the course because she had con-cluded that she was an artist and contemplative. I pointed out that we need plenty of pioneers who are artists and contemplatives as they have developed ways of seeing and imagining that are essen-tial. I am glad to say she stayed. She most definitely has the gift. I have since begun to recognize a strand of pioneer mystics.[6] We have also discovered that there is no blueprint, no manual to pull off the shelf that tells you how to see and build something new, though there is a growing body of wisdom around practice. The ways that new things emerge are as full of surprises and diversity as the range of people. It is an extraordinary gift!

A mission-shaped gift

Whatever else it is about, the pioneer gift is about mission. The mission of God that we seek to discern and join in with is like the magnetic force of true North around which pioneering orients itself.[7] When navigating landscape that is not mapped, a compass and a needle that shows this overarching direction is an invaluable tool in the kit bag. This is a helpful picture for the current moment because the landscape is unmapped in a number of ways. It is unmapped in that there have been such huge changes in the wider culture in the West over the last 50 years or so that it seems like we are literally in a new world. It has been described in multiple ways often with a 'post' on the front – postmodern, post-Christendom, and postcolonial are three big posts. While writers describe the new world differently they are almost all agreed that in substantial ways reality is not what it used to be.

The gospel is always culturally robed and the Church itself is embedded and embodied in time and space in particular ways (Bosch, 1991, p. 297). But navigating this new world has proved something of a challenge in the West for the churches. Their identity, imagination, theologies and practices have been more shaped by modernity than perhaps at first we realized or like to admit. When the wider culture changes and churches do not, over time they can seem wedded to a bygone era. This is certainly not to make an argument for changing everything at a whim or to denigrate what is ancient, or to suggest that the Church has not changed, but rather how to prolong the logic of the ministry of Jesus in a new era (Bosch, 1991, p. 34), or orient to true North, has become a pressing question, especially when there is an over-all pattern of decline in attendance in the main denominational churches and growing economic pressure. Doug Gay suggests that one of the outcomes of debriefing the western missionary enter-prise has been a growing awareness within western churches of how their own beliefs and practices too were inculturated (Gay, 2011, p. 16). The pioneer gift may be needed for such a time as this.

One of the pluses in this difficult climate has been a growing awareness that the UK (and Europe) is a mission context itself. Mission is not just something that happens overseas. The lens, imagination and practice of ministry called for is a cross-cultural one (Cray (ed.), 2004, p. 147). This is the reason I joined CMS several years ago as I recognized they had a deep well of experi-ence and nous in this area, which I was keen to draw from. It is also why CMS as a mission community is so well placed to encourage, nurture, train and form pioneers. Cathy's chapter creatively weaves together contemporary themes in missiology alongside CMS's founding story.

One of the jargon words in theological education is *formation*, which is a recognition that it is about much more than knowledge; it is forming people to be mature disciples of Christ and for ministry. I have been very helped by Gerald Arbuckle's thinking in *From Chaos to Mission* where he looks at refounding formation (Arbuckle, 1996). He contrasts formation in religious communities that are cloistered, where the focus is on predictability and stability, with formation in the communities of friars who are spread out and live in the world. For them the purpose of formation is inculturation and prophetic ministry to the world, with a focus on flexibility and the ability to adapt to rapid change. Further, for a Franciscan, say, if their ministry is to be among the poor, then that is where they must be formed. Jesuits had to develop the ability to be open to the presence of God in the world where they found themselves, to find God in all things rather than withdrawing into cloisters to find God (Arbuckle, 1996, pp. 18, 24). You could say that for one the emphasis is a con-formation to the ecclesiastical status quo and traditions, and for the other trans-formation in and of the world. He is writing about a different era but I think it helped me see that there are various formations at play that are contested, and often they are both invisible or assumed and not critiqued or reflected upon. The formation of pioneers is very much about the latter. There is so much creativity and energy in a learning community of pioneers that this second kind of formation takes place. It is also why it is essential that pioneers are trained in a context rather than residentially, which thankfully was an insight and recommendation in *Mission-Shaped Church* (Cray, 2004, p. 148). How much it has been heeded is a different question.

These are some of the contours we navigate that help pioneers develop the ability to imagine and build. Every pioneer is in a *context*. This is one of the words we use most I suspect. The turn to context in global Christianity is massive. To make sense of that context will involve, for example, exploring of notions of identity, reading cultures, economics, religion, locale, myths, texts, symbols, power relations, gender, ethnicity. Each pioneer is unique and has particular gifts and calling that they will relate to the context, so we spend time working on *who you are*. That includes personality, calling, story, identity, brokenness, character, posture, self-awareness. We study *mission* – this is such a rich vein for pioneers with its themes of ecology, liberation, hospitality, the five marks of mission, discernment and joining in with God's mission, evangelization, inculturation, migration, healing, prophetic dialogue, ecclesiology and so on. To both see and build something requires tools and *skills* such as theologizing, reading culture, crossing culture, resourcing, strategies and tactics, communication, pastoral care, fundraising. Some of those skills will relate to the particular pioneering such as church planting or building social enterprise. They are not the first people to do such a thing so there is lots to learn from *history*, including various paradigms of mission, both good and bad, imperialism, contextual approaches, stories, ethnography, tradition as local theologies, women's movement, CMS, doctrine. The *Bible* is an amazing resource for understanding God's mission in the world and working creatively to communicate that story in the contexts pioneers are in. The romantic ideal of pioneering is not quite like the actual experience on the ground so those in training need to work out how to fuel a life of mission with support, friends, prayer, spiritual direction, retreat, appropriate rhythms – a *mission spirituality*.[8]

In many places missiology is not a discipline in the academy in its own right. So it ends up located in practical theology, world Christianity or intercultural studies. When you consider these themes you can see why – it is integrative, multidisciplinary and at its core is an ability to embody a life lived that draws on these areas as a contemplative activist, a reflective practitioner. But for the formation of pioneers prophetic mission is the organizing principle, the true North. Kim Hartshorne's chapter is a lovely reflection on one pioneer's journey in mission. The pioneer gift is mission-shaped.

A difficult gift

It would be so much easier if the journey to the new was straight-forward, if you could be in the old place and then at the appropriate moment simply jump across to the new. But the journey from the old to the new seems always to go through wilderness, liminality, desert, darkness, chaos or Gethsemane. I wish with all my heart that this was avoidable but we have not yet worked out a way to bypass it. Beth Keith's chapter plots and reflects helpfully on this pioneer journey, perhaps giving some clues as to why it is important to go through this space. I do not want to be overly dramatic and am not looking for sympathy votes for pioneers but the pioneer gift is a difficult gift to carry. I have talked about it as a gift but several pioneers have expressed that at times it feels more like an impossible curse, or a pathology they cannot shake off. Life would be so much easier if they could accept things the way they are. A quick read of almost any of the prophets in the Scriptures is a reminder that this has nearly always been the case for those with prophetic calls, imagination and speech. Evoking grief as well as energizing hope is the prophet's way.[9]

It has equally been a difficult gift for the Church to fathom. It is one thing to create a new designation for pioneer ministry but it is another challenge to then make sense of what that is and means, along with surrounding questions of how to discern, select, train, deploy and resource pioneers in the wider mixed economy of the Church. The kind of pioneering understood most readily involves an outcome that looks something like what we have already, namely a community of disciples in a church building with worship, singing, preaching and money being paid back into the centre – preferably all happening within a very short space of time. Of course there is nothing wrong with that as an outcome and some strands of church planting have done it very well, though the experienced wisdom on this is that it might well take five to ten years (Hollinghurst, 2013, p. 26). But it is as though there is an invisible gravitational pull that is always seeking to pull pioneers back into business as usual. It takes great imagination, courage, tenacity and resilience (and indeed velocity) to resist that pull. These challenges are not new. The history of mission is a mix of stories of sharing the gospel while unwittingly imposing the culture of missionaries in the bargain, along with wonderful examples of contextual approaches. Simon Sutcliffe outlines in his chapter why contextual theology and practice is such an important resource if there is to be deep engagement in pioneering, rather than simply stylistic change or tweaking of the old. He also throws down the gauntlet to pioneer theologians to do some work in particular areas, one of which is sin. Emma Nash and Andrea Campanale both address this question in different ways in their chapters. Emma outlines her research in this area and she begins to redefine sin. Andrea's chapter on the gospel and shame is an example of this sort of contextual theological reflection and ecclesiology arising from her pioneering. The forms of church themselves are cultural so to pioneer in a new space and community will require an imaginative approach that is able to let go some of the old shape, structure, culture and, dare I say, theology in order to allow something new and indigenous to be born. One of the most important spiritual disciplines required for the pioneer will be this letting go.[10] Outcomes will be important but this journey in mission involves quite a period of discernment of where God is at work, exploration on the way to the new, and surprises. Fruit sometimes comes in places you did not think to look.

The nature of ministry itself is also part of what needs reimagining. This plays out differently in different denominations and traditions. What the ministry of an ordained pioneer might look like is more easily understood by the Church if it does not look too different from what we know already, what some have termed 'priest plus'.[11] In his chapter, Doug Gay observes that the Church gets the vocations it calls for, and this has been such a difficult area for both pioneers and the Church. I keep hearing the suggestion that everyone is a pioneer, which patently is not true though of course every leader in the Church does need to be shaped by mission and have some awareness of pioneering. And it is equally common to come across the assumption that pioneer is a phase people go through before becoming a proper vicar! There are many gifts given and the pioneer gift is one among many. I was with some selectors in the Church of England discussing pioneer ministry and have been haunted ever since by one of the comments, which summed up in one short statement the scale of difficulty we face. She simply said that she 'can't be faffed!' She has good reasons. She is unclear what a pioneer is, the selection process is more difficult for pioneers, who have to go through a discernment around pioneering as well as ordination, and it requires more paperwork. She has to find a way to get them trained in a context, and she has worked out that if they go as a regular ordinand they are more likely to get through the process and can be deployed in pioneer roles afterwards. Furthermore, where are the jobs, and who is going to pay for them? I am sympathetic – I could reel off a whole host of stories of the difficulties pioneers have found who have heard the Church saying that they recognize the vocation of ordained pioneer ministry but in responding to that call have faced hurdle after hurdle. The gravity and imagination is such that many end up in roles as parish priests pioneering alongside what they are doing. It is without doubt fraught with difficulty.

Anthropology has some real insights in processes of change, how the pioneer gift plays its part and experiences such challenge.[12] Almost any business, culture, organization, institution or system faces these issues. The Church is not unique. Every organization has a culture, a status quo. Inevitably lots of people like it the way it is either because of vested interests or fear of what change might bring. But unless an organization or church cultivates innovation it risks getting stuck and may have no future. There are always those who are innovators, who see the world differently, who dream new possibilities, and they need to be encouraged to dream their dreams. However, if they are put in an environment with guardians of the status quo, the chances are they will put a lot of their energies into justifying themselves, and be under constant critique from those who perceive them as a threat, which can sap a lot of energy. That energy would be better served in mission. So the smart tactic for newness is to create space for the new to grow elsewhere, alongside the old, away from the status quo. In business this is likely to be located in the research and development department. In the Church the newness that has emerged has been a lot more fruitful where the new has been elsewhere, starting a new congregation alongside the old, in the margins, in community spaces and venues.

The pioneer gift at times calls for leadership as dissent. 'There can be no constructive change at all, even in church, unless there is some form of dissent. By dissent I mean simply the proposing of alternatives, and a system that is not continuously examining alternatives is not likely to evolve creatively' (Arbuckle, 1993, p. 1). Arbuckle suggests that for newness to take root, there are two kinds of dissenters – authority dissenters and pathfinding dissenters. There is a parallel here in the language that has been used in the Church in various places, with permission-givers, loyal radicals and sponsors perhaps being the equivalent of the authority dissenter and pioneers the equivalent of pathfinding dissenters. Pathfinding dissenters devise ways to bridge the gap between gospel and culture, imagining and implementing new strategies. Pathfinding dissenters are needed within the Church to critique or dissent from the conventional and ineffective wisdom of the present. Without these courageous people the Church simply cannot fulfil its mission. The task and position of the authority dissenter is somewhat different. They are somewhere in the structures of an organization or church, able to make decisions with responsibility. Their challenge is threefold. They need to spot, encourage and recruit pathfinding dissenters. This in itself is not always easy. It is amazing how often safer options are chosen in leadership with whom business as usual is just fine. Then, second, they are to use and deploy the gifts of the pathfinding dissenters for the benefit of the organization, culture or church. Finally they need to broker space for this dissent so that it can flourish without being forever under the glare and critique of those who like things the way they are. Real change and newness has a much better chance of taking root if it has this interplay between these two. Cultures of organizations are often much more powerful than people assume. As Arbuckle points out in his chapter of this book, culture eats strategies for lunch! Jesus and all the prophets before him were dissenters who made the world new through their dissent. This aspect of the gift is tricky. It can be fractious, and new worlds do not come through any old dissent. Those who carry the gift need to dissent out of love – for people beyond the edges of the Church, for Jesus Christ and for the Church. All the grief and seeing must come from a place of love and commitment. Newness that has depth is found by driving to the heart of the tradition and reclaiming it over and against itself, by refounding, and not by rubbishing it and leaving it. In the light of these anthropological insights perhaps it is not surprising that the Church has found that this gift is as difficult as it is essential.

There is a stereotype of a pioneer as a lone individual who goes off to stick their flag in the land to begin something new, or of a prophet who lives alone in the wilderness communing with God and appearing occasionally to deliver their message. But these are really unhelpful pictures. The kind of seeing out of which genuine newness might emerge is much more likely a communal one. In the case of prophets in the Old Testament there were schools of prophets, and I suspect pioneers were rarely alone. So as well as seeing and dissent the nurturing of this gift also requires community – new possibilities will come through dreaming and reflecting with others, knocking around ideas, eating together and conversation. It has certainly been amazing with the pioneers we have had at CMS to see the impact of people with this gift being in a community with people who get it and encourage it. Community is where dreams of new possible worlds are nurtured and enacted and where grief is shared. Both Karlie Allaway's and Jim Barker's chapters explore the importance of community in the pioneer gift, both as mission community in context and also as spread-out communities and networks of practice and support that enable the pioneer gift to remain true.

A storied gift

Every gift has a story. Families often relive memories of particular gifts through storytelling. The pioneer gift did not come from nowhere.[13] This latest emergence of pioneering began in youth ministry, which is still absolutely crucial to the well-being of the Church into the future. Youth ministers who were working among young people outside of church cultures found it was straightforward enough to begin to share Christ with young people but getting them to join existing churches proved almost impossible. The cultural gap between the two was simply too large. Pete Ward was very much the pioneer leading the way. He drew on stories of cross-cultural mission blended with a model of youth ministry developed by Young Life to suggest that a relational model of youth ministry with young people was called for that developed church in their culture as an outcome.[14] There were books, papers, conferences, networks, a training programme and a sense of excitement at this new approach. It became apparent that what was being named was also an issue for many youth ministers and their friends. I am pleased to say that there is still lots of pioneering taking place in and out of youth ministry. For example, Anna Ruddick reflects in her chapter on the impact over time of the Eden network. Alternative worship was a movement that sought to do something similar, particularly in relation to the postmodern turn. Various other waves followed – emerging church, new monasticism, missional communities and so on. Because of the connectivity available the same practices and questions were and still are circling in many other western contexts. It has largely been a lay movement. *Mission-Shaped Church* was published in 2004 and this report from the Church of England and Methodist Church stated that it was seeing and describing practice that was already happening at the edges, recognizing it as a good thing and welcoming a new mixed economy in the Church, to build on what the Spirit was doing. As outlined above, this was where the language of pioneer came to the fore.

This did not come from nowhere in CMS either. One of CMS's core values is pioneering. CMS was founded by pioneers. A small group, the Eclectic Society, was founded in 1783 to dream ways in which the world might be changed. They imagined other possibilities to business as usual and went on to build things that made that happen. They are perhaps best known for their involvement in the abolition of slavery. But one of their endeavours was to set up CMS in 1799 to send people in mission to share the good news of Jesus Christ cross-culturally in places, countries and cultures beyond the then reach of the Church. Two hundred years later those places have become the heartlands of Christianity worldwide. This is not the place to explore that history but it is ironic that Europe perhaps is now the most challenging context for mission. CMS responded to the challenge of mission in Europe and the UK in a number of ways, which included introducing mission partners in Britain and setting up a team to engage in mission in Britain through practice, catalysing, networking, resourcing and training alongside and in partnership with others. Two of the CMS staff were on the writing group for the *Mission-Shaped Church* report and the latest initiative has been the setting up of the CMS pioneer training. Against the odds, I think, the environment has changed. Mission is on the agenda of the Church in Britain and certainly of the Church of England. There are inspiring leaders, networks, resources, training and creativity. I was speaking with Colin Smith, who has been a CMS mission partner in Nairobi for 14 years and is joining the CMS pioneer team. We discussed the changes in the Church, the wider culture and in CMS while he has been away. It was a reminder of just how much has changed that is easy to take for granted. CMS has shifted radically its self-understanding during this period, becoming an acknowledged mission community with a vision for mission and transformation of the world through that community of mission disciples. At the heart of the community is a mission spirituality that fuels a life of mission locally and in interchange globally. CMS as an ecclesial community now finds itself uniquely poised as a fresh expression of church, not gathered but spread out. Religious orders have often been the places that have sustained and nurtured missionary vision in the Church (Cray et al., 2010, p. 7). Their primary task is prophetic ministry to the world and the purpose of formation in them is to foster the art of inculturation (Arbuckle, 1996, pp. 4, 36). So while it has been something of a surprise to find ourselves in a religious order or mission community, it makes perfect sense that this would be a natural home for the pioneer gift.

A gift that takes time

After the resurrection of Jesus, the newness that comes through the outpouring of the Spirit is extraordinary. Reading the first few chapters of Acts there is hardly time to take a breath as the gospel ripples outwards from Jerusalem along the trade routes of the empire, crossing borders and boundaries. New communities of disciples are begun. It is a huge shock to the religious system and the powers that be. The practices of healing, deliverance, baptism, preaching the resurrection of Jesus, meeting in homes to share fellowship, teaching, possessions, bread and wine are simply not the way things have been done or indeed are done in the tradition. There are several occasions where the clash of the new and the old comes to a head. One such occasion is in Acts 5 when the apostles who are supposed to be locked up in jail are found preaching in the Temple having been let out by an angel! When confronted about it, the ringleader Peter has the audacity to say that they will keep doing so and obey God rather than the wishes and dictates of the religious leaders. The incensed council is about to put them to death when Gamaliel, a Pharisee, intervenes and persuades them not to, but to let them go. His argument is simple. If what is happening is not from God it will dissipate and go away, but by implication if it is from God, which is possible, it will flourish. Only time will tell. So the council should wait and see. They take on board his advice and the apostles are freed after a flogging.

Steven Croft drew a parallel between this story and the pioneering that was being done through the Fresh Expressions movement in 2009 (Croft and Mobsby, 2009, p. 38). He suggested that as he travelled round to share the vision for fresh expressions of church, he thought that about half of those he encountered adopted the Gamaliel position. Others were either already on board or against it. He respected this position and understood that it was too early to say whether what was going on was something from God that would last or something that would dissipate as simply new ideas being done by people on a whim in their own strength. As with Gamaliel, the Church needed to wait and see, keeping open permission and possibility for the new, which to its credit it has done.

The Church of England commissioned a large piece of research into church growth. The research was conducted between 2011 and 2013.[15] One of the reports researched pioneering fresh expressions of church and its impact. Its findings from ten dioceses are that there are lots of fresh expressions of church which if put together have added the equivalent in numbers of an additional diocese to the Church, while the overall picture in the Church has been one of decline. There are at least 20 types. Over half meet in spaces other than traditional church buildings, and over half are lay led. They genuinely are reaching people who were not followers of Christ before. If you extrapolate from the data, something like one new community of disciples is being birthed each week. And this is just in the Church of England, not counting all the other places where this is taking place. Part of me is very resistant to measuring because I think it is fraught with challenges. Many of the things being done by pioneers would not be counted as they are participating in the mission of God in the world to bring healing and transformation and making real impact, but in this research the criteria for impact being looked at is solely growing fresh expressions of church. However, it is hugely encouraging to have confirmed what many of us have sensed for a long time – pioneering is not just a nice gift in and of itself, it is a gift that gives and grows the kingdom of God and the Church of Jesus Christ. Perhaps we are now at a point where those who have adopted the Gamaliel position will be persuaded. 'There comes a time when Gamaliel himself needs to be challenged and persuaded. His position may be a good place to visit but it is an unhelpful place to live permanently' (Croft and Mobsby, 2009, p. 39).

Keep the gift moving

In his book *The Gift* Lewis Hyde explores the notion of when something is genuine gift (Hyde, 1988). His particular interest is artists who are trying both to be artists, which is their call, passion and focus of their energy, and to make a living at the same time. They operate in the gap between commerce and art and need to navigate both a gift economy and the market economy. Art flows in both but he says that art always has to carry a notion of gift and not be collapsed into simply a market exchange or it loses its giftedness. The relationships between the two can be quite tricky to tease out. The same could be said of pioneering mission – where there is no gift there is no mission.

Mission begins with and in God. Mission is the overflow of God's self-diffusive love creating, redeeming, reaching out to, challenging and healing the world (Bevans and Schroeder, 2011, p. 10). It is given through love and not earned. God's gifts of Godself through Jesus Christ and through the Spirit are overwhelmingly generous. Mission is joining with this overflow of gift, receiving and participating with God in his gift economy and giving away again to others. The best gifts have no strings attached. In some cultures there is a reciprocity of expectations attached to gift-giving – for example, if someone comes for a meal we invite them back. But there are other cultures where when a gift is given it moves onwards elsewhere as if it goes round a corner, blind or out of sight as it is given to another party (Hyde, 1988, p. 16). It is no longer controlled. You have to trust the process and trust that the recipient will keep the gift moving. I think this is a lovely picture for the spirit of gift that the Church can embody at its best – always keeping gifts moving, being generous, being prepared to let the gifts go blind and trust the Spirit.

In many ways it still feels like we are at the beginning of something with pioneer training, but after a few years we have learned so much and yet got so many more questions. It seems so important to reflect on what is going on and to talk about it, learn from it and dialogue about it in the wider Church as well as among pioneers. This book is a collection of research and reflections arising out of pioneering mission. Several of the papers were first presented at a pioneer research and conversations day in Oxford. This will be an annual event and we hope this book will be the first of many. I hope that this series of reflections sheds a little light on and provokes further thinking and conversation about the pioneer gift. It is clear that there are many questions to ponder and a huge agenda for research and reflection. It is particularly encouraging that four of the chapters in the book are written by students publishing for the first time. It is early days still for the pioneer gift in its latest guise. But it surely is a gift that has been given, a gift of the Spirit for our time. Yes it is a difficult gift to carry and to fathom, but its mystery and ambiguity are part of its appeal. It is also one whose pleasure is unfolding over time, a gift that changes and moves on and will not be boxed. It refuses to stand still. It is a surprise that keeps surprising. I hope that the wider Church has the courage to keep the pioneer gift moving.

References

Arbuckle, G., 1993, *Refounding the Church: Dissent for Leadership*, London: Geoffrey Chapman.

Arbuckle, G., 1996, *From Chaos to Mission: Refounding Religious Life Formation*, London: Geoffrey Chapman.

Arbuckle, G., 2010, *Culture, Inculturation and Theologians: A Postmodern Critique*, Collegeville, MN: Michael Glazier Liturgical Press.

Bevans, S. and R. Schroeder, 2011, *Prophetic Dialogue*, Maryknoll, NY: Orbis Books.

Bosch, D., 1991, *Transforming Mission*, Maryknoll, NY: Orbis Books.

Brueggemann, W., 1978, *The Prophetic Imagination*, Philadelphia, PA: Fortress Press.

Cray, G. (ed.), 2004, *Mission-Shaped Church*, London: Church House Publishing.

Cray, G., I. Mobsby and A. Kennedy (eds), 2010, *New Monasticism as Fresh Expression of Church*, Norwich: Canterbury Press.

Croft, S. and I. Mobsby, 2009, *Fresh Expressions in the Sacramental Tradition*, Norwich: Canterbury Press.

Gay, D., 2011, *Remixing the Church*, London: SCM Press.

Goodhew, D., A. Roberts and M. Volland, 2012, *Fresh*, London: SCM Press.

Hollinghurst, S., 2013, *Starting, Assessing and Sustaining Pioneering Mission*, Cambridge: Grove Books.

Hyde, L., 1988, *The Gift*, New York: Vintage Books.

Male, D. (ed.), 2011, *Pioneers 4 Life*, Oxford: Bible Reading Fellowship.

Moynagh, M., 2012, *Church for Every Context*, London: SCM Press.

Passmore, R. and L., 2013, *Here Be Dragons*, Birmingham: Frontier Youth Trust.

Scott, Rev. J., 1827, *Life Letters and Papers Of The Late Thomas Scott*, New Haven, CT: Nathan Whiting.
Skreslet, S., 2012, *Comprehending Mission*, Maryknoll, NY: Orbis Books.
Ward, P., 1997, *Youthwork and the Mission of God*, London: SPCK.

Notes

1 This was a report published by the Church of England and Methodist Church in 2004 to reflect on the emerging church planting and fresh expressions of church in the changing context in Britain.

2 See www.freshexpressions.org.uk/pioneerministry (accessed January 2014).

3 This was at Aston Sandford in Buckinghamshire. Thomas Scott was the vicar and had written an esteemed Bible commentary. He had a large vicarage and potential missionaries came to stay and learn biblical knowledge. They then had a college in London for many years and then one in Birmingham. See Rev. John Scott, *Life Letters and Papers Of The Late Thomas Scott*, 1827, New Haven, CT: Nathan Whiting, p. 191.

4 See www.pioneer.cms-uk.org.

5 George Lings points this out in his extremely helpful chapter in Male (ed.), 2011, p. 31.

6 There are many, for example, whose journey has grown and been inspired by new monasticism and the likes of the 24/7 prayer movement, which is pioneering mission in and out of a mission spirituality.

7 I came across the metaphor of true North in this way in Passmore and Passmore, 2013, p. 14.

8 Skreslet (2012) maps the questions, methods, themes, problems and prospects of missiology, and these themes are fairly close to the way he groups areas of curriculum.

9 Brueggemann (1978) says that evoking grief and energizing hope are the two tasks of the prophet.

10 Bevans and Schroeder (2011) elucidate this brilliantly in chapter 7, 'Letting Go and Speaking Out'.

11 I first heard this term at a gathering of theological educators who were involved in training pioneer ordinands.

12 Gerald Arbuckle is an anthropologist who has introduced me to many of these insights through the books listed in the bibliography.

13 Gay (2011) is a good reflection on the story.

14 This approach is best summarized in Ward (1997), though this approach to youth ministry had begun in the late 1980s and early 1990s.

15 Several reports were part of this research. A summary report and the Fresh Expressions report are available at www.churchgrowthresearch. org.uk.

2

Pioneering Missiologies: Seeing Afresh

CATHY ROSS

The Eclectic Society

Although pioneer mission leadership training is only in its fourth year at the Church Mission Society (CMS), it has a long history. I believe we can date it back to the early discussions of the Eclectic Society, founded in 1783. The Eclectic Society was an Anglican discussion society that met fortnightly in the vestry of St John's Chapel, Bedford Road, London and discussed a wide range of topics such as: the nature, evil and remedy of schism; what can be done to counteract the designs of Infidels against Christianity; what is meant by the 'wedding garment' in Proverbs; ways of conducting private prayer; what lessons may be learnt from the dispensations of providence.[1]

There are several important points to note concerning the founding of the Eclectic Society. First, it was founded by both clergy and lay. This has always been part of the DNA of CMS. CMS is not a clerical club. CMS encourages the involvement and engagement of both lay and ordained people. Second, the Eclectic Society took its context seriously. They had serious discussions on the role and place of faith in their world. They were grappling with how to understand and communicate the realities of faith in their own context, time and place. While most of their topics related to theological and biblical matters, they were keen to apply these subjects to their lives together in society. Third, they were activists – they made things happen. In 1799, one of their members, Josiah Pratt, proposed the following question for discussion: 'How far may a periodical Publication be made subservient to the interest of Religion?' The discussions led, two years later, to the starting of the *Christian Observer*, which became a valuable journal of evangelical principles and work for much of the nineteenth century. So they did not merely discuss theology and engage in debate; they then did something about it. Their fortnightly discussions, their research and their faith led them to action. Finally, they were also a praying community – or, in those days, a Society. They drew strength, encouragement and support from being together and praying together. Therefore they were able to take action with the support of a close and prayerful community.

These are all values that we take seriously, appreciate and try to replicate in the pioneer training at CMS. We welcome both lay and ordained. We grapple with the realities of our current context as we try to understand and live out our faith in our time and place. Careful listening and immersion in the context are foundational mission approaches for us. We tend to be activists and desire to get things done. We value the CMS community as a praying community, and as a place where we can be nurtured, strengthened and challenged together. I believe that our ancestors in the Eclectic Society are good role models for our missional approach to pioneering.

These ancestors first discussed foreign mission in 1786, three years after they were founded, and the subject arose again in 1789 and 1791. Finally on 18 March 1799 they became more specific, addressing the following question: 'What methods can we use more effectually to promote the knowledge of the Gospel among the Heathen?' At this meeting it was resolved to form a society to achieve this end. At a public meeting in April 1799, the Church Missionary Society for Africa and the East was formed. It was also supported by members of the Clapham Sect, a group of activist, evangelical social reformers with such luminaries as William Wilberforce, Henry Thornton and Hannah More. Activism, social engagement and awareness of context were there at the very beginning.

This is some of the rich heritage that we in CMS can offer to the pioneer. I would like to outline three missiological approaches that I have experienced in my work with the pioneers at CMS. Then I will offer some reflections on theological homelessness and little theologies.

A missiology of sight

Pioneers are generally good at reading culture and context. I believe they have the gifts of sight and insight, which are gifts of the Holy Spirit. The Holy Spirit is the Go-Between God who opens our inward eyes and makes us aware of the other. 'The Holy Spirit is that power which opens eyes that are closed, hearts that are unaware and minds that shrink from too much reality' (Taylor, 1972, p. 19). We need the Holy Spirit to give us this gift, as without the Spirit's presence, and as T. S. Eliot reminds us, 'human kind Cannot bear very much reality' (Eliot, 1974, p. 190).

The concept of sight and recognition of the other are clear in the parable in Matthew 25 when the righteous say to Jesus, 'Lord, when did we *see* you hungry and feed you, or thirsty and give you something to drink? When did we *see* you a stranger and invite you in, or needing clothes and clothe you? When did we *see* you ill or in prison and go to visit you?' (Matt. 25.37–39). And we all know Jesus' answer. When we do what Jesus commended in Matthew 25 – visit those in prison, feed the hungry, clothe the naked, entertain the stranger – we are living out a very different set of values and relationships. We are according dignity to others, we are breaking social boundaries, we are including those who are so often excluded; we are engaged in transformation. All this begins with *seeing* the other person, the act of recognition – a powerful act indeed. Looking the other in the eye – the establishment of the 'I–Thou' relationship – is fundamental because it acknowledges people's humanity, accords them dignity and denies their invisibility. As Christine Pohl writes in her superb book on hospitality:

> Hospitality resists boundaries that endanger persons by denying their humanness. It saves others from the invisibility that comes

from social abandonment. Sometimes, by the very act of welcome, a vision for a whole society is offered, a small evidence that transformed relations are possible. (Pohl, 1999, p. 64)

Think of the good Samaritan who refused to pass by or pretend that he had not *seen* the wounded man. His vision and action crossed ethnic boundaries, caused him personal cost and inconvenience, and saved a life. When we see the other person, we see the image of God, as well as our common humanity, which establishes a fundamental dignity, respect and common bond. It helps us to see rightly. The parable in Matthew 25 reminds us that we can *see* Christ in every guest and stranger.

If we had been able to 'see the other' and to see rightly, might the genocide in Rwanda or Cambodia never have happened? If we were able 'to see the other', might the ethnic cleansing in Bosnia-Herzegovina, the civil war in Northern Ireland, the ignorance and apathy concerning Sudan and Congo, apartheid in South Africa, tribalism, caste and class systems, oppressive colonialism – might all this have been avoided if only we could see? Who are we blind to in our contexts, which prevents us from seeing the other person and, wittingly or unwittingly, means that we practise a theology of exclusion rather than of embrace? Might it be the Dalit, the untouchable, the homeless person selling *The Big Issue* whom we have never noticed before, whom we have never seen before, whom we have always passed by in the street and never looked in the eye nor exchanged a greeting. Might it be the differently abled person who is awkward and difficult or the person with mental-health issues who is unpredictable and unreliable? Have we paused to see our own brokenness reflected there, and asked ourselves what we could learn? Might it be those migrants who never learn our language, who never even try to integrate, who take over whole streets and suburbs in our cities – have we ever had them in our homes, offered them hospitality and tried to 'see' their culture?

So Christianity is a way of seeing the world which may go against the grain. This is what Jesus offers us – an upside down kingdom, an alternative reality, a remedial perspective. The parables of the great banquet and of the sheep and the goats do indeed mean a reconstruction of reality. God's universal welcome is displayed and as we see the other we are welcoming Jesus. This is indeed a new way of seeing and makes me think of one of the OCCUPY slogans, 'Another world is possible'. The pioneers help us to see differently by living and working with spiritual seekers, people with learning difficulties, unemployed and disenfranchised youth, for example. It is in these contexts that the pioneers learn a new way of seeing as God's Holy Spirit enables them to see and to learn from the other. The pioneers learn to see with expectancy, with love, to see prophetically and rightly, to see the other as a human being with gifts to offer as well.

A missiology of emptiness and hiddenness

A missiology of emptiness was first suggested by Korean woman missiologist Chun Chae Ok in 2004. A missiology of emptiness is about emptying self to the point of self-sacrifice. It is about *kenosis* as expressed in Philippians 2.5–11. Scholars debate two possible meanings here: Jesus' taking on the form of a servant by becoming human, known as the incarnation, and Jesus' self-surrender and the giving of his life on the cross, self-sacrifice (Brown, 1976, p. 548). Much of the pioneering mission of our students is small, fragile and sometimes unseen or even hidden. It involves listening, learning, being alongside, building relationships and being present. This approach is what Jesus modelled to us in his incarnation. Jesus poured himself out for the sake of the world. Jesus befriended disreputable people and refused to condemn the unrighteous. Jesus loved women and children and the poor – the hidden ones, the little ones, the marginalized, the outsiders. We need to recover these perspectives in our missiology. This was the approach of Jesus in his ministry, where he emptied himself for the sake of others, where he sometimes even asked people to keep his healing miracles secret, where he declared that the first would be last and told his disciples that we all need to take up our cross to follow him.

By contrast, so much of our current missiology is focused on the drive for growth, expansion, projects, strategies and numbers. The recent Church Growth Research Programme, with which I was involved, is partly a testimony to this focus.[2] This research uncovered some excellent and new findings, already referred to by Jonny Baker in the opening chapter of this book. One of the key findings was that there is no single recipe for growth. Others included involvement of laity and those in the community, importance of retaining young people, willingness to change, readiness to learn and reflect, robust welcoming systems, commitment to nurture new Christians, having a clear mission and vision – all helpful and worthwhile findings. However, a deeper consideration and reflection on what exactly is growth would be helpful. Where do our assumed understandings of growth come from? Is all growth necessarily good growth, and how do we evaluate this? Is success in church growth and mission simply a matter of finding the right techniques, approaches and people? This is certainly a discussion that we need to have. For example, are we just in thrall to modern capitalism's obsession with seemingly endless and infinite growth? Has growth become an end in itself? The agrarian parables of Jesus – perhaps especially the parable of the sower – suggest that different rates of growth, and success or failure, may be dependent on the contextual soil in which the seeds are planted. It is important to appreciate that growth may wax and wane, that faithful presence is important and that fragility is inherent. Where is the language that expresses our mission engagement in terms of weakness, vulnerability, relationships, service, compassion, meekness, caring?

If we consider the Christian Church from both historical and global perspectives, we see clearly that Christian expansion is not linear but serial, unlike other world religions. What was a centre of Christian vitality in one generation may become a wilderness in another. Christian advance is not a steady line of success. Advance may not produce further advance. Christian advance is serial – rooted first in one place and then in another. Therefore, it seems that there is a vulnerability at the heart of our faith; indeed the cross stands as a reminder of that vulnerability. Each manifestation of growth has the fragile status of an ingrafted olive branch, which, by its very nature, can be removed. Much of Jesus' teaching on the growth of the kingdom is about its veiledness, its unpredictability and the sheer length of time maturity can take. Yes we can have confidence that the kingdom grows, but we may need a greater humility when we talk about particular manifestations and whether they are expressions of growth or decline. It is also vital to remember that the effectiveness of Christianity within a culture depends on proper translation and contextualization.

However, I would like to issue a warning note about this missiological approach from feminist theology. Christian attitudes of service and self-sacrifice can be taken too far and therefore result in unhealthy oppression, particularly of women. Culture can certainly be a source of oppression and this was readily acknowledged by early missionaries – footbinding of women in China or *sati* in India being obvious examples. There are also more subtle examples, such as tribalism in the majority world or 'old boys' clubs' in the western world, which can deeply embed male power. Moreover, we can become blinded by this as the prevailing culture and fail to see and name this oppression as sin. And then, as feminist theologian Serene Jones writes, 'we must strain hard to see, given the powerfully destructive ways in which oppression structures our thinking and makes even the most profound forms of brokenness seem normal' (2000, p. 109). Oppression works like a blinder preventing us from seeing that we are caught in sin. Therefore relations of domination begin to abound; women become disempowered and invisible, and so we have to be extremely careful that a missiology of emptiness and a missiology of hiddenness do not ultimately work against women.

Sadly, we continue to see this throughout many cultures in our world. Marilu Salazar reminds us of the invisibility of women in Latin America in the Roman Catholic context. She quotes Brazilian theologian Ivone Gebara whose critique of the Latin American Conference of Bishops, held in Aparecida in 2007, was, 'we women were the great disappeared ones in Aparecida.' (Salazar, 2010). The official documents from the conference made no mention of indigenous women, religious women, feminist theology, nor women's organizations 'that in Latin America have dedicated their labours to fight against the different faces of violence and to offer alternatives of survival' (Salazar, 2010). A Roman Catholic sister from India once told me that 'women are like curry leaves. Curry leaves are used in cooking to give a nice flavour and taste. When people eat food they throw the curry leaves away. Like this, women are used and thrown out.' She grieved over the plight of women in her church. After women give flavour they are discarded as they have served their purpose. Sometimes it is difficult not to become overwhelmed by attitudes and structures that prevent women flourishing. A lack of proper and thorough gender analysis can therefore lead to a truncated understanding of the gospel that is oppressive for women. This then clearly begs the question as to why Christian mission, at times, did not challenge cultural practices that were discriminatory or harmful towards women.

A missiology of hospitality or a missiology of the kitchen table

Hospitality is one of my favourite metaphors for mission. It is such a rich metaphor for mission because it incorporates all the fundamentally important virtues in mission of reciprocity, mutuality, surprise, welcome, eating together and receiving from the other.

The very etymology of the word hospitality is illuminating. In Latin the word that signifies host is *hospes* and the word for enemy is *hostis*, from which we derive hostile. This suggests ambiguity and tension around the concept of hospitality. However, the derivation from the Greek offers us something slightly different. There is an interesting and intriguing conundrum around the Greek word *xenos*, which denotes simultaneously guest, host or stranger. The Greek word for hospitality in the New Testament, *philoxenia*, refers not so much to love of strangers but to a delight in the whole guest–host relationship and in the surprises that may occur. Jesus is portrayed as a gracious host, welcoming children, tax-collectors, prostitutes and sinners into his presence and therefore offending those who would prefer such guests not to be at his gatherings. But Jesus is also portrayed as vulnerable guest and needy stranger who came to his own but his own did not receive him. (John 1.11). Pohl comments that this 'intermingling of guest and host roles in the person of Jesus is part of what makes the story of hospitality so compelling for Christians' (1999, p. 17). Think of Jesus on the Emmaus road as travelling pilgrim and stranger, recognized as host and who he was in the breaking of bread during a meal involving an act of hospitality. Or think of the Peter and Cornelius story – who is the host and who is the guest? Both offer and receive, both listen and learn, both are challenged and changed by the hospitality of the other. So we can see the importance not only of the ambiguity but also the fluidity of the host–guest conundrum. We offer and receive as both guest or stranger and host. In fact, strangers may enhance our well-being rather than diminish it. The three major festivals of the Church – Christmas, Easter and Pentecost – all have to do with the advent of a divine stranger. In each case this stranger – a baby, a resurrected Christ and the wind of the Holy Spirit – all meet us as mysterious or strange visitors, breaking into our world, challenging our world-views and systems, and welcoming us to new worlds (Koenig, 2001, p. 5).

As we welcome people into our homes, share food with them around our kitchen tables and spend time with them, our perspective begins to change. When we eat together we are 'playing out the drama of life' as we begin to share stories, let down our guard, welcome strangers and see the other (Hershberger, 1999, p. 104). Rebecca Nyegenye, chaplain at Uganda Christian University, Mukono, explained that in Uganda hospitality goes with both elaborate meals and listening to the visitor. Ugandans believe that for any relationship to be strong, food and intentional listening must be shared. Eating together is a great leveller. It is something that we all must do, so it has a profoundly egalitarian dimension. Jean Vanier, of l'Arche community, confessed that when he started to share meals with men of serious mental disabilities, 'Sitting down at the same table meant becoming friends with them, creating a family. It was a way of life absolutely opposed to the values of a competitive, hierarchical society in which the weak are pushed aside' (Pohl, 1999, p. 74). When we eat together, as we let down our guard and share stories, we begin to create relationship and this is at the heart of mission – our relationship with God and neighbour. Listening is an important part of honouring the guest. In both hospitality and mission, listening to the other is the beginning of understanding and of entering the other's world. In a unique moment in the book of Ephesians, we see Jews and Gentiles coming together. The test of their coming together was the meal table – the institution that once symbolized ethnic and cultural division now became a symbol of Christian living. Eating together locates us at the heart of the *missio Dei* (Katangole, 2012).

Offering food and drink to guests is central to almost every act of hospitality. This takes time. It requires attention to the other, it requires an effort. It requires us to stop and focus. As a Benedictine monk once observed, 'In a fast food culture, you have to remind yourself that some things cannot be done quickly. Hospitality takes time' (Pohl, 1999, p. 178). This is a challenge in our time-starved culture. Hospitality emerges from a willingness to create time and space for this to happen.

The theme of banqueting, of food and drink is central in the ministry of Jesus. Was he not accused of being a glutton and a drunkard and of eating with sinners? Jesus was celebrating the messianic banquet but with all the wrong people! Bretherton even goes so far as to state that 'This table fellowship with sinners, and the reconfiguring of Israel's purity boundaries which this hospitality represents, signifies the heart of Jesus' mission' (2006, p. 128). Jesus and his followers here are also celebrating the abundance of God – think of all the stories of food and drink overflowing, of parties enjoyed, of the feeding of the 5,000. God's household is a household of superabundance, of extravagant hospitality, where food and wine is generously shared and the divine welcome universally offered. Jesus' rejection of social and religious categories of inclusion and exclusion was offensive to the authorities. As one theologian expressed it, 'Jesus got himself crucified by the way he ate' (Karris, 1985, p. 47).

Jesus was unambiguously clear about who should be around the kitchen table:

> When you give a luncheon or a dinner, do not invite you friends or your brothers or your relations or rich neighbours, in case they may invite you in return, and you would be repaid. But when you give a banquet, invite the poor, the crippled, the lame, and the blind. And you will be blessed, because they cannot repay you. (Luke 14.12–14)

This is, of course, the prelude to the parable of the great banquet, a powerful metaphor for the kingdom of God, where all are universally welcomed. When the expected guests turn down the invitation to the banquet, the same four groups are to be invited, 'the poor, the crippled, the lame, and the blind' and then everyone else from the highways and byways.

Perhaps this meal is most powerfully expressed in the Eucharist, where this ritualized eating and drinking together re-enacts the crux of the gospel. As we remember what it cost Jesus to welcome us into relationship with God, we remember with sorrow the agony and the pain, but at the same time we rejoice and celebrate our reconciliation and this new relationship made possible because of Christ's sacrifice and supreme act of hospitality. We rejoice in our new relationship with God, made possible through the cross, and we rejoice as we partake of this meal together in community. When we share in the Eucharist, we are not only foreshadowing the great heavenly banquet to come but we are also nourished on our journey towards God's banquet table. Jesus is, quite literally, the host as we partake of his body and blood and we are the guests as we feed on him by faith with thanksgiving. In this way, the Eucharist connects hospitality at a very basic level with God and with the *missio Dei* as it anticipates and reveals God's heavenly table and the coming kingdom. This is beautifully expressed in one of the Eucharistic Prayers from *A New Zealand Prayer Book* (1989):

Most merciful Lord,
your love compels us to come in.
Our hands were unclean,
our hearts were unprepared;
we were not fit
even to eat the crumbs from under your table.
But you, Lord, are the God of our salvation,
and share your bread with sinners.
So cleanse and feed us
with the precious body and blood of your Son,
that he may live in us and we in him;
and that we, with the whole company of Christ,
may sit and eat in your kingdom.

A missiology of hospitality or a missiology of the kitchen table is essentially a missiology of relationship. It conjures up images of intimacy, homeliness, warmth, comfort, rootedness, safety and community. It resonates with the community focus of the Eclectic Society and the current status of CMS as an Acknowledged Community within the Church of England.

In my experience, pioneers are good at hospitality. They like to loiter and listen, enjoy food and drink. They are often with people on the edge of church or society, people who may not easily fit in. This takes time, intentional listening, patience – an ability to know when to wait and when to act. As Vanier reminds us, sharing food together is a great leveller and relationship builder as we linger over the kitchen table.

Theological homelessness

Pioneers experience a certain amount of theological homelessness. I think that this is linked to the gift of not fitting in. For many, the theology that they grew up with, or have been introduced to, does not seem to engage with reality as they experience it. I suspect this is because we are all trying to take our contexts seriously and some of our theology may not. So a kind of theological 'leaving home' begins to take place. This means that home and the theology with which we were nurtured is never quite the same. Theological homelessness can be painful. It may leave us stranded between two or more worlds. It forces us to look at our theological upbringing with new eyes.

However, perhaps a certain amount of theological discomfort is a good thing. Certainly the themes of exile, pilgrimage and even homelessness are biblical themes. Our ancestor Abraham was uprooted from his home by Yahweh to discover new things about God, the people of Israel were forced to adapt to new cultures and strange ways while in exile, and Jesus knew pilgrimage and homelessness even while in his mother's womb. And so pioneering can be uncomfortable – unable to return home as T. S. Eliot so eloquently expressed it in his poem *Journey of the Magi*, 'no longer at ease here, in the old dispensation, with an alien people clutching their gods'. But the new place is hard also – just as for the Magi, 'this Birth was hard and bitter agony for us, like Death, our death'.

Theological homelessness may also be linked to the theme of dissent. Jonny Baker has encapsulated Gerry Arbuckle's insights about dissent in the first chapter. Jonny differentiates between pathfinding and authority dissenters. Both have a role to play and it can be painful. But both are needed to help create change by reclaiming the heart of the tradition – much as I imagine the Eclectic Society were doing in birthing the Church Missionary Society for Africa and the East back in 1799. They clearly saw a need for a mission impetus overseas, and could see no way of doing this within the already existing structures so they dissented and refounded at the same time – by founding a Society outside the existing Anglican structures but by also remaining faithful to the Anglican tradition, ethos and structures. This takes some courage and genius, to challenge the tradition but remain loyal to it simultaneously.

So in what new directions might this theological homelessness lead us? Some of the chapters in this book are a start as we begin to wrestle with our contexts and discover not only how the gospel speaks into them but also how gospel insights may be drawn out of them. What does sin and shame mean in twenty-first-century UK? How do we live in community? What support structures are needed for pioneers? What does transformation look like today?

CMS wisdom is helpful here. How do we learn from our surrounding context and be shaped by the contexts in which we live? Andrew Walls reminds us that a missionary (or pioneer) 'has to live on terms set by other people' (Walls and Ross (eds), 2008, p. 197). This is a crucial insight. We do not approach other contexts with a ready-made gospel and with God in our pocket; rather we go in all humility and gentleness. Max Warren, former General Secretary of CMS, expressed it beautifully,

> Our first task in approaching another people, another culture, another religion, is to take off our shoes, for the place we are approaching is holy. Else we may find ourselves treading on people's dreams. More serious still, we may forget that God was here before our arrival. (Warren, in Taylor, 1963, p. 10)

Or another image is of entering another's garden where there is much to learn about that garden. This can only be done by developing a relationship of trust and respect (Bevans and Schroeder, 2011, p. 76). How is Christ understood in the new context? How might Christianity best be expressed in this new soil? How will Christianity flourish in this new soil? And how may this new soil enhance the understanding and depth of Christianity? One of the key things that was learnt from the reception of Christianity in Africa, for example, is that it was not what western missionaries said that mattered in the long term but rather how African Christians appropriated Christ in ways that made sense to them, utilizing African spiritual maps of the universe. This is a lesson for us here and now when we consider pioneering. Are we able to engage in ways that are truly contextual, allowing faith communities to flourish in indigenous soil using local spiritual maps? And do we find our own understanding and appropriation of the faith challenged and enhanced by deep engagement in this particular context?

And so further images and metaphors of midwife, companion, treasure hunter, cartographer come to mind. As pioneers, are we able to be in the context 'birthing' theological ideas and insights without imposing our own expectations, agendas, assumptions? Can we stand alongside as a friend – or literally one who breaks bread with another (from the Latin *cum-* + *panis*), resonant of the kitchen table again. Are we able to find the treasure that is already there? We need to study local maps with care to find the local treasure. As Bevans and Schroeder remind us, '[we] need to befriend people, engage them as guides, be taught by them' (Bevans and Schroeder, 2011, p. 32). This is indeed a high calling. Can we allow the 'locals' to develop their own cartography, their own local maps to make sense of their own particular universe to find their own way home?

This is the challenge before us. We can learn from our CMS ancestors in mission, many of whom laid down their lives to make this approach possible. It seems that this is what John the Baptist modelled when he diminished himself as Jesus came to be acknowledged as Lord. So as Jesus becomes embedded in the local culture and context, then the pioneer can not only make way for the local to flourish but also discover new ways of understanding and appreciating the gospel.

Little theologies and reciprocity

'Little theologies' is a concept I like very much, developed by Austrian theologian Clemens Sedmak. He defines it as follows: 'little theologies are theologies made for a particular situation, taking particular circumstances into account, using local questions and concerns, local stories and examples as their starting point. People should be able to recognize themselves in little theologies' (Sedmak, 2002, p. 119). He claims that little theologies point to the 'richness and goodness' of local contexts, challenge the local context to go beyond its limits and open eyes and ears to new perspectives (Sedmak, 2002, p. 125). To construct little theologies we need to know the local context well so that we can construct theologies with local materials – local knowledge, rituals, arts, songs, stories, proverbs, graffiti, music, architecture. Sedmak challenges us to be creative and to dig deep into the local to communicate gospel insights.

> Which image would you use to illustrate entering the Christian way, of being reborn? A good shower, after a long, hot day? Falling in love? Being able to see after successful surgery? ... Can we use the image of a great farm on which everybody earns the same as an image for the kingdom of God? (Sedmak, 2002, p. 148)

This is the hard work we need to do when engaging in mission in different contexts – discovering the depth and richness of the local context while also exposing the local context to difference and newness. This is the mutuality and reciprocity of mission; the excitement and the engagement, offering change and being changed.

In a lecture last year hosted by CAFOD, Agbonkhianmeghe Orobator, the Jesuit Provincial for East Africa, suggested four principles that should characterize how individuals and organizations work to develop the African continent. I believe that these principles can equally apply to how we engage in pioneering mission. The first is solidarity, which means that we do not engage with the other as 'worthy object or other' but rather as partner. Second, he suggests subsidiarity or empowerment, which enables people to take charge of their own future and destiny in a dignified manner. Third, there is mutuality. Orobator challenges us to ask ourselves the simple question, 'What's in it for me?' This helpfully emphasizes the mutuality and reciprocity of our engagement in mission. Mission is not a one-way street. It is about giving and receiving, 'and where the progress of some is not bought at the expense of others' (*Populorum Progressio*, no. 44, 1967). Vanier asks poignantly, 'How can Christian men and women be persuaded to turn towards the weakest of our societies, not simply to look after them and evangelize them, but to meet them and be evangelized by them, to receive from them the Gospel we need today?' (Vanier, 2013, pp. 117–18). We are shaped, challenged and transformed by our encounters in mission. Finally, relationality – it is about people, 'their dignity, their humanity, their rights, their values, their gifts' (Orobator, 2013). This is a valuable reminder not to objectivize people and to remember that mission is always about relationship – with God and our neighbour.

Reciprocity is a principle that also applies to our relationships with the world Church. As we listen to and learn from the world Church, we learn much from new voices speaking out of radically different perspectives and contexts from our own. We need this engagement and conversation to challenge our blind spots and enlarge our understanding of Jesus.

Conclusion

What would our ancestors in the Eclectic Society make of this approach to mission and to pioneering? I think they would recognize it and rejoice in it as we tread in their footsteps. They too were pioneers when they initiated a discussion society, founded not only a Christian periodical but also CMS, which is still thriving today. They found strength in community and in prayer. They were activists and wanted to make a difference. They challenged the Anglican tradition while remaining within it and faithful to it. In many ways we draw from their wells. So it may be that pioneers have the awkward gift of not fitting in, that we experience a kind of theological homelessness, that we are learning anew to live on other people's terms; but we have hope because we have ancestors who have been before us, and because we have the message of hope, we have the promise of life.

References

A New Zealand Prayer Book, He Karakia Mihinare o Aotearoa, 1989, Auckland: William Collins.

Bevans, S. and R. Schroeder, 2011, *Prophetic Dialogue*, Maryknoll, NY: Orbis Books.

Bretherton, L., 2006, *Hospitality as Holiness: Christian Witness Amid Moral Diversity*, Aldershot: Ashgate.

Brown, C. (ed.), 1976, *The New International Dictionary of New Testament Theology, Vol. 1*, Exeter: Paternoster.

Eclectic Society Papers (CMS/ACC11), Cadbury Research Library, Special Collections, University of Birmingham.

Eliot, T. S., 1974, *Collected Poems, 1909–1962*, London: Faber & Faber.

Hershberger, M., 1999, *A Christian View of Hospitality: Expecting Surprises*, Scottdale, PA: Herald Press.

Jones, S., 2000, *Feminist Theory and Christian Theology: Cartographies of Grace*, Minneapolis, MN: Fortress Press.

Karris, R., 1985, *Luke: Artist and Theologian*, New York: Paulist Press.

Katangole, E., 2012, 'Mission and the Ephesian Moment of World Christianity: Pilgrimages of Pain and Hope and the Economics of Eating Together', *Mission Studies*, 29:2.

Koenig, J., 2001, *New Testament Hospitality: Partnership with Strangers as Promise of Mission*, Eugene, OR: Wipf and Stock.

Ok, Chun Chae, 2004, 'Integrity of Mission in the Light of the Gospel: Bearing the Witness of the Spirit: An Asian Perspective', unpublished paper, Eleventh Conference of the International Association for Mission Studies, Port Dickson, Malaysia, August.

Orobator, Agbonkhianmeghe E. sj, 2013, 'A billion reasons to believe in Africa – The long march from "the hopeless continent" to the "spiritual lung" of humanity', Greenwood Theatre, King's College, London, 18 October.

Paul VI, Pope, 1967, *Populorum Progressio, On the Development of Peoples*, March; http://www.papalencyclicals.net/Paul06/p6develo.htm.

Pohl, C., 1999, *Making Room: Recovering Hospitality as a Christian Tradition*, Grand Rapids, MI: Eerdmans.

Salazar, M., 2010, 'Education and Violence: A Reflection from the Perspective of Latin American Feminist Theology of Liberation', unpublished paper, 'Women in Mission', Bossey workshop, 15–18 October.

Sedmak, C., 2002, *Doing Local Theology: A Guide for Artisans of a New Humanity*, Maryknoll, NY: Orbis Books.

Taylor, J. V., 1963, *The Primal Vision: Christian Presence Amid African Religion*, London: SCM Press.

Taylor, J. V., 1972, *The Go-Between God: The Holy Spirit and the Christian Mission*, London: SCM Press.

Vanier, J., 2013, *Signs of the Tines: Seven Paths of Hope for a Troubled World*, London: Darton, Longman & Todd.

Walls, A. and C. Ross (eds), 2008, *Mission in the 21st Century: Exploring the Five Marks of Global Mission*, London: Darton, Longman & Todd.

Notes

1 The Eclectic Society Papers (CMS/ACC11), Cadbury Research Library, Special Collections, University of Birmingham.

2 See http://www.churchgrowthresearch.org.uk/.

3

Prospective Practitioners:
A Pioneer's Progress

DOUG GAY

In this chapter I do some thinking aloud about my own journey through three different 'pioneering' situations and, in particular, about a move in 2013 partly to reduce my academic work and re-enter the world of practice in a paid, ministry role. Within my discipline of practical theology, the common shorthand for our work is theological reflection on practice. This suggests that we will normally be looking back at past experience. However, Elaine Graham's key book *Transforming Practice* (2002) also asserts an important role for the forward look in practical theology. The practice of reflection is not just about introspection, it is about future prospects. Reflective practice is for the sake of prospective practice. Mission is often said to be the mother of theology, but reflexive theology also has its broody moments and properly so as it looks for transformation and renewal.

In my case, I had already written up a fair number of reflections in my book, *Remixing The Church* (2011), in which I looked back on two decades of involvement in alternative worship/emerging church practice and conversation. I have been encouraged by how that book was received across the theological spectrum. What has been less encouraging has been the coolness in my own denomination, and in Scotland more generally, towards what we now tend to call fresh expressions or mission-shaped church. The Church of England and Methodist Church in the UK (joined more recently by my former denomination, the United Reformed Church) have seen a permission-giving moment, substantial investment in creating hundreds of new congregational initiatives, new (Pioneer) ordination pathways and training initiatives and the passing of enabling provisions within canon law, but the Church of Scotland has been much cooler about the same themes. Writing in early 2014, arguably the permission-giving has still not happened, there have been too few new initiatives on the ground, there is no equivalent to pioneer ministry and no Bishop's Mission Order type provision to address the legal problems of intrusion.[1] A formal connection to Fresh Expressions was developed in late 2013, but it is seen by many as still having a lot to do in order to prove its worth. It is the object of as much scepticism as hope.

The prospect of pioneering involves a forward look. In my 2011 analysis, I described a hermeneutical spiral, beginning with auditing, moving through retrieval, unbundling and supplementing, ending in *remixing*.[2] Here I want to share some reflections and projections related to the project of remixing that I have just become involved in and to explore some of the challenges it presents.

The politics of pioneering

Our family moved back to Glasgow in January 2006. Since 2009, after an inspirational sabbatical among Canadian Mennonites, we have been part of a small, intentional but low-key community. Just a few households, a mix of couples with kids and singles, we chose to move close to one another in the same area of Glasgow. Some of that time we have lived in shared houses, although that was never central to our aims. We have met each Wednesday night for food and, until small children came along, for regular worship. Since 2011, we have had a community fund, which we pay into monthly. There are no designated leaders and no formal criteria for membership. Our key values are faith, art, justice and community.

Over the years it has been clear that, for some of us, becoming involved in a new church plant was part of the project. We kept the two ideas of community and church separate – the church plant was to be taken forward by a coalition of the willing. One factor, which has sometimes been controversial, is that as a Church of Scotland minister I was clear that I wanted to do this within the Kirk and with its blessing. That meant respecting parish boundaries and rules about intrusion.

It is fair to say that other folk in the community were much less bothered about working within Presbyterian structures. They have borne with it because of me. They were more anarchic, more willing to work independently – and, above all, less persuaded about 'membership' of an institution. Until this year we have had four years of frustration; something for which I take a good deal of responsibility. I was convinced that we could persuade the local parish and presbytery to take us on and make room for us. I wasn't a young buck any more, I was the Principal of Trinity College, I was on the Church's Emerging Ministries Group, I wrote reports for the Church. 'Trust me, I'll fix this for us.' And I couldn't. We couldn't make it work in our home parish.

Approaching the then parish minister with an offer of working alongside the parish church, we had a core team that was full of gifted folk: two ordained ministers, a trainee doctor and two psychologists, a teacher working full time for Christian Aid, community workers, artists and musicians. We were a threat because we wanted to plant rather than assimilate. I was described by the local minister as a big beast, with the implication that we had tanks on his lawn, despite our having approached him in the most supportive of terms. After two years of negotiations – and begging to be allowed to take over one of the scruffiest redundant church halls you have ever seen – we got nowhere. Without the patronage of a parish minister we were basically stymied. There was no equivalent of a Bishop's Mission Order for us to turn to.

I had reassured people that the Church would come through for us, I had asked them to be patient; it was a big disappointment. To cut a long story short, after being knocked back for one other city-centre project, from this autumn, I have just gone back into the system and become the locum minister one day a week for a neighbouring congregation, which had been in decline for

30 years. The deal I struck with them was this: evolution in the morning, revolution in the evening. Continuity in the morning, pioneering in the evening; nurturing the existing congregation in the morning, planting a new one in the evening.

Our experience has been a salutary reminder to me of the importance and the difficulty of negotiating power and obtaining permission, when pioneers seek to work within the structures of an established denomination. Within the Church of England, the publication of *Mission-Shaped Church* and Rowan Williams' subsequent public support for a 'mixed economy' vision of the Church's future have regularly been described as 'permission-giving moments'. Future research might benefit from exploring how far such moments are necessary and how they are constituted. For those of us outside the Church of England, the examples of pioneer ministry and the Bishop's Mission Order seem like crucial institutional instruments to move beyond the confines of existing arrangements. Research to evaluate their effectiveness will be important in coming years. From the other side of the fence, there is a research agenda around the whole question of 'joining' churches and committing to institutions. It has become commonplace to observe that we are in an anti-institutional era, but there is still a need to unpack the why and how of that. My own hunch (and research projects often begin with a hunch) is that, on the whole, emerging church groups/fresh expressions have been more enthusiastic about communion than about baptism, confirmation or membership. The open and hospitable table hosted by the Christ who eats with tax-collectors and sinners has been an easier sell within contemporary culture than practices that draw lines, identify thresholds and create 'others' who are not yet fully part of the body.

In a way that parallels the early influence of the charismatic renewal of the 1960s and 1970s, much of the most creative leadership of 'missional' initiatives in the past two decades has been coming from non-ordained women and men. Research is needed into whether and how those leaders and pioneers make or resist moves towards ordination and why. My own experience has been that a growing commitment to ecumenism and a waning enthusiasm for 'independency'[3] has seen me view my own role as an ordained minister in terms of being a broker, mediator, human shield, bridgehead between a more restless, post-denominational laity and the denominations I have worked within (URC and Church of Scotland). At times I have found that very uncomfortable. Certainly in my own denomination, it still feels hard to create spaces to incubate the new without first being a steward of the inherited and traditional. This takes us back to power, permission and resourcing. It also limits the spaces on offer to do the new thing. If the traditional pattern of Sunday morning worship has to be protected and resourced, then a new initiative will have to find another non-competing slot and a pioneer may have to support and enable both old and new forms.

Serial pioneering

The second thing I want to reflect on is being in a situation of what could be called serial pioneering. I notice that the London-based alternative congregation Grace has just had its twentieth birthday. Jonny Baker, one of its early members, has done well at living out the old monastic practice of taking a vow of stability. I have been a more unstable character.

The work to establish a new congregation that I am involved with now is the third such project I have been involved in over the last 20 years, beginning with the Late, Late Service (established as an independent congregation in Glasgow in the early 1990s), then setting up Host in Hackney (the newly planted evening congregation of a URC church in Hackney, East London, in the late 1990s). When our family moved back to Glasgow in 2005, my wife and I agreed we wanted to join something already there and not get involved in another start-up. We have been part of a church in Glasgow for the past seven years, but somehow we found ourselves in a part of town where the choices were between traditional and liberal forms of church which were struggling and declining and a few conservative evangelical churches, of either the traditional or the charismatic kind.

Over time, I felt the pull of the kind of projects that we had been part of before to be still as strong as ever. We often spoke of four strands: faith, art, justice, community. It was a mix of things which all felt both obvious and essential and yet which felt hard to find in the church landscape we were living in. I was conscious of a familiar tension returning. On the one hand there were conservative evangelical churches which could bring people to faith in Christ and cement strong bonds of fellowship, but could not seem to embrace the political or the artistic. On the other, there were more liberal churches which got the arts and politics, but did not have the missional imagination or the belief that they could grow and were often resigned to a future of decline.

As I reflected on the experience of the Church of Scotland, the Church in Scotland and the local churches around me, I realized that I retained a strong conviction about the need to plant new congregations alongside the old. I often hear rallying calls within the churches, which say that we are not just in the business of managing decline. I sympathize with that, although if we are declining (and most Church of Scotland congregations are) then, for pastoral reasons, that has to be managed. The difficult thing is that we have to work within a changing system where, to use economic metaphors, we need a balance of ecclesial austerity and missional Keynesianism. Developing new alongside old is something the institutional church is struggling to get its collective head round. The legacy of Victorian church planting is a difficult one for Scotland. Divisions within Presbyterianism in the nineteenth century led to waves of competitive church planting, with rival denominations vying for prestigious locations in towns and cities.[4] Churches were planted very close together, sometimes even across the street from one another. Not only that, the perceptions of church planners/planters within Victorian and Edwardian Scotland about ideal locations for church buildings reflected cities that were inhabited differently at that time than they are today. A vision for mission and the future of the Church in Scotland/ UK will have to combine hopes for re-growing congregations on traditional sites with new initiatives that are positioned differently within the communities of which they are part. For the Church of England and the Church of Scotland, mapping this on to their parish structures is proving a challenging task. The parish system has many virtues and I do not believe the commitment to reach out in mission and service to a particular geographical area should be consigned to the past. However, given the complex ecology of twenty-first-century living, with new flows and networks, we need pathways for mission that supplement these older 'domains'. So long as structures of governance, resourcing and permission are tied tightly to parish structures, those interested in new ways of working are going to struggle. The instincts of Bishop's Mission Orders, to allow supplementary patterns of working that are authorized and overseen at a wider geographical level of the diocese (in Scotland the parallel is the Presbytery), seem to me to be exactly right. The mixed ecology of our towns and cities calls not only for a mixed economy but also a *mixed polity*, which does not sweep away the parish system but supplements it.

These conclusions, judgements and instincts about the future of churches and of mission have been explored by a wide range of commentators in the past two decades within the UK. They were given their most strategic and influential early articulation in the Church of England's *Mission-Shaped Church* report and are still being developed and refined across denominations, mission agencies and academic centres.

A mixed economy of response, unless it is profoundly out of step with both the Spirit and the institutional church, will be accompanied by a mixed economy of vocation, as denominations, dioceses/presbyteries/districts/synods, congregations and individuals respond to the varieties of ministry needed by the mixed economy.

I am learning to live with my own unease about being something of a serial pioneer and trying to see it positively as an attempt to understand my own calling. I have never been a 'career-minded' minister in the sense of wanting to move on to bigger and better things. I do not claim any virtue for this. I have always been more excited about the possibility of starting something new than running something big. I don't mind the idea of starting small or of working at the edge. I like the freedom you get at the margins. In

2013 I found myself both turning 50 and involved in another new initiative; trying to figure out how to approach planning and practice in another new context. In the low moments, I get worried that I am just an old guy stuck in the past and unwilling to let go of my old-school vision. Am I deluding myself that a new generation of younger people or even my own generation of church deserters are still hungry for the vision of church I am still hungry for? The academic and the personal agendas are morphing into each other and mapping on to each other.

Theologies of 'call', and the practices associated with them of ministerial selection and authorization, represent key areas where the institutional and the personal intersect. They also represent areas where it can be difficult for the institutional and the personal to keep pace with each other. Pioneers are often people who sense a new calling and explore it before the institutional church knows how to test it, approve it or endorse it. What happens if I feel called to a ministry my own denomination does not seem to recognize, or to be able to equip me for or to be ready to ordain me to? It seems likely we will need to develop research and reflection into how denominations like the Church of England, Church of Scotland, Methodist Church and so on have responded to the mixed economy in terms of recognizing and responding to vocations.

In missiological and ecclesiological terms, we may need to return to theological questions around innovation. The writers Alan Hirsch and Michael Frost have been influential in emphasizing the importance of recovering the apostolic, but this is not entirely straightforward.[5] Inhibitions about resorting to the apostolic may be linked both to its cavalier overuse and sometimes self-important use within charismatic evangelical circles as well as to the weight of its having often been reserved historically for founding and authorizing ministries within the life of the Church catholic.[6] On the other hand, the frequent resort to the language of *entrepreneur* among some who are supportive of emerging/ fresh expressions/pioneering leaves me uncomfortable about its embrace of a term soaked in an individualistic vision of market capitalism. Perhaps the language of *pioneering* bridges the gap, but all of these 'ministry' terms need to be tested theologically and asked about how they dock with our ecclesiology as well as what effect they have on the perennial problems involved in thinking lay–clergy categories.

Worship and mission

Fatal attraction?

My third reflection is about the relationship between worship and mission. In preparing for the conference where a first version of this chapter was shared, I realized there was a confession I had to make. I had listened for years to powerful and challenging calls to move away from an attractional vision of church, but my missional instincts are still very attractional. Maybe fatally so. This was something that I had become very aware of in relation to the prospect of a new ministry in 2013.

I will try to unpack what I mean by that. For a start, I remain fairly attached to church buildings. I find their oddity and their set-apartness missionally useful, especially when they are architecturally beautiful, but not only when that is the case. I like the aesthetic scale and the physical space of a non-domestic 'community building' that a larger number of people can gather in. I don't relish a world of café churches and messy churches, or praise gatherings in hi-tech warehouses or seeker-friendly services in converted cinemas. One major reason for that is that I also seem to be drawn, when I am thinking with others about planning and planting a new congregation, to start with worship. Some of this I freely admit is my own stuff. I carry a restless longing to create a worshipping community that feels like home to me and that might become a hospitable home for others. I have struggled over the years to find that.

I have also long struggled with the idea, painfully common within evangelicalism from the mid-nineteenth century onwards, that missional practice should take a purely pragmatic approach to issues of culture and aesthetics. This seems to me to lack integrity and to encourage a lack of integrity among disciples and also fatally to misunderstand the ways in which the medium is always part of the message (Gay, 2011). At a personal level, while I can put up with a lot out of love for the Church, if I give up on a vision of aesthetic and cultural integrity in worship, of what I recognize as authentic practice, then I fear for my own heart and soul and, with that, for my own ability to witness to anyone else.

Peter Neilson is a Church of Scotland minister who has been a wise and patient mentor to many of us in Scotland: a kind of unofficial Presbyterian flying bishop for folk working in emerging and pioneer contexts. I remember him saying to me several decades ago that a church plant could start with worship or with evangelism or with pastoral care or with prophetic action. In a way it didn't matter, he said, as long as it got round, in time, to growing into the rest, to covering the other three bases.

That I have always tended to start with worship may reflect something of a Field of Dreams mentality – 'if you build it they will come'. It does not mean that I do not see the crucial importance of those other areas. It does mean that I recognize where some of my own strengths and limitations may lie and that I have an acute sense of the need within any church plant for a variety of complementary ministries and a variety of women and men to share and lead in them.

In my thinking, worship is always understood as a centring point for any new expression of church, the place where the gathering pull of ecclesia and the sending impulse of mission are felt and known. Lesslie Newbigin used to say that you could define the centre of the kingdom, but not its edges. In worship, we pray again and again: Jesus be the centre, triune God be the centre.

A key research question is how far, contra Hirsch and Frost, pioneers can embrace a continuing vision of the attractional power of the church's life and worship. Do pioneers often gravitate to one pole or another of a church's life and give it priority in the establishment of something new? Are these largely personality-driven decisions on the part of leaders? Do pioneers tend to be one-trick ponies, who get stuck with one model and try to replicate it regardless of context, or is this about individual calling and gifting along with appropriate contextualization?

Is Peter Neilson's insight an important one for church planting – start with any of these four dimensions to the fore and grow into the other three? If we do more research into these areas, how could this lead to transforming practice, without creating a falsely mechanistic approach? How do pioneers protect authenticity against a reductive pragmatism? What helps us to guard against the dangers of an instrumentalist view of art and culture as they work to attract or reach people outside the Church?

Fresh adaptation?

In the final part of this chapter I want to ask you to humour me, to allow me to develop my attractional model and to allow me to start with worship. The questions I have been wrestling with recently as I moved from reflective into prospective mode were about how to structure this new thing, this next thing. It is notable, I think, that these types of question, as questions about the 'design' and the 'style' of a new initiative, have been common preoccupations of alternative worship and emerging church groups. Aside from critical concerns being raised about whether this kind of thing was evidence of superficiality or of an obsession with creating cool church, my sense is that we have not done enough reflection on why the redesign, the restyling of certain features of church were so important to my generation of 'pioneers' and to some of the new/next generations.[7] It may of course be that we are less different from previous generations than we imagine. The aesthetic shifts of a Zwingli or a Pugin were also key features of their 'ecclesiological' projects.

Planning for a new project prompted me to reflect on other examples of what we could call the ecology of worship. With a nod to Calvin's Genevan habits, conservative evangelicals in the Kirk worked with a pattern of two Sunday services of conservative expository preaching and a Wednesday-night prayer meeting. The patterns of praying certain prayers at key times of the day and night developed by monastic traditions were not handed down on tablets of stone. They were created by human beings to reflect particular understandings and serve particular needs. The weekly rhythm of night prayers in Iona Abbey when I first went there was Sunday: Communion; Monday: Peace and Justice; Tuesday: Healing Service; Wednesday: Communion; Thursday: Act of Commitment. All of these very different examples time were once new. All were contextual.

In the autumn of 2013, a few of us worked on a new pattern for monthly worship. What we came up with represented an attempt to discern how we could evolve an ecology of worship services that reflected our sense of the missional context we were working in.

This new pattern is scarcely in place. It is unproven. It is not based on research into what works. It is the product of a much rougher matching of what we are doing in worship to a set of theological, missional and pastoral instincts. I probably struggle as much with the idea of anyone calling themselves prophetic as apostolic, but we can all seek to hear the call to become a prophetic community – to have a word and a way for our time.

The new congregation we are trying to plant on Sunday nights is working with a cycle of four services. It is based in a middle-class parish, very near the university, with a lot of students, professionals and people working in arts and media living within the parish bounds. We have chosen to work with four themes: peacetime, healthservice, commontable, still life. The themes are an attempt to contextualize the shape and focus of our worship services in relation to four key features of a Scottish society that is undergoing rapid secularization.[8]

Peacetime is a response to a widespread withdrawal from and objection to religion in Scotland because it is seen to be a source and cause of conflict and division; both sectarian conflict in Scotland and Ireland and terrorism and war internationally. In recent years several factors have shaped my thinking about a response to this, including our own family's involvement with Mennonite traditions and churches and the influence of Stanley Hauerwas and Sam Wells on my theology. This has led me to a growing understanding of the importance of discipleship as formation in peacemaking. Could we take as one of the basic components of a new worship ecology a service in which we take time to pray for peace and justice and to which we bring a commitment to learn skills and practices linked to non-violence and mediation?

Healthservice is a response to the conflicted and confusing sense many people have of how to relate suffering and pain to the existence of a good and loving God. While strong in every age, in a secularizing age, reactions to 'the problem of pain' have a particular poignancy and ambivalence to them. Suffering can pull believers towards doubt and doubters towards belief. For months before we started out, I brooded on a Sam Wells remark about our not talking enough about physical illness and health in church, alongside a Giles Fraser *Guardian* column about churches as (rare) places where together we are (sometimes) able to hold one another's pain and distress. Henri Nouwen's classic thinking about wounded healers finds powerful expression in the Healing Liturgy of the Iona Community, with its simple somatic solidarity shown in laying on of hands. Could we set within our basic pattern a service in which we practised this and explored some dimension of health, while negotiating the over-believing of power-evangelicalism and the under-believing of insipid liberalism? Could this somehow be missional?

Commontable is a communion service set in the context of a shared meal, with no written liturgy. Developed from earlier Maundy Thursday experiments at St Luke's Anglican church in Holloway and Clapton Park URC church in Hackney, it stages a proper meal and enriches and disrupts it with storytelling. Returning to the reality of a shared supper is a response to increasing social isolation, to a city in which more people live in smaller households and more people eat alone. In our context, the presence of a more classic Scoto-Catholic[9] morning communion liturgy each month disperses the burden of liturgical expectation. The final story is what Presbyterians sometimes call the warrant: 'on the night he was betrayed our Lord took bread ...'. We are right to be wary when stressing the 'therapeutic' dimensions of the gospel; that we might lose the sense of Jesus at the centre. Communion resists that. It remembers Christ's death and resurrection. It sets his story at the centre of our stories. Could this be a meal others might want to come to? Could they share the first food and stories, even if they held back from the final story and the final eating and drinking? Could they get a taste for the goodness of the Lord?

Still life for me represents a continuing thread reaching back to the early days of alternative worship. It is a therapeutic response to the wordiness of Presbyterianism and to its lack of space and time for visual media. But 25 years later, it also promises a response to media overload, to the tyranny of social media and the ubiquity of mobiles. So this is a service in which we are learning the practices of silence, alongside single or slow images or installations. We are teaching ourselves to be silent and to be attentive as a way of waiting on God. We are learning to breathe and to wait and see. It marks out a new space into which we can invite visual artists to curate different services throughout the year. Could something so simple still be attractive/attractional?

If that is our prospective practice, our attempt to think out a new ecology of worship, we are already aware of its imperfections and lacks. The presence of associated morning church provides a diet of preaching and children's liturgy which this pattern lacks. Another potentially large lack is a more obviously ecstatic/celebratory format.

Research might choose to probe ancient–future comparisons between different liturgical ecologies. It might draw on missiological thinking to reflect on how worship is appropriately contextualized. It might reflect on the size and scale of the contexts we respond to and think which variables might drive liturgical differences. It might ask about the danger of 'liturgical miserabilism' and the advantages of a more upbeat and celebratory pattern. It might explore that alternative worship/emerging/pioneer chestnut of how to balance creativity and sustainability. It might reflect on how long to maintain a single pattern: should liturgical time always be slow or does that only work when the fine filters of tradition have already done their work?

Conclusion

This chapter deliberately raises a lot of questions as it considers prospective/pioneering practice. I often think of a prayer of the Iona Community which asks God that we will find 'new ways to touch the hearts of all'.

One of the burdens of the alternative worship/emerging church era was that in making its 1990s post-charismatic moves, in reaction to the banality of some praise and worship cultures within the churches, it left itself unsure of how or what to sing. Some groups and congregations simply fell silent. The possibilities of dance music and dance within worship were fewer than was supposed at the beginning. Had we created worship for critics or even cynics? So my final research questions focus on the prospect of what to sing this Sunday in worship. How can we keep from singing? There won't be one, but if there were to be a pioneer hymnal, what would be in it? And why? What kind of affective spirituality will pioneer congregations be able to live with? Could there be expressive practices that will touch not just our hearts but the hearts of those we hope will come into our pioneer churches, our alternative congregations and fresh expressions? One we have been trying out, with our few, mixed voices, is the Lightnin' Hopkins song 'Now is the needed time'. Our reflective practice aims at transforming practice. The goal of our research is to feed our prospective practice. Right now is the needed time.

References

Frost, M. and A. Hirsch, 2003, *The Shaping of Things to Come*, Peabody, MA: Hendrickson.

Gay, D., 2011, *Remixing the Church*, London: SCM Press.

Graham, E., 2002, *Transforming Practice: Pastoral Theology in an Age of Uncertainty*, Eugene, OR: Cascade.

Hirsch, A., 2009, *The Forgotten Ways*, Grand Rapids, MI: Brazos.

Moltmann, J., 1977, *The Church in the Power of the Spirit*, London: SCM Press.

Wright, N. T. and D. Stancliffe, 2008, in J. Rigney (ed.), *Women as Bishops*, London: Mowbray.

Notes

1 Intrusion is the term used to describe initiatives that might undercut the prerogative of a parish minister in Scotland in respect of the work of their own denomination within the bounds of their parish, e.g. planting a new congregation.

2 As with most hermeneutical circles/spirals, the process should be thought of as ongoing – remixing gives way to a fresh audit of practice, and so on.

3 That is, the evangelical habit of simply establishing a new, free-standing congregation with little or no authorization or recognition from other parts of the Church catholic.

4 In England and Wales there are some parallels with the nineteenth century rise of Methodism and Congregationalism, where there were strong currents of ecclesial competition running.

5 See both Frost and Hirsch (2003) and Hirsch (2009).

6 Jürgen Moltmann suggests in *The Church in the Power of the Spirit* (1977, pp. 312ff.) that as well as thinking about apostolic succession, we need to think in a more open-ended way about apostolic *procession* – the Church is able to take on new forms as it looks to the future and participates in the *missio Dei*, the mission of God. For an interesting appropriation of this term within ecumenical dialogue (in the context of debates around women becoming bishops), see the response to Walter Kasper's June 2006 paper to the Church of England's House of Bishops, written by N. T. Wright and David Stancliffe (2008).

7 Here I am following the assumption that in today's culture a generation is simultaneously longer and shorter, that is, rapid change means that we should perhaps think in terms of ten-year generations; but it also means that those less tied to the past have more capacity to keep reinvesting in new projects which then have an intergenerational dimension to them. The examples include Hendrix, Led Zeppelin and The Stones – Jagger at 70 represents a pop generation whose tastes can in some broader senses stay young, even while they may lose awareness of decadal differentiation.

8 In the recently released census results, this Glasgow West End parish rates one of the most secular in Scotland.

9 Common descriptor for High Church Presbyterians within the Kirk.

4

Transformation: A 'How To' Guide

ANNA RUDDICK

'It's like making an egg.'
'Like making an egg?'
'Yeah.'
'What do you mean?'
'Cos you watch it go from just the white and the yolk into an actually fully formed egg.'
'Ok?'
'You watch it transform.'
'Oh like boiled do you mean and harden?'
'Yeah.'

These are the words of a qualitative research conversation between myself and 19-year-old Susie from East Manchester in answer to the question 'What is transformation?' Susie's response demonstrates the slippery nature of transformation as a category. This conversation forms part of a programme of research into perceptions of transformation in urban communities focused on the work of the Eden Network,[1] which has been my sphere of professional practice for the last eight years. In this chapter I introduce some reflections emerging from my experience and research and ask key questions about the language and nature of transformation.

I argue that transformation requires a combination of a supportive environment of anticipation, contrasting experiences and affirmed identity. Furthermore I argue that achieving these core conditions requires paying attention to the 'how' of ministry, developing an ordinary methodology that can enable the core conditions for change. These conclusions have arisen from my doctoral research among the urban communities of the Eden Network and I will begin by introducing my research before discussing the discourse of transformation and allowing the voices of my research participants to illuminate it further. I will then introduce my proposal for an ordinary methodology and offer some initial methodological hunches on 'how' we can best create the conditions for transformation.

Perceptions of transformation in urban communities

The Eden Network is a family of missional communities born out of the schools work of The Message Trust.[2] In partnership with local churches or church planters, the Eden Network recruits teams of Christians to move into Britain's 10 per cent most deprived communities, to live there long term as salt and light. The Network began in Greater Manchester in 1997 and since 2008 has developed teams across the country focusing on regions of concentrated deprivation. There are currently 20 Eden teams nationally, in Greater Manchester, Yorkshire, the North East, Humber and London.

In addition to working for Eden, most recently as Director of the Eden Associates scheme,[3] I also live within an Eden community, Openshaw in East Manchester, and have done so for seven years, becoming a participant observer and experiencing first hand some of the complications of being an incomer into an urban community. My doctoral research has arisen from my work supporting Eden team members, alongside my own experiences of urban life and ministry, and is summarized in the following research question:

> How is Eden Network's distinctive approach to urban ministry perceived to be transformative by participants in the Eden Network (both team members and community members); and do these perceptions embody a scriptural model of salvation and discipleship?

To answer this question I have used a purposive sampling strategy to conduct 16 qualitative, semi-structured interviews with a combination of Eden team members and urban community members who have encountered Eden teams in their neighbourhoods. It is beyond the scope of this chapter to fully develop the results of this research, but I intend to offer some initial reflections, beginning with an exploration of the concept and discourse of transformation within the Eden Network.

A discourse of transformation

The research data indicates issues relating the language of transformation to the narrative of the Eden Network and the wider Christian tradition. Community member participants in general comfortably used the language of transformation to describe positive changes they had identified in their lives and in others. For them, transformation is perceived as an abstract concept – 'it changes something within yourself' – whereas Eden team members, for whom transformation language is central in articulating their expectations for ministry, consider it to be our surrender to God's activity – 'how God would take you and mould you into the person that he really wants you to be'. However, when community members were asked whether they felt God was involved, all responded positively to some degree even if all they could claim was 'I'd like to think he was'. The ease with which community members talked about transformation contrasts strongly with their struggle to find a connection with the more conventional Christian language of salvation: 'Salvation Army! This is just what's in my head.' The introduction of discipleship language unlocked the extent to which the language of community members had been shaped by Eden teams: 'I've done a lot with Eden discipleship groups … I think the discipleship is the journey, the following God.' There is evidence too that Eden team members have had their own theological language challenged. One participant, when asked about salvation, replied: 'I can't believe that God's a God who just does one mould fits all because that would just be impossible, and that would be terrible to think that as well ... it's much more about relationship.'

The choice of language of my research participants and their responses as I asked them specifically about transformation, salvation and discipleship has been important in this project. The data indicates that transformation is a more compelling discourse, accessible and familiar to community members, than traditional Christian categories for change, suggesting the need for some investigation into the discourse of transformation within the Eden Network and its influences in the wider Christian tradition. The Eden Network began in 1997 as a response of The Message Trust to the success of a week of schools' mission in Wythenshawe, a large estate in South Manchester. Young people were gathered to a small local congregation; however, it became apparent that the challenges of their estate context meant that, for these young people to develop their own Christian faith, a new approach to ministry would be required. In response, a team recruited by The Message Trust relocated into Wythenshawe with the intention of remaining long term to reach out to the young people and families living around them.

The Message Trust is a charismatic evangelical organization focused on the gifting of the evangelist, primarily that of its founder and CEO Andy Hawthorne. Evangelical commitments to conversion and activism are expressed in the language of 'words and deeds evangelism', which shaped the early years of The Message Trust's work, alongside an entrepreneurial spirit, inspiring concerts seeking to present the gospel relevantly to teenagers across Manchester using hip hop and dance music.

Into this context came the influence of an international movement within Pentecostalism and charismatic evangelicalism, the 'Transformation' films. Created and distributed by Ed Silvoso, these recaptured the revival spirit of early evangelicalism, depicting the movement of God in mass salvation and the miraculous across the world. Ed Silvoso was influenced by the church growth movement spearheaded by Peter Wagner, and during the 1990s travelled the world encouraging church leaders and congregations to unite in prayer and evangelism to 'take their cities for God'

(Silvoso, 1994, p. 15). He advocated a strategy of united prayer and local community evangelism by lay Christians, combined with larger 'crusades' (Silvoso, 1994, p. 270).

Inspired by Ed Silvoso's visit to Manchester in the mid-1990s, the language of transformation was established in The Message's culture, with strong associations with mass salvation, revival and structural transformation. Into this context the first Eden team was launched in 1997, inspired by the words of Isaiah 43.19–21:

> See, I am doing a new thing! Now it springs up; do you not perceive it? I am making a way in the wilderness and streams in the wasteland. The wild animals honour me, the jackals and the owls, because I provide water in the wilderness and streams in the wasteland, to give drink to my people, my chosen, the people I formed for myself that they may proclaim my praise.

The wastelands of Manchester's estates were to become streams and the wild animals, Manchester's teenagers, were to proclaim praise.

Eden Network has used the strapline 'Transforming communities from the inside out' for the last five years, and this language remains at the core of Eden's hope. In an earlier article I reflected on the 'transformation' undergone by Eden team members and the Eden Network itself as the rhetoric of mission encountered the faces and places of urban young people. Contrasting an early emphasis on mass salvation with team members' current reflections, I wrote: 'The hope for transformed lives in which belonging, faithful practice and gratitude are expressed in the ordinary, has become the prophetic expectation of Eden teams' (Thompson, 2012, p. 54). Matt Wilson, former National Director of Eden Network, articulates this more nuanced understanding when he describes transformation as 'rather like percolation – there's a lot of coughing and spluttering before anything good appears' (Wilson, 2012, p. 132). In his book *Concrete Faith* he devotes a chapter to 'Trans-formation', unpacking the necessity of formation in ourselves as urban practitioners in the transformation of those we seek to come alongside.

This change has been brought about not only by the challenge of practice but also by the influence of alternative discourses of transformation. Arguably the most significant influence has come from liberation theology. I suggest that movements such as Eden are part of the worldwide legacy of liberation theologians who put God's concern for the poor front and centre. For Eden, however, there were specific lessons to learn. Paulo Freire articulates transformation in pedagogical terms: people are changed when they are enabled to perceive their oppressed situation and to believe that they hold the power to act to overthrow it. Two important connecting points are evident here with the evolution of Eden and my research: first, Freire's commitment to a pedagogy formed 'with not for the oppressed' (Freire, 1996, p. 30), which is expressed in the language of Eden teams as to/for/with, meaning that teams learn to avoid doing things *to* people, even to avoid the temptation of doing things *for* people, but to do things *with* people in their communities; second, Freire's methodology of conscientizing by re-presenting a world-view to people as a problem (Freire, 1996, p. 90). The research data, as I will show, demonstrates the importance of a challenge to perspective in transformation. Eden team members are, as they settle into an urban community, themselves a re-presentation of the world-view of that community, and by their difference they problematize it.

A second discourse of transformation that has influenced the Network has been that of David Bosch, who understands transformation as the work of the *missio Dei*, God acting in the world by his dynamic Spirit (Bosch, 2011, p. 401). Eden's early discourse of entering in to transform has been replaced by joining in with God's activity. Wilson writes: 'as [Eden team members] have followed Jesus in this way thousands of lives have been touched and transformed' (Wilson, 2012, p. 26).

A final influence has been the prevalence of transformation discourse within government regeneration rhetoric throughout the last decade. The hope for Christian change held by Eden, salvation and discipleship, was confronted in practice by vast social and systemic problems. Salvation took on a here-and-now urgency and discipleship a new holism. As teams began to engage with systemic issues in their communities – health, education, addiction, housing – they needed a discourse that could enable the Local Strategic Partnerships and New Deal committees to understand their aims and enter into partnership. Transformation fits the bill, representing the desire for individual change encompassed by holistic salvation, and community change in the systemic 'kingdom coming'.

This exploration demonstrates that 'transformation' is a *pragmatic* discourse, positive, easy to use and flexible. The commitment to activism and experience in evangelicalism and liberation theologies, and The Message Trust as a fruit of these, results in an entrepreneurial pragmatism, a 'whatever it takes' approach. Swinton and Pattison argue in relation to spirituality discourse that language can have meaning in terms of its functionality: 'thin, vague and useful' remains valid (Pattison and Swinton, 2010, p. 226). Transformation discourse has been expansive and generous to accommodate Eden's theological diversity as an ecumenical network, the need for an acceptable face to government and community agencies and the theological shifts of team members in response to their practice.

Conceptualizing transformation

To conceptualize transformation in the context of my research I began with the Eden Network discourse outlined above and have set it alongside the work of Raymond Paloutzian writing in the field of the psychology of religion. Paloutzian uses the language of transformation to articulate the scope of religious change. He writes: 'a spiritual transformation constitutes a change in the meaning system that a person holds as a basis for self definition, the interpretation of life, and overarching purposes and ultimate concerns' (Paloutzian, 2005, p. 334). For Paloutzian, conversion is a subcategory within the larger picture of spiritual transformation (Paloutzian, 2005, p. 333) and this is borne out in my data, for example in community member Paul's thoughts about conversion:

I don't wanna take that path, I'm happy doing what I'm doing by helping people along with these but stay as how I am, I don't want to transform that way. But they have transformed me, you know being an adult more and respect more people that's how they have changed me but they won't change me that way, I don't know, I don't think it'd suit me that way.

Paloutzian's definition of spiritual transformation illuminates Paul's explanation of his personal change. It acknowledges the profound changes to his meaning system that he describes as 'being an adult more' and 'respect more people' but also allows for his decision not to convert to Christianity. Paul is an example of the complex interplay between faith and change in urban communities. He described his regular church attendance, volunteering and interest in the Bible. He also describes his sense that

God's probably that one rung ahead of me, you know until actually something happens and I meet up with him. Yeah and until that day, I'm always going to be one behind him, and I won't find it until that happens.

In the light of this complexity I suggest that transformation discourse equips those in urban communities to articulate their own change. It also equips us theologically to engage with contextual conceptions of salvation and discipleship. It is liminal language, mediating language, with a flexibility and fluidity that enables us to fill and refill more traditional theological language of salvation, discipleship and sanctification.

Having traced the transformation discourse in the practice of the Eden Network and proposed spiritual transformation according to Paloutzian as a change in one's meaning system which underpins self-definition, I will now use three of the voices of my participants to highlight three core conditions for transformation emerging from my research.

Core condition 1: A supportive environment of anticipation

Susie explains it like this:

> I think more having the support, and the support of people saying 'look you can do it, you can do this you can do that if you put your mind to it' cos at home my dad was, well a lot of the time he was in the pub so I didn't have the support at home, so I end up getting it from the Eden team ...
>
> It made me realize that people had faith in me to do things. That they can say actually 'oh look you are old enough and you can do it' and having the support saying 'look we trust you to do this' it changed my thought on the way adults were cos I only got used to my dad saying 'yeah do it if you want to' I actually got trusted with a responsibility that I needed to do within a set time, so it taught me how to keep into time limits so ... it boosted my self confidence quite a lot. Then I started caring about how I was dressed, how my hair was then people started noticing that I was a person so I weren't getting bullied as much ... so offered me the security and safety net that I needed.

The thread of personal change runs throughout Christian theology, particularly in the evangelical tradition where conversion and sanctification are defining elements of Christian faith (Bebbington, 1989, p. 5). Along with the expectation of change comes a language of change within Scripture, liturgy and culture, so my research highlights the importance of this language and the anticipation it perpetuates in creating the environment for change. However, Susie and others demonstrate that this anticipation requires an environment of supportive relationships that provides a safe context in which change can happen. As Charles Gerkin describes, the Christian community can be a 'living community of faith and care' in which a person can be 'nested' (1997, p. 100).

Core condition 2: A confrontation of the familiar with the new

Clare described her first experiences of coming to church:

> I think it was the people who went there as well, it wasn't like
> the people you'd normally meet d'y'know what I mean, they
> thought a lot of theirselves they thought a lot of their health
> you know of each other, things like that and I think that was
> like the positive thing yeah.
> *Right, did you find yourself ...*
> Wanting to be like that, yeah, yeah, there's some, live here
> there's a lot of drugs there's a lot of all sorts and you can find
> yourself being in there ... and you have to get yourself away
> from it d'y'know what I mean but I think going to church
> helped me do that, to think this is not all of you, don't have to
> be like this to be cool, to be good. I mean I know I'm grown up
> and it shouldn't be like that but it does still y'know.

Paloutzian writes: 'Spiritual transformations, religious and otherwise, occur because people are confronted with discrepancies in
life that require them to construct a new meaning system because
the old one no longer works' (Paloutzian, 2005, p. 334). A confrontation of the familiar with the new emerged throughout
the data as a core element in enabling change. For community
members like Clare, meeting an Eden team member began a process of exposure to a different way of life which challenged their
previous experience and called into question their meaning system.
Equally, for Eden team members, transformation was effected
through contrast experiences, often the same relationships with
community members that they had hoped would enable change
in them also brought, sometimes unexpected, change in the Eden
team members themselves.

Paloutzian writes that doubt and discrepancy 'between the
"ought" and the "is" of a person's life' are the key categories
of contrast experience (Paloutzian, 2005, pp. 334–7). However,
his diagnosis is primarily negative, focusing on life experiences
that create disillusionment. I would add the possibility of positive
contrast experiences embedded in supportive relationships, which

create the same dissonance and enable the same re-evaluation of meaning systems.

Core condition 3: Some staying the same

This is articulated across the data, but Jack, a 16-year-old from Manchester, in his description of transformation, brought it to the fore:

> [I]t's kind of like as a plant grows it just grows one way but as a human grows ... yeah it broadens it's like a tree different branches on a tree and that changes it from going like a long stick or just, and it's just added so many branches on a tree that it's just made a more full person if that makes sense.
>
> ... when you think about transforming you think about transformers and how it's the same thing but it just expands or becomes smaller. And like the tree it starts off as just like a little thing and just expands so maybe it doesn't change much in particularly apart from just getting bigger and bigger and bigger and broadening itself. Erm and I think whether that's your mind, whether that's your heart, whether that's your soul, whether that's your relationships with God or something erm transformation is just not necessarily, maybe not changing completely but broadening.

Transformation *sounds* like radical, cataclysmic change, and is often expected to be so. However, the importance of staying the same evidenced in my research would suggest that this expectation is misplaced. The data concerning staying the same indicates that for transformation to be coherent and lasting an individual must have a sense of self that is positive and affirmed. Security in the core issues of identity and acceptance enables the challenge brought about by encountering the new to be embraced, and change to be integrated in such a way that the individual becomes authentically different. Transformation is not about learning to 'fit in' to a different cultural group, rather it is about renegotiating one's meaning system based on new information and allowing it to evolve, bringing about change in 'one's interpretation of life, overarching purposes and ultimate concerns' (Paloutzian, 2005, p. 334).

Through the above urban voices I have suggested that transformation requires three core conditions: a supportive environment containing an anticipation of change, the surprise and confusion of new meeting old, and the affirmation of personhood brought about by staying the same. I will now build on this by offering some reflections from my professional practice in urban ministry as to how these core conditions can be created by making use of an 'ordinary methodology'.

Ordinary methodology

Jeff Astley defines 'ordinary theology' as 'the theological beliefs and processes of believing that find expression in the God-talk of those believers who have received no scholarly theological education' (Astley, 2002, p. 1). He describes the learning process of such 'ordinary theologians' as having three stages: first, learning about religion second hand; second, embracing the faith as authentically one's own; and third, 'moving on', the self-motivated exploration of faith undertaken both corporately and independently (Astley, 2002, pp. 25–34). In the language of the Eden Network this third stage is often referred to as 'self-sustaining discipleship'.

In my use of the phrase 'ordinary methodology' I indicate a way of going about ministry activity that cultivates that 'moving on' stage of learning in relation to the full breadth of spiritual transformation. How and why become the pivotal questions that enable practitioners to make good decisions about the 'what' of urban mission.

The importance of how

Methodology describes the logic that flows through a project (Mason, 2002, p. 30). It provides the bridge between beliefs about the world, God and people, the purpose of the project and the actions undertaken in executing it. The experience of the Eden Network demonstrates that what resources are used in small groups, mentoring or other activities are less important than how they are used and why. In Eden's evolution, change has not primarily been in methods; the most fundamental changes have been in methodology, shifts in theological and sociological understanding that have challenged the Network's purpose and therefore changed the way teams go about their work.

Reflection on my research, my experience within the Eden Network and my own urban ministry has led me to conclude that how ministry is undertaken will dictate the outcome and, importantly for my research question, whether it has the potential to enable transformation. The 'how' is the shade and tone of our actions, making an invitation to an Alpha course appear patronizing or a genuine offer of friendship, a community café a place vulnerable people avoid or the one place they feel safe. I will now outline three methodological issues that relate to the core conditions for transformation. Each of these issues requires further investigation; however, I offer initial methodological 'hunches' for approaches that may enable spiritual transformation.

Overcoming dependence – ministry that creates significance not empowerment

The experience of dependence as a fact of life is widespread among marginalized communities (Green, 1997, p. 118). Above I have advocated a supportive environment with a discourse and anticipation of change as the first core condition for transformation. However, the experience of Eden teams indicates that building relationships without an awareness of the structures of dependence leads not to transformation but to 'fitting in', making it a critical methodological issue to be addressed by urban practitioners.

The response to dependence within statutory and community agencies has often been the language of 'empowerment' (Local

Government Association, 2012). However, reflection on my urban practice suggests that the concept of 'significance' provides a more robust basis for a language of anticipation that can enable transformation. There are three risks inherent in an empowerment approach that lead me to question its usefulness: first, the tendency towards individualism, emphasizing the personal journey of an increasing sense of power; second, the language of power is deeply contested, holding associations of 'power over' and placing us in a combative rather than collaborative stance towards others (Walsh, 1995, p. 57); third, I suggest that the concept of empowerment struggles in the face of the uncontrollable situations of life. By introducing people to a sense of their own power as a solution to dependence we can make them vulnerable to disillusionment when the events of life demonstrate their actual powerlessness (Paloutzian, 2005, p. 336).

I suggest that the concept of personal significance may offer a better hope and route out of dependence and towards transformation. Significance is defined by Brian Zinnbauer and Kenneth Pargament as 'a phenomenological construct that involves the experience of caring, attraction or attachment' (Zinnbauer and Pargament, 2005, p. 33). For an individual to find themselves to be significant enables an ongoing process of self-care and the ability to act.

Zinnbauer and Pargament argue that significance is a critical feature of spirituality. Therefore finding oneself to be significant in relation to God and others can be a powerful feature of growing faith (Zinnbauer and Pargament, 2005, p. 33). Significance then is corporate and inclusive; it is also collaborative rather than competitive, we can accept our own significance as children of God alongside that of others (Morisy, 2004, p. 38). It can also be resilient in the face of the uncontrollable in life. Rather than rendering us passive, significance emphasizes the importance of our responses and actions in the midst of potentially overwhelming life events. I suggest that a focus on personal significance may enable dependence to be overcome in such a way that change is authentic and sustainable.

Overcoming the 'wall in the head' – ministry that ushers in the new

The 'wall in the head' is Lynsey Hanley's phrase and in *Estates* she writes

> The wall is about not knowing what is out there, or believing that what is out there is either entirely irrelevant to your life, or so complicated that it would go right over your head if you made an attempt to understand it. (Hanley, 2007, p. 153)

Corresponding to the need for a confrontation between old and new I suggest that the 'wall in the head' consists of reinforced assumptions about one's capacity to understand the world. In order to overcome this, practitioners must first expose and surrender their own assumptions concerning the abilities of those they seek to come alongside (Green, 2009, p. 134). Practically, therefore, ministry must begin with a question addressed to God and to people: where are you? By listening first to uncover what your community already knows and to discern where God is already at work we can prevent our ministry reinforcing the 'wall in the head' (Green, 1987, p. 91).

Second, in order to overcome the 'wall in the head' we need to address the issue of complexity. The perception of theology as complicated is perpetuated by the monopoly of the academy (Green, 2009, pp. 1–7). By accepting this complexity as inherent to Christian theology we construct barriers to learning biased towards a middle-class, western epistemology. From this position attempts to contextualize Bible study and other ministry resources for urban or non-book culture can result in simplistic materials focused merely on building familiarity with biblical facts. As an alternative I suggest that we might see our understanding of Christian truth on two axes: simple to complex and superficial to deep.

An approach that seeks to enable transformation might focus on the simple and deep corner of the axes. For example, Janet Lees' 'remembering the Bible' (Lees, 2007) technique enables people with all levels of literacy to work together to discover truth for life in the Bible. This group approach involves compiling people's memories of a biblical incident to create their own version of the narrative. Through this creative process, personal interpretations and meaning emerge from the stories and everyone benefits from the shared experience. Approaches such as this may provide the resources to go beyond comprehension of biblical facts by considering empathetic resonance with biblical characters, an imaginative, experiential dimension to learning and the possibility of the Spirit speaking through all who are present.

Overcoming inaction – ministry that cultivates personhood

To cultivate personhood, the kind of sense of self that Susie described, '... then people started noticing that I was a person so I weren't getting bullied as much, and I had friends ...', ministry must be equipping in nature and the minister a facilitator. Laurie Green writes: 'I now try to distinguish clearly between what it is to have "expertise" and what it is to be an "expert". The first makes one a servant, the second a trapped status-seeker' (Green, 2009, p. 162). In practice this often means leaving gaps for others to participate. Astley defines learning as 'any enduring change brought about by experience' (2002, p. 4); without participation there can be no learning experience. Previously I have written about the experiences of Eden Fitton Hill as they sought to plant a new expression of church in their estate: 'The team began to be mentored by the kids of Fitton Hill, who showed them how Fitton Hill did life, social events and worship' (Thompson, 2010, p. 123). Making room for others not simply to receive but to bring their skills and insight cultivates personhood, providing the basis for their future action.

Transformation: a 'how to' guide

In this chapter I have explored the capacity and usefulness of the language of transformation in the urban ministry of the Eden

Network, offered the core conditions for transformation arising from my research and made some suggestions for approaches to ministry that can enable spiritual transformation. I have outlined three critical issues for urban practitioners and suggested an ordinary methodological approach to each: overcoming dependence through a focus on significance; overcoming the 'wall in the head' by ushering in the new; and overcoming inaction by cultivating personhood. I have argued that these initial hunches offer resources to create the core conditions needed for transformation.

As I have noted above, the ambiguity of transformation as a concept allows it to be contextually and functionally useful in articulating the experiences and aspirations of urban people. My research indicates that in the context of the ministry of the Eden Network transformation is the process of a change in meaning system, which both constitutes and results in a stronger love of self, a more positive approach to life choices large and small, increased ability to act and an awareness of the involvement of a good God in a person's world. The experience of ministry in urban communities suggests that by paying attention to the 'how' of our practice it is possible to enable this transformation more effectively.

References

Astley, J., 2002, *Ordinary Theology: Looking, Listening and Learning in Theology*, Aldershot: Ashgate.

Bailey, G., 2010, 'Entire Sanctification and Theological Method', in T. Greggs (ed.), *New Perspectives for Evangelical Theology*, London: Routledge, pp. 63–74.

Bebbington, D. W., 1989. *Evangelicalism in Modern Britain*, London: Unwin Hyman.

Bosch, D. J., 2011, *Transforming Mission: Paradigm Shifts in Theology of Mission*, Maryknoll, NY: Orbis Books.

Freire, P., 1996, *Pedagogy of the Oppressed*, London: Penguin.

Gerkin, C. V., 1997, *An Introduction to Pastoral Care*, Nashville, TN: Abingdon Press.

Green, L., 1987, *Power to the Powerless*, Basingstoke: Marshall Pickering.

Green, L., 1995, 'Blowing Bubbles: Poplar', in P. Sedgewick (ed.), *God in the City*, London: Mowbray, pp. 72–91.

Green, L., 1997, 'Gospel from the Underclass', in C. Rowland and J. J. Vincent (eds), *Gospel from the City*, Sheffield: Urban Theology Unit, pp. 117–25.

Green, L., 2009, *Let's Do Theology: Resources for Contextual Theology*, London: Mowbray.

Hanley, L., 2007, *Estates: An Intimate History*, London: Granta Books.

Lees, J., 2007, *Word of Mouth: Using the Remembered Bible for Building Community*, Glasgow: Wild Goose Publications.

Local Government Association, 2012, *Benefits of Investing in Community Empowerment*, available at http://www.local.gov.uk/localism-act/-/journal_content/56/10180/3510417/ARTICLE (Accessed 16 January 2014).

Mason, J., 2002, *Qualitative Researching*, 2nd edn, London: Sage.

Morisy, A., 2004, *Journeying Out: A New Approach to Christian Mission*, London: Continuum.

Paloutzian, R. F., 2005, 'Religious Conversion and Spiritual Transformation: A Meaning-System Analysis', in R. F. Paloutzian and C. L. Park (eds), *Handbook of the Psychology of Religion and Spirituality*, London: Guilford Press, pp. 331–47.

Pattison, S. and J. Swinton, 2010, 'Moving Beyond Clarity: Towards a Thin, Vague, and Useful Understanding of Spirituality in Nursing Care', *Nursing Philosophy*, 11.4, pp. 226–37.

Silvoso, E., 1994, *That None Should Perish*, Ventura: Regal Books.

Thompson, A., 2010, 'Eden Fitton Hill: Demonstrating and Becoming in Oldham', in A. Davey (ed.), *Crossover City: Resources for Urban Mission and Transformation*, London: Mowbray, pp. 120–4.

Thompson, A., 2012, 'Holy Sofas: Transformational Encounters between Evangelical Christians and Post-Christendom Urban Communities', *Practical Theology* 5.1, pp. 47–64.

Walsh, M., 1995, 'Here's Hoping: The Hope Community Wolverhampton', in P. Sedgewick (ed.), *God in the City*, London: Mowbray, pp. 52–71.

Wilson, M., 2012, *Concrete Faith*, Manchester: Message Publications.

Zinnbauer, B. J. and K. I. Pargament, 2005, 'Religiousness and Spirituality', in R. F. Paloutzian and C. L. Park (eds), *Handbook of the Psychology of Religion and Spirituality*, London: Guilford Press, pp. 21–42.

Notes

1 www.eden-network.org.
2 www.message.org.
3 www.eden-network.org/associates.

5

Pioneer Mission in Community

KARLIE ALLAWAY

Cold loneliness

I have unravelled

And I try, I try

To knit a suit of armour
With these ragged cords
That could connect me to others

Warm bandage words wrap comfort around friends
But applied to contain my own pain
They shrink, thin and tangle in my trailing self

Isolated by what ifs
Reaching out is risky
I search for a way to tidy up, alone

Community, family, relationship
Moth words
Eat my newest self-sufficient cloak

Compassion reveals a fake shawl of pride
Real grief threads through its holes
Seen by those who trail pain too

There is no choice, again
I have to meet their eyes
Let my loss try to find theirs

As the laughter of relief empties self
Until love begins the untangling
And I unwind safely in the shelter of trust

There, friends patiently, reverently
Crochet me back into the larger warmth
Of beautiful unfinished communion

Why a chapter on community?

The word community is generally so overused it is like a ball
of dough that has been rolled out thinner and thinner until it is
difficult to make anything with it. If you try to create anything
with the sense stretched that far it breaks apart. So first I will
ball the meaning back up into a definition we can work with. A
community is a group of people with shared values, intentionally
creating a context for belonging, solidarity, mutual care, collaboration and authentic relationship.

That settled, why community? Much of the following results
from questions formed over the years in various contexts of community. These questions have emerged through both difficult and
transformative experiences. As well as questions, I have carried
aspirations, but often wondered if these are naive and romantic,
or imaginings that can be turned into reality. Can we move the
biblical idea of being the body of Christ from the bare bones of
theory to a tangible enfleshed possibility? What exactly does it
mean to add the word *Christian* to community? What does this
look like and what does it mean for mission? But among the
reasons I reflect on and pursue community there are more personal motivations at work. Sensitive souls like mine often head
for isolation, while still longing for healing and belonging. As I
have sought help in my own struggles and tried to help others in

theirs, out of necessity I have asked what role community plays in growth and healing.

I am part of several communities and have reached the conclusion that, for me at least, this is healthy. Being asked to contribute this chapter emerged from belonging to the CMS pioneer mission community. I am grateful to experience the supportive learning environment of the pioneer course. Through it I am part of a small network of relationships that have helped sustain me through some very difficult times. These friends have also been crucial in supporting the explorations of a peculiar sense of vocation that the wider Church usually struggles to understand, nurture or utilize.

My family is a community. We are a microcosm of the issues explored here. I am married to a wonderful/infuriating man (I own an old 'grumpy but gorgeous' t-shirt that he still insists really suits me!). After 18 years, a marriage come of age seems to mean loving each other enough to keep learning how to handle both of us still being a work in progress. We also have those occasional out-of-the-body experiences where we realize again we have become parents to three unique human beings, who bring constant change and, as their sense of humour develops, lately more and more laughter. My mum also lives with us at the top of the house, where she has her own mini annexe. It works – honestly! We have worked out a rhythm to our overlapping lives and close relationships that significantly enhances life for all of us. These are the people I am most grateful to know. I want to get better at loving them well. Hospitality is very important to us and we really enjoy allowing family to mean a little more than the core members I have just described.

It is also almost three years since we became Roman Catholic, with a wider group, who now make up a community that explores what it means to be prayerful and missional within the sacramental and contemplative traditions. We are Eastbourne Ordinariate Mission, formed by a group seeking to bring the best of their faith nurtured within Anglicanism into full relationship with Roman Catholicism. This is a group that aspires to prayerful rootedness in a living tradition (with an awareness that we need to avoid dead traditionalism), enabling creative stability and stable creativity. I hesitate to try to communicate how important these relationships have been for my family and our healing and spiritual growth. This is partly because some experiences should remain hidden treasure and come from the intimacies of authentic relationship. I can say we are very grateful for these friends and a much needed place of belonging. But before things get too sentimental or suspiciously romantic sounding, let me tell you, occasionally some of these people, whom I love dearly, also drive me nuts. (They do not mind my telling you that as long as I mention how annoying I too can be!) This is where I do community at its most raw and transformative, with lots of grounding laughter and occasional tears. Attached to our house we have a prayer space with its own entrance, which allows people connected to the community to drop in there to pray or occasionally stay the night as a kind of mini retreat (it is self-contained). Twelve- and 24-hour prayer vigils there have been an important way for the community to develop, reflect on its identity and prepare for mission.

I am also energized by being part of an emerging group of Christians from different church traditions across Eastbourne, who seek to engage in dialogue and relationship with spiritual seekers in a variety of respectful and creative ways. We do this mainly by working together in temporary community as a Christian presence at festivals for pagan groups. Engagement with a Steam Punk group, a community café and culturally sensitive Christ-centred outdoor worship have also happened through the connections of this group. This team believes that people who are spiritually searching should be able to explore the Christian gospel and its related spirituality in a culturally sensitive, safe and non-judgemental way. So we go to where they will be, knowing they are for the most part unlikely to come to us. We spend our time talking about Jesus and the way of life he calls us to, listening to a lot of struggle and praying with people. Many people we speak to are very open and positive about hearing about Christ even if they have no interest in church.

These contexts mean I have had to get better at articulating the issues of community. Through the course I am held to account by some pioneer people who push me on these subjects. I need to know how to describe effective collaboration if asked searching questions like these: Is our community bearing fruit? What kind? Are we becoming more human? Less selfish? Are we grounded; resisting pretence, denial and the superficial as strategies to make life and relationships easier? How effectively do we work together? What are we achieving as a group that we could not do and be alone? How do we experience grace? What rhythms of prayer do we adopt? I welcome these penetrating questions.

As I write this I am currently reading *Forest Church*, which is rooted in the idea that nature is the second book of God (Stanley, 2013). At one time, I would have argued that people and relationships are the second book of God. Before I ever opened and read the Bible but was hanging around Christians, I was reading people and their relationships to see what Christianity was about. Our faith needs to be embodied. We need to be a visible sign of the invisible realities of grace.

Pioneers and community

Are you born a pioneer? I am not sure. Some natural talents help but often people identified as pioneers are people with a passion, which then leads them to need to cut a new path. Their dedication drives looking for a new way to do things, alongside the will to develop the skills to do this. They put their natural talents in the service of whatever they are passionate about, which is why pioneers are a diverse group of people, approaching their challenges in different ways.

There can be a pioneer stereotype and we can sometimes limit ourselves in discussions around pioneering. This type of pioneer is an entrepreneurial loner, off doing their own thing at the frontier where the majority would not go. I always want to push back against this, mostly because, at my best, I am naturally relational and try to follow my passions in community. At heart I do not want to be a lone missionary, I want to be part of a missional community. I think we all hold a piece of the wisdom and I love to collaborate within that approach. Even though it is harder to try to do things by consensus and to wait for others to understand my point of view, I would much rather work within a team. It is difficult to keep trying patiently and vulnerably to find ways to communicate passions born out of hopeful struggle, but I have never been happy just getting on with what I whole-heartedly believe in alone, even if it is easier. It is also challenging for a loving dissenter to have their motives misunderstood for a while, or even to encounter seeming indifference to something we passionately want to prioritize. However, I am grateful that our Catholic community has persevered in a process of engaging in discovering a *communal* sense of mission. We have spent valuable time and energy discovering a collective charism (grace-given vocational gift) of compassionate hospitality. Each of us fits our individual sense of vocation with this communal charism. In our context there is also a clear sense in which we are pioneering together in a unique situation with new challenges, which requires working together to cut a new path.

Pioneers, by nature or nurture or both, understand the power of imagination and of the prophetic role of being able to see differently and influence, both at the margins and in the centre of traditions and institutions. They do this within their communities but also call their communities to embrace the prophetic aspect of Christ's call to energize and criticize where needed, in whatever context they are found.

Missional community

Having wrestled in changing contexts with the question, 'What is mission?', what can I conclude? I have found some help-ful definitions that have resonated. For example, that mission happens when Christianity becomes 'a catalyst for new identity formation rather than a fixed institution' (Robert, 2009, p. 2). Or that missional church is simply a community of Jesus' disci-ples, making disciples (Hopkins, 2000). These descriptions appeal because they add in what can often be missing from Christian community: genuine transformation for the better. But as I have enthusiastically explored the belief that the essence of church is to be engaged in mission, I have realized there can be problems in thinking this way. Mission becomes unhealthy if the nature of the Church is completely defined by its task: 'It is precisely because [the church] is not merely instrumental that she can be instrumental' (Newbigin, 1953, p. 147).

Mission is a natural consequence of concepts more fundamental and ultimately mysterious: faith, love and hope. The outworking of an encounter with God, and the reality of love and hope in my life, has led to a transformative struggle that I am compelled to share with others. As we experience the love of God, our world-view and view of self radically changes and we grow into embracing life's struggle, with hope and faith, not fear and despair. On a good day, that love and hope then flow out to others. Community, when embracing this corporately, is potentially a powerful embodiment of this full spectrum of reality. As individuals, but more fully together, we are a work in progress, pointing beyond ourselves to the reconciliation of the whole of humanity and creation with the reality of God's transforming love. Our focus should not really be on mission at all, but on being a community of prayerful love from which we bear witness to this beautiful now and not-yet relationship in Christ. In the words of Rowan Williams, church is 'what happens when people encounter the Risen Jesus and commit themselves to sustaining and deepening that encounter in their encounter with each other' (Gray, 2004, p. vii). Mission flows naturally, in an uncontrived way, from this. I love Walter Brueggemann's conclusion:

At base, biblical faith is the assertion that God has overcome all that threatens to cheapen, enslave, or fragment our common life. Because the power of death is so resilient, this triumph of God is endlessly reiterated, reenacted, and replicated in new formats and venues. As a result of that always new victory, we are left to do our most imaginative proclamation and our most courageous appropriation. (1993, pp. 129–30)

Missional communities, in their common life, commit to being intentional about communicating *and* embodying the reality of the resurrection. Missional communities embrace both the imaginative expression of this triumph over death as well as the outworking and witness of its courageous appropriation.

So mission ought to be an unnecessary word. But because it often needs adding back where it is missing, we have to find ways to lift our eyes from our own churchy preoccupations and look out to the wider community. We need to listen to the call of Christ to be visible in our wider communities as light and salt, peacemakers and justice-seekers, carers of orphans and widows, and passionate pursuers of life, wholeness, equality, dignity and ultimately fully developed humanity in all its beautiful guises. In my context, where we can easily become overly preoccupied with refining the liturgy and all things relating to it, we have challenged ourselves with the orthodox idea of the liturgy *after* the liturgy. In the words of Stephen Bevans and Roger Schroeder:

> Liturgy (The Eucharist) is always the entrance into the presence of the triune God and always ends with the community being sent forth in God's name to transform the world in God's image … Mission is conceived, in other words, as the 'the liturgy after the liturgy', the natural consequence of entering into the divine presence in worship. (2004, p. 295)

Periodically I reread Mark Berry's meditative words which remind me that:

> There is no breathing out without breathing in,
> There is no flow without ebb,
> There is no outpouring without drinking deep of life.
> We cannot be love for the community without being drawn
>   deeper ourselves into God,
> We cannot bring change to the world without our lives being
>   realigned,
> We cannot forgive each other without knowing the freedom of
>   forgiveness ourselves. (Berry, 2010)

But the acid test for mission is love. As we are loved by God so we are to flow with God's loving action in the world. Mission happens because God loves people. Within any activity we call mission, is love our motive, is love the way we go about it and is love the fruit of it? Or as Orthodox priest and writer Alexander Schmemann put it: 'The church constitutes itself through love and on love, and in this world it is to "witness" to love, to re-present it, to make love present' (1973, pp. 36–7).

Love is …

Jesus said, 'A new command I give you: love one another. As I have loved you, so you must love one another. By this everyone will know that you are my disciples, if you love one another' (John 13.34–5).

Any community exploring together what it means to follow Christ will ask questions about love. We may talk a lot about love, but what do we really know about putting it into practice? Misunderstanding what love is and looks like has caused me many problems on the way up a steep learning cliff face. I have heard the same struggle echoed in many conversations with those involved in intentional, missional community. Knee deep in the nitty-gritty of pursuing 'authentic' relationship and/or caring for people who are hurting, we have to work out what love is and is not. Morgan Scott Peck's *The Road Less Travelled* deals comprehensively with this subject. He concludes that love is 'the will to extend one's self for the purpose of nurturing one's own or another's spiritual growth' (Peck, 1990, p. 81). Love is not to be confused with the feelings and choices of dependency or being needed, and it is not about strong feelings, though these may accompany loving action. It is about effort, discipline, courage and commitment. He describes real love as requiring the regular painful collapse of ego boundaries in order to grow into being able to nurture better the spiritual growth of ourselves and others. I recognize that! It also speaks to me of the profound connection between love, and death and resurrection. When those helpful initial feelings disappear (which Peck suggests always happens because they are at least partly rooted in an illusion) and everything does not seem as special any more, then the authentic task begins of better recognizing our own and others' limitations *and* potential. Real love reveals where we *all* need to keep growing. Community that resists hanging out in superficial ease knows this. Jean Vanier, founder of the L'Arche communities, echoes Peck's conclusions: 'If we are to grow in love, the prisons of our egoism must be unlocked. This implies suffering, constant effort and repeated choices' (Vanier, 1979, p. 74). In Christian community, forgiveness will become a necessity which resurrects the will to love, not just a theological concept. We will also realize we cannot love everyone. Choices have to be made. This has been one of the most difficult but practical things I have learnt about love; trying to love someone who cannot benefit from your love with spiritual growth is a waste of energy. As Peck says, 'Genuine love is precious, and those who are capable of genuine love know that their loving must be focused as productively as possible through self-discipline.' We must learn to say yes and no, to see where to invest our limited energy, by asking, 'Will it help both me and them grow?' Boundaries help us protect our own and others' actions as leading to spiritual growth. A collective commitment to this kind of practical, everyday effort to love can slowly reveal the ordinary wonder of humanity over time. Peck tells us that real love does slowly bear fruit in feelings of gratitude and joy. This reveals the temporary feelings of the honeymoon of early relationship as a poor relation to those born and nurtured over time in the reality of the long-term effort to love.

The fires of community

Community is hard. The poem at the beginning of this chapter is included because I wrote it out of the ambivalence of my feelings about community. The groups of people I belong to are like fires that both warm me with their relationship and humanity *and* burn away those things that make us less than human. I am grateful for both, but the latter is always painfully difficult. These difficulties have grounded my aspirations for and expectations of community. I have moved from aiming for romantic ideals, to testing ideas for tangible substance. Most importantly, experience, and insights from those wiser and longer in community, has taught me that we should not hold a vision of community without embracing the pain of actualization. Thus birthed, authentic community emerges.

Community can be a crucible in which we can do the hard work of growing up. Yeats' poem 'To a Child Dancing in the Wind' (it is short, if you want to stop, find it on the web and read it) describes how those in the second half of life face the consequences of accepting difficult realities they encounter. Echoing the poem, Richard Rohr argues that we are just not able to handle this when we are younger. I think it is almost impossible to handle this alone. We need others to help us with what Rohr calls 'falling upwards' (Rohr, 2012). Many of us seek tested relationships of enough depth, authenticity and permanence within which to recover from passing into some of the second half of life reality described by Yeats and Rohr. Community is often created when people come together to try to make sense of the regret, disillusionment and loss of growing up. There are times when we are overwhelmed by feeling, as Yeats puts it, 'how despairing/ The moths are when they are burned' or the bewilderment and senselessness of 'the best labourer dead/ And all the sheaves to bind' (Yeats, 1994, p. 99). What do we do when life turns out to be much harder than we had been able to imagine it could be? It takes empathy and compassion from others to face the disillusionment and loss and begin to recover and ask, 'How do we get through this and live fully again in the light of it?' As we look hard at Christ on the cross at these times, we may ask with more necessity to understand than we ever had before, 'What does the resurrection really mean?'

I can remember vividly being compelled to look for people who also wanted to learn how to hold their brokenness in one hand and hope in the other. Some of our help in all this can be found outside community in spiritual accompaniment, pastoral support or forms of therapy. This kind of support may be essential in certain circumstances. There can also be problems with expecting one community to meet all our needs. But we all need equal relationships with friends who over time have paid attention to who we really are and who know the deeper story carried unseen by the person whom others encounter in the superficial ease of a less challenging relationship. My repeated experience has been that sharing mutual wisdom, and the giving and receiving of compassionate empathy within tested friendship, is just as, if not more, important for healing and growth as the professional distance and unequal relationships of pastoral care or therapy.

Emerging Catholic

I have travelled a fair bit of the Christian landscape on my faith journey. From first calling myself a Christian at 17 with a full immersion baptism at a Bible-focused 'Free Church', to attending a 'Baptist' youth group, to a decade as a youth worker for a 'charismatic house church', to disconnected, disillusioned deconstruction and 'alternative worship', to a long hard look at joining 'incarnational mission' in the 'Salvation Army', to an ecumenical project for the homeless and 'High Anglicanism', and now to 'Catholic'. But I was not raised a Christian and until recent years I found the constant pigeonholing of the Christian world annoying. I did not want to be called anything other than a follower of Christ, so internally I never settled underneath the label of one tradition. In the end we recognized our need as a family to put spiritual roots down somewhere. So we prayed and looked for a home. We were open and would have gone anywhere where Christ, mission, prayer, grace and real relationship were prioritized, but we did not expect that to be Roman Catholic. It has not been the easiest label to finally embrace. But it is a good home. Through the ecumenical nature of CMS I still visit other 'homes' and I am kept from feeling my home is better than others. I strive to retain an attitude that says, this is my spiritual home and this is what is good about it but I am interested in where you live and what is good about that. Now Catholic, I have begun to look at what Catholic teaching has to say relating to community. So as to integrate my previous experiences and story, this new perspective is put into dialogue with any wisdom gleaned from journeying across traditions.

For the purposes of this chapter I have picked a few examples of Catholic teaching to explore. In a section of the Catechism on the communal character of the human vocation the following is found:

> There is a certain resemblance between the unity of the divine persons and the fraternity that men are to establish among themselves in truth and love. Love of neighbour is insepar-able from love for God ... Through the exchange with others, mutual service and dialogue with his brethren, man develops his potential; he thus responds to his vocation. A society is a group of persons bound together organically by a principle of unity that goes beyond each one of them. As an assembly that is at once visible and spiritual, a society endures through time: it gathers up the past and prepares for the future. (Catholic Church, 1999, p. 145)

This echoes Shane Hipps' summary that effective community requires four elements: proximity, permanence, a shared history and a shared imagination of the future (Hipps, 2005). Hipps also explores at length the idea that the medium is the message. Applied to community, this means a bit more than actions speak louder than words. It is more like the community itself is a sign of something. Christopher Jamison, former Abbott of Worth Abbey, reminds us community is a place for individuals to be formed and protected and for those individuals to contribute in ways that form and protect the community. 'Community is in this way sacramental, that is to say the material realities of community are the means by which the hidden grace of Christ is given to its members' (Jamison, 2006, p. 129).

The Catholic principle of *subsidiarity* holds that 'a commu-nity of a higher order should not assume the task belonging to a community of a lower order and deprive it of its authority' (Catholic Church, 1999, p. 145). The principle is based upon valuing the autonomy and dignity of individuals, calling all other forms of society, from the family to the state, to first be in the service of the human person. Subsidiarity emphasizes the importance of small communities as mediating structures that empower individual action and join the individual to society as a whole. *Positive subsidiarity* creates the social conditions necessary for the full development of the individual. I have found this teaching helpful for affirming small grassroots communities of Christians as they understand and explore their potential responsibilities, influence and mission tasks. It also gives communities connected to institutional hierarchy confidence to be an effective empowered group, and consider the development of each individual within them. When difficulties for an individual or family lead to temporary dependency on others, this teaching affirms wisely setting people back on their feet again at the right time. We must foster autonomy and responsibility in each other, in tension with mutual care. The ideal is a community in which every individual can flourish and contribute their talents, without fostering any unhealthy dependency or passivity. Subsidiarity also reminds us that we have an autonomy, authority and responsibility that must not be undermined or discouraged by those in authority above us. This would be in contrast to congregations that remain quite passive in relation to the authority of their priests, bishops and diocesan bodies (or the equivalent hierarchy of other situations) and seem unaware of their responsibilities and potential as empowered agents for transformation and growth, both for the benefit of individuals and for the influence of good at the grassroots of local society.

A growing disillusionment around ten years ago focused my enthusiastic interest in the deconstruction of church practices and community life done by those loosely grouped and labelled as the emerging church movement.

Emerging churches dismantle many forms of church ... [to] create a space for the Kingdom to enter their midst ... They abhor the idea of church as a meeting, a place, a routine. Clearly, for these communities church is a people, a community, a rhythm, a way of life, a way of connectedness with other Christ followers ... These communities are small, missional, and offer space for each individual to participate ... It is through living as a community that emerging churches practice the way of Jesus in all realms of culture. (Gibbs and Bolger, 2006, pp. 96, 115)

If I now put this into dialogue with Catholic contexts and teaching, what conclusions can I draw? Many emerging communities have little structured time for gathered worship or a service, because they have intentionally sought to be relational and organic and to emphasize living *as* church over going *to* church. I understand well the desire to look at church as a 24/7 organic process rather than a one-hour event. In the past I have done giving up church to follow Jesus. I understand well why people do this. As a family, we tried to follow Christ out of communion both in the sense of without community and without the sacrament. Over time I felt their absence keenly and realized their essential place when we re-engaged with both. Now Mass, though much more than this, is like a ritual rehearsal for mission and a window to the inspiration for authentic community. In its sacramental nature it is a visible sign of the invisible grace that makes communion, as the deepest expression of lived Christian community, possible. During Mass I prayerfully enter into the grace that potentially enables deeper community. As Jonathan Campbell, an emerging church leader says:

> In our current cultural crisis, the most powerful demonstration of the reality of the gospel is a community embodying the way, the truth and the life of Jesus. Healthy community is the life of Jesus living in us and through us. For community to last, our love for one another must be surpassed only by our love for Jesus. If the relationships are grounded on anything other than Jesus, the community will fail. (Gibbs and Bolger, 2006, p. 89)

And though his community has deconstructed away gathered worship in an effort to organically reach these goals, for me Mass is the foundational way I root my imagination in Jesus and nurture the kind of prayer that pumps spiritual life into my actions, so that I can become part of this kind of community. It is the time and place set aside to receive the 'life of Jesus living in and through us'. Within the Eucharist, I silently pray to be made like him, to be nourished and healed by his presence, to be made more fully a part of his body, to live his way, truth and life. A group of people doing this are potentially grounded in love for Christ in a way that will enable them to flourish as community. Deeper relationship requires much forgiveness to keep resurrecting love. Gathering together for this sacrament is the time and place where grace enables this to happen for me. 'Emerging churches raise basic questions about the nature of church. Is it the place where weekly services are conducted or is it a network of relationships?' (Gibbs and Bolger, 2006, p. 96). I would say that I experience it as both, each making the other a more real communion as they mutually interpret and reinforce each other: 'In her whole being, and in all her members, the Church is sent to announce, bear witness, make present and spread the mystery of ... communion' (Catholic Church, 1999, para. 738).

In missional community we desire to become the body of Christ, Christ visible in the world. But there is an intimate link to becoming this in receiving the body of Christ in the Eucharist. The Eucharist has become fundamental to anchoring myself in Christ, in community and in mission. I have encountered different views on the significance of communion in our various contexts. One aid to partly reconciling conflicting views on the term 'body of Christ' is described by Steve Bevans, referring to the work of Catholic theologian Henri de Lubac. De Lubac researched early texts, discovering that while originally the Church was considered as the true body of Christ and the Eucharist as the mystical body whose purpose was the building up of the Church, in the tenth and eleventh centuries the focus shifted to the Eucharist as the true body and the Church as peripheral mystical body. For the Church to become renewed for mission, she does not need to reverse this understanding but instead recognize that 'The church and the eucharist make each other, every day, each by the other.

Celebrating the Eucharist is the way that Christians are nourished to be the body of Christ in the world' (Bevans, 2009, p. 305). In this way we are open to and entering into the grace that transforms us:

> we will grow to become in every respect the mature body of him who is the head, that is, Christ. From him the whole body, joined and held together by every supporting ligament, grows and builds itself up in love, as each part does its work. (Eph. 4.15–16)

Prophetic and sacramental

St Augustine describes a sacrament as 'an outward and visible sign of an inward and invisible grace'. Does community itself have the potential to be sacramental and inspire us to ask, what are we a sign of? In my late twenties, after eventually getting desperate enough to start telling the truth when I was praying, I began to encounter God in a much deeper, transformative way. As I began to experience what I eventually identified as grace, I looked for ways to centre myself prayerfully through practices that sustained a new openness to the transformation of my soul. Before I properly explored the significance of the sacraments I sought to engage with the mystery of love and grace by every means I could. I encountered its mysterious reality across all areas of my life. As a result, I 'knew' intimately much about grace before I understood any theology or ecclesiology relating to it. This means I have a generous understanding of the possibilities for those outside the sacramental traditions to experience and root themselves in a sacramental world-view – even if they never call it that.

But what is a sacramental world-view? Sacramentality sees the *whole world* as a potential means for grace, a means for knowing and loving God more fully and growing into who God has made us to be. There is no sacred and secular divide. In creation (including humanity), the spiritual and divine are made visible. As someone who writes poetry and therefore loves metaphor, it makes total sense to me that the whole world is a metaphor for God. So I approach the sacraments as wells of transforming grace from which I draw with gratitude. But this overflows into the sacramentality of all of life, which then comes back with me into prayerful engagement with the sacraments again.

So what does this have to do with pioneer mission and community? I find this hard to express but a sacramental world-view does something profound to your imagination. When you can see how beautiful everything is meant to be, or rather actually is, this makes you look differently. You pay attention to the beauty, and anything that mars this starts to cause a kind of grief. Walter Brueggemann, who writes so compellingly about the prophetic imagination which resonates with many pioneers, touches on sacramentality as he envisions a particular kind of community:

> Sacramentalism is a cogent alternative to despair, an awareness that even here and now we are in God's demanding and assuring presence ... In our time of dislocation the church can offer ways of speaking and acting that the dominant society regards as subversive, but without which we cannot for long stay human. It can express sadness, rage and loss as an alternative to the denial that inevitably breeds brutality. It can be a voice of holiness that counters the trivial commodity-centered world by the practice of disciplines that make communion possible. It can be a voice of imaginative, neighborly transformation, focused on those in need ... Before us is the choice between succumbing to a fearful self-preoccupation that shrivels the spirit or heeding God's call to re-enter the pain of the world and the possibility of renewal and salvation. (Brueggemann, 1997)

Brueggemann helps me understand how and where sacramentality can permeate the stability of a living tradition essential for making a certain kind of community possible. Perhaps sacramental Catholic communities, feeling marginalized and increasingly exiled from the surrounding culture, could increasingly, as they embrace a faithful, hopeful newness, become more dangerously prophetic than we might have previously imagined. For many, particularly non-Catholic observers, Pope Francis seems to embody this potential. Michael Frost's *Exiles*, which is fairly dismissive of institutional church, calls Christians to become 'the living breathing promise to society that it is possible to live out the values of Christ – that is, to be a radical, troubling alternative ... a community of generosity and selflessness ... pursuant of justice, flushed with mercy' (Frost, 2006, p. 15). I want to encourage those of us integrated into the institutionalism that comes with most sacramental tradition to be open to the possibilities perhaps uniquely there. To those free to experiment outside these boundaries – OK, I admit it, sometimes I still wish I was there. But do not dismiss the discipline and constraints, which, if wisely negotiated, can allow the stability that enables a genuinely surprising organic fractal creativity. This too might just be a way to make a window into a better kind of world.

A prayerful community

Catholic writer and monk Thomas Merton writes, under the heading 'Learn to be alone', 'We do not go into the desert to escape people but to learn how to find them ... to find out the way to do them most good. But this is only a secondary end. The one end that includes all others is the love of God' (2003, p. 82). If we are seeking to be more fully, lovingly present to others, especially those who are suffering, this compassionate love flows from a love for, in and from God. This is nurtured in contemplative prayer.

'Within a context of belonging there can co-exist a cave of the heart, where the full mystery, hiddenness and interiority of life in Christ can be contemplated' (Roderick, 2010, p. 104). If we shape our lives by choices and imagination grown in this place in our soul, we see differently, we become vulnerable, open and awake, fully present to people in a way we cannot be without being fully present within ourselves to God. This is prayer echoing the sacramentality explored earlier. Mark Yaconelli sums this up beautifully by drawing a thread through the writings of many contemplatives:

Ignatius of Loyola referred to contemplation as 'seeing God in all things'. Brother Lawrence called it 'the pure loving gaze that finds God everywhere'. Jean Pierre de Caussade defined contemplation as the 'sacrament of the present moment'. Teresa of Avila referred to this experience as 'awareness absorbed and amazed' ... Walter Burghardt ... said contemplation is 'a long loving look at the real'. (Yaconelli, 2006, p. 6)

Many of the Christians whose writings on prayer I have found most helpful have been contemplative activists, whose actions embodied compassion flowing out of a life of prayer. Their prayer is like the heart that pumps life and love through their actions. They lived their prayers. Dorothy Day, Henri Nouwen and Jean Vanier are prayerfully compassionate Roman Catholics who inspire me by their example. Each of them writes of the deep value of community. They remind me that it is possible to live from a place of engagement with people, where our actions *are* prayers, flowing wordlessly from a heart fully open both to love from and for God, and love for people as God's image bearers. This is experienced incarnation; life is transfigured in a balance of the transcendence and immanence of the presence of God. I believe Day, Nouwen and Vanier when they tell us that a community of sustained, disciplined, prayerful love remains flawed but becomes beautiful. Love covers over a multitude of sins. By grace we may also grow into this.

Conclusion

As I have been writing this chapter I have asked myself: Why has community been such a constant fascination for me? There is something much deeper focusing me than an academic interest or even the subtle, or not so subtle, pressure of circumstances. I have just finished reading a book written by a young Zimbabwean woman who moved to the USA. She creates a vivid sense of her connection to her birthplace and its people. In the acknowledgements she begins, 'a person is a person because of other people'

(Bulawayo, 2013, p. 292). The effect of her writing on my reflections on community was like sunlight when I have stayed too long indoors, and this phrase made me weep. It took effort to work out why, but I realized I have been looking for community made up of relationships that would help me become who I was created to be. I have also wanted to give this back in return.

Currently, through counselling, I am being supported in facing a fundamental loss, the reality of which I was pushed into by the difficult circumstances of the death of a family member. I have been feeling the painful absence, for most of my life, of a rich and abiding sense of the value of who I am. I have skirted the edges of this absence for many years. I am now the most ready I have ever been to embrace who I am and really live, by acknowledging the full pain of the half-life this loss caused. Christianity, at its best and most life-giving, slaps me awake every now and then with the realization that all of us, everyone, should see and know the full worth and dignity of who they really are. Now I want to stay awake. I think this must be why I held out, sometimes incredulous at myself, for a *Christian* community as a place of healing and becoming, rather than leaving the hurts and disillusionment of church groups behind for good.

Like the author of the book I have just closed, I am profoundly grateful to the people who have shown me who I am. I am proficient at hiding my real self, having for most of my life felt revealing it would lead to rejection. In recent years some ordinarily wonderful people have kept trying to connect with the real me and demonstrated a healing empathy and patience. I have pushed some of them to the limits of trying to demonstrate care and connection, while the false part of me formed in shame refused to die. Love is gently to bring to light and make known the beauty of another person to themselves. I am deeply grateful to each person who has done this for me by beautifully, and occasionally very vulnerably, being who they really are. Some of them do not even know how life-changing seemingly small kindnesses have been. Wherever we discover it, may we nurture and protect community like this.

A prayer of becoming

As the body of Christ, together becoming like him, we pray:

We ask to see the beauty in our brokenness
To be enabled to receive, uncover and use all our gifts and talents
To see how to use them in the most selfless way to serve others
    also broken.

As a dwelling place of God, his kingdom displayed increasingly among us, on earth as it is in heaven, we pray:

We ask to find a place of becoming, a place of home and
    community
Discovered in shared memories and shared hope for the future
A common place from which to live and love well
To know that is where we belong and that Christ is with us
    there.

As followers of Jesus, becoming more and more committed and faithful to him, we pray:

We ask to see the radiance of our God of love
Whose name is more treasured to us than any other
In real encounters with Christ
To see it in his words as we meditate on them
In his presence with broken, forgotten people
And in the light shining in those who love him.

As part of the Church of Jesus Christ across time and throughout the world, we pray:

We ask to become a community who are being transformed by
    their love for God, one another and those who suffer
We ask for increasingly transparent relationships, grown in
    honesty and kindness

Relationships strong enough to enable us to demonstrate love
from our deepest selves
We ask to become people known for a love that comes from
renewed minds and hearts and souls
A love that seeks to offer all that we are and have
A love that brings hope and peace
A love that sees the scars of sacrifice and compassion as beautiful
And points to the day when all things will be beautiful again.

Amen.

References

Berry, M., 2010, *Liturgy after the Liturgy ... some words for tonights 'table'*, http://markjberry.blogs.com/way_out_west/2010/03/liturgy-after-the-liturgy-some-words-for-tonights-table.html (accessed 9 September 2011).

Bevans, S. B., 2009, *An Introduction to Theology in Global Perspective*, Maryknoll, NY: Orbis Books.

Bevans, S. B. and R. P. Schroeder, 2004, *Constants in Context: A Theology of Mission for Today*, Maryknoll, NY: Orbis Books.

Brueggemann, W., 1993, *Biblical Perspectives on Evangelism: Living in a Three-Storied Universe*, Nashville, TN: Abingdon Press.

Brueggemann, W., 1997, *Conversations among Exiles*, http://www.religion-online.org/showarticle.asp?title=26 (accessed 31 January 2014).

Bulawayo, N., 2013, *We Need New Names*, London: Chatto & Windus.

Catholic Church, 1999, *Catechism of the Catholic Church*, London: Geoffrey Chapman.

Frost, M., 2006, *Exiles: Living Missionally in a Post-Christian Culture*, Grand Rapids, MI: Baker Books.

Gibbs, E. and R. K. Bolger, 2006, *Emerging Churches*, London: SPCK.

Gray, G., 2004, *Mission-Shaped Church*, London: Church House Publishing.

Hipps, S., 2005, *The Hidden Power of Electronic Culture: How Media Shapes Faith, the Gospel, and Church*, Grand Rapids, MI: Zondervan.

Hopkins, B., 2000, *Introduction and Background to Cell Church*, http://www.acpi.org.uk/Joomla/index.php?option=com_content&task=view&id=53&Itemid=65 (accessed 2 February 2014).

Jamison, C., 2006, *Finding Sanctuary: Monastic Steps for Everyday Life*, London: Orion.

Merton, T., 2003, *New Seeds of Contemplation*, London: Shambhala.

Newbigin, L., 1953, *The Household of God*, London: SCM Press.

Peck, M. S., 1990, *The Road Less Travelled*, London: Arrow.

Robert, D., 2009, *Christian Mission: How Christianity Became a World Religion*, Chichester: Wiley-Blackwell.

Roderick, P. D., 2010, 'Connected Solitude: Re-Imagining the Skete', in G. Cray, I. Mobsby, A. Kennedy (eds), 2010, *New Monasticism as Fresh Expression of Church*, London: Canterbury Press.

Rohr, R., 2012, *Falling Upward: A Spirituality for the Two Halves of Life*, London: SPCK.

Schmemann, A., 1973, *For the Life of the World*, New York: SVS Press.

Stanley, B., 2013, *Forest Church*, Llangurig: Mystic Christ Press.

Vanier, J., 1979, *Community and Growth*, London: Darton, Longman & Todd.

Yaconelli, M., 2006, *Contemplative Youth Ministry*, London: SPCK.

Yeats, W. B., 1994, *The Collected Poems of W. B. Yeats*, Ware: Wordsworth.

6

Participation in Waiting: An Inquiry into the Practice and Development of Pioneers as a Community of Practice

JIM BARKER

As a population we are becoming increasingly conscious that the most impactful learning encounters are when we participate with peers in our practice, whatever our particular practice might be. Going further with this, the truth for many of us is that the impact of the more formal or structured learning interventions, such as degree courses, skills-based learning (such as information technology) or theological training, can be quite minimal in comparison to the less formal day-to-day interactions with friends, colleagues and peers. This is no great shocking revelation and many authors have explored this. David Boud and Heather Middleton (2003) are a good start. I hope this assertion could be a good starting point from which we can begin to explore the environment, process and impact these less formal learning environments can have on us, especially among pioneers.

So far several interventions have been made to support pioneers in the development of their practice, ranging from interventions developed by existing theological colleges, through to more context-based courses such as the Pioneer Leadership course at the Church Mission Society, which demands that participants are engaged in practice, and in context, throughout the course. With the exception of a few courses, current models for learning in the Church are predominantly didactic (teacher centric), cognitive (aimed towards changing reasoning and/or reasoning processes) and individualistic (assume that the changed cognition of the individual is the most effective pedagogy).

The broad field of social learning can be explored through a number of different lenses, including: networked learning (Steeples and Jones, 2002), social learning (Bandura, 1977) or, as in this case, communities of practice (Lave and Wenger, 1991). I have specifically chosen to explore communities of practice as a field because, in some way, it seemed to describe the community of pioneers developing in the UK.

What are 'communities of practice'?

The term 'communities of practice' and communities of practice theory became a throwaway term at the end of Jean Lave's and Etienne Wenger's (1991) study into, what they call, legitimate peripheral participation. This is a way of describing social learning not as a pedagogy in itself, but rather a 'lens through which to view and study many forms of social learning' (Lave and Wenger, 1991, p. 40).

Many of us might point towards the practice of apprenticeship as the most commonly understood form of social learning, and suggest that the idea of communities of practice is simply an extension of an apprenticeship process. My challenge to this is that apprenticeship itself has a predetermined pedagogy that fails to capture the width and breadth of the social learning experience. Legitimate peripheral participation becomes a way of describing how people learn, not simply through social interaction, but through a process of gradual and, in some ways, graded participation. Lave and Wenger argue that the primary place for legitimate peripheral participation is within a particular and situated *community of practice* (hereafter CoP). 'In summary, rather than learning by replicating the performances of others or by acquiring knowledge transmitted in instruction, we suggest that learning occurs through centripetal participation in the learning curriculum of the ambient community' (Lave and Wenger, 1991, p. 100).

This idea, that the primary place of learning for most situated activity was a CoP, took hold very quickly, but it took another seven years for Wenger (1998) to follow up Lave's and Wenger's (1991) original work, and propose a deeper thesis on the traits, components and practice of these CoP. Perhaps the most succinct and comprehensive definition of a CoP is provided by Wenger: 'communities of practice are groups of people who share a concern, a set of problems, or a passion about a topic, and who deepen their knowledge and expertise in this area by interacting on a ongoing basis' (Wenger et al., 2000, p. 4).

Communities of practice and social learning

Almost since its identification as a field for exploration and research, learning has been situated within the field of psychological theory. This ties well with those who argue that, as a society, we give precedence to the abstract over the practice, in the belief that the practice will work itself out in light of the better or purer abstract theory. For many it appears that CoP theory comes out of a growing dissatisfaction with that particular paradigm. (See Hughes et al. (eds), 2007; Engeström, 1987; Marsick and Watkins, 1990; and Nicolini and Meznar, 1995.)

So, the concept, model and theory of communities of practice comes out of the idea that learning is not solely, or even primarily, a personal and cognitive process, but rather that it fundamentally consists of social participation. CoP theory argues for a 'shift away from a theory of situated activity in which learning is reified as one kind of activity, and toward a theory of social practice in which learning is viewed as an aspect of all activity' (Lave and Wenger, 1991, pp. 37–8). This proposal somewhat ridicules the idea that to learn properly you need to remove yourself from the day-to-day practice of work, receive teaching somewhere else, to then take back into day-to-day practice.

It could be simply summed up if we said that the theory of CoP is primarily a theory of learning through socialization, but Wenger (1998) adds depth to this by proposing that learning, as a social process, occurs in the junction between four points: community, meaning, identity and practice. In the figure below (Figure 1), Wenger shows how each of these four elements provides the make-up of social learning, arguing that the power of the CoP is that it integrates these four components, giving equal strength to each, rather than privileging one over the others. He goes on to argue that learning through participation occurs in the tension between these points, the individual identity 'against' the community, the experience of doing 'against' the collective meaning of the doing.

Of course there is no 'against' here, rather it is more accurate to say that learning happens within a thorough and tenacious negotiation between the points, as shown in Figure 1 below.

Figure 1: Wenger's social theory of learning

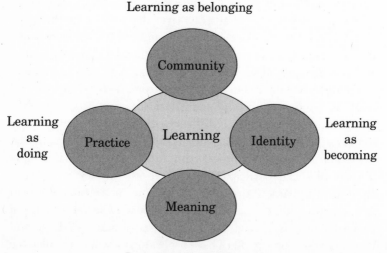

Source: Wenger, 1998, p. 5.

To help summarize all of this, in a way that we all might be able to identify CoPs with which we engage, Wenger provides a list of what he considered indicators, which would show that a CoP has formed. These are listed in Table 1 below.

Table 1: Indicators that a community of practice has formed

• Sustained mutual relationships – harmonious or conflictual
• Shared ways of engaging in doing things together
• A rapid flow of information and propagation of innovation
• An absence of introductory preambles, as if conversations and interactions were merely the continuation of an ongoing process
• Very quick setup of a problem to be discussed
• Substantial overlap in participants' descriptions of who belongs
• Knowing what others know, what they can do, and how they can contribute to an enterprise
• Mutually defining identities
• The ability to assess the appropriateness of actions and products
• Specific tools, representations, and other artefacts
• Local lore, shared stories, inside jokes, knowing laughter jargon and shortcuts to communication as well as the ease of producing new ones
• Certain styles recognized as displaying membership
• A shared discourse reflecting a certain perspective on the world

Source: Wenger, 1998, pp. 125–6

I think each of us could reflect on this list and identify ways in which particular communities that we know exemplify these traits. Whether we are priests, accountants, architects, designers, cooks, lecturers, cleaners, fundraisers or management trainers, it is my conviction that these traits apply.

Developing communities of practice

In the process of following my own curiosity I was keen to discover how CoPs develop, and specifically what clues might help to resolve the question I had about the challenges this community of pioneers will face in its development. I was struck by Wenger's reflection:

> Learning cannot be designed. Ultimately it belongs to the realm of experience and practice. It follows the negotiation of meaning; it moves on its own terms. It slips through the cracks, and creates its own cracks. Learning happens, design or no design. (Wenger, 1998, p. 225)

Despite this assertion, Wenger et al. (2000) appear keen to suggest agency can be applied to the development of CoPs, and present five stages in the growth and development of any particular CoP. These are: Potential, Coalescing, Maturing, Stewardship, and Transformation. Wenger et al. argue that 'progressing through these stages, communities typically undergo several changes in their focus, relationships, and practice' (Wenger et al., 2000, p. 111). They continue to argue that CoPs move around in their focus and develop from simple practices of sharing reflections, thoughts and ideas and move towards developing their relationship between each other, and understanding each other, in a more formal way. So my question now became: What did this process of development have to say to how pioneers might develop as a community of practice, and what challenges might they face?

Who was engaged in the research?

I took a sample of 11 people who, in some way, self-identified as 'pioneers' among whom I conducted semi-structured interviews. The interviewees were four women and seven men, five ordained and six non-ordained, and six full-time, four part-time and one unpaid 'volunteer'.

Each interview had three or four sections:

1 What's the story of how you entered into this work, and this community?
2 How would you say you 'learned' to do the work you do?
3 What does learning mean for you now?
4 How does participation and learning happen for the people in your 'situated' community?

Alongside the data provided from these interviews there is a raft of data available on this community of pioneers, thanks in part to the period in which this CoP was birthed. A significant number of members are authors, bloggers and speakers on the subject at hand, which provided an invaluable resource.

To preserve the anonymity of respondents, while using real quotations, I have created pseudonyms for the participants: they are Alex, Bailey, Hayden, Justice, Rowan, Kennedy, Tyler, Devon, Sage, Everly and Cameron. If you find this somewhat tiresome then please forgive me; I simply found it less tiresome than constantly writing 'as one respondent said ...' or 'as summed up by another respondent ...'.

So what emerged?

From the process of analysing the transcripts five themes emerged from the data, which I believe had something to say in this conversation between CoP literature and theory, and the experienced practice of this group of pioneers. These were:

- What do we mean by pioneer?
- Different CoPs with different practices
- Constellations of practice
- Processes of reification
- Deep learning, empirical learning.

What do we mean by 'pioneer'?

It was no great surprise to me that in almost every interview we had to face the question: 'What do we mean by pioneer?' Perhaps from the time the word was first used by people to describe pioneers until today there has been an enormous amount of ambiguity around the name: what does it mean, how do we recognize one, what particular practice denotes someone as a pioneer? This ambiguity has been helpful in some ways, as it has left the group or community to determine its own meanings, but unhelpful in others. Bailey recounted a story that has been common among many people I have worked with and spoken to, where she has often been asked '… aren't we all pioneers?'

This is where the ambiguity of the term starts to impact upon how this group behaves as a CoP. If 'we're all pioneers' then what is distinct about the practice of this group of people, and how, as a newcomer, would I be able to participate in something different if, fundamentally, there is no difference between my practice and the practice of others who happened to call themselves pioneers? It might be tempting to join with Bailey, who continued with further thoughts on this: 'So I guess we need to be more rigorous about what this actually is so we can push further into it, be more precise with our terminology. But I don't think this makes us better pioneers, or better practitioners.'

I would agree with Bailey on the first point, that we need to have better definitions of what we mean by pioneer if we are to move deeper into the practice of pioneering, but I would challenge the second assertion that it would not make us better pioneers or practitioners. Lave and Wenger (1991) write at some length of the importance of 'learning to talk' as part of the process of participating in a CoP. If this group is struggling to find expression that could in some way 'define their practice', it becomes difficult for others to take initial steps towards participation, and identify, even loosely, what participation looks like.

To try to get some idea as to whether this group was, in some way, a CoP, I used Wenger's list in Table 1 above, as a guide. I showed the list to the first five interviewees and asked if they saw any of the traits Wenger (1998) identifies as signs that a CoP has emerged within this group. Most people recognized the group in the list of attributes and behaviours, some more enthusiastically than others. Alex was perhaps the most vociferous: 'It's all there … I recognize a lot of that. It's horrible when you can look at a piece of paper and say, yes that is what we are.'

During conversations a general term began to emerge around what this particular group of people identified as being unique to being a pioneer as they understood it. Fundamentally it was about the 'contextual thing'. This group of people held a common understanding that to be a pioneer was to embrace and work out their own practice of being a minister from the understanding that they were 'practitioners of contextual theology'.

Although each of the people I spoke to easily identified this 'network of pioneer leaders' as a CoP, there was another supposition to be questioned, namely, 'Which community are you talking about here?' From my conversations, a number of different communities of pioneers were presented and discussed, aside from this group who identified themselves as 'contextual practitioners'. Very few organizations are single institutions; most are a collection of different groupings, an informal confederation if you like. Likewise most organizations comprise a collection of different CoPs. The Church is no different, and each of the interviewees identified different CoPs within the groupings of people currently identified as pioneers, within which were this group of 'contextual pioneers'. As Hayden reflected, '… it's like all this stuff really, for better or worse, it creates camps'. Wenger et al. help us further with this when they add that 'as communities of practice focus their domains and deepen their expertise, they inevitably create boundaries. This is a natural outcome of the focus, the intimacy, and the competence they share' (2000, p. 150).

Constellations of practice

In addition to the question concerning which community we were talking about, the interviewees also asked another qualifying question, neatly summed up by Alex, when he asked, 'Are you meaning a broader network of people who are involved in this kind of thing, or are you meaning a local group of people who are working it out?'

This question suggests two levels of what is going on here: a 'local' level that, as it were, delivers something on the ground, alongside some kind of 'holding' community, or a broader network of people who are in relationship with one another in some way. Wenger et al. (2000) come close to describing what is going on here when they identify global CoPs, proposing that communities that exist beyond national boundaries, that are restricted by geography or lack the intimacy of proximity, take on a different form.

It is clear there are two 'layers' to the learning activity within this CoP. On one level there is the activity of a 'base community' – the CoP at the local level – in which people are involved in their local practice. But, at another level, there is also a 'prime community', which in some way is the 'holding' community. This 'prime community' somehow holds, or expresses, the bigger context of these dispersed, or local, communities. This mode was affirmed by Alex who noted:

There is a whole spread-out group. It's much easier to explore [my local community] as a community of practice, but I am equally fuelled by that spread-out set of relationships and set of connections; it's not one or the other, in fact the practice of the local is informed by the wider thing.

Figure 2: System of practice (1)

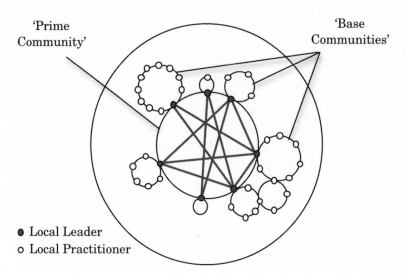

Source: adapted from R. McDermott and J. Jackson, 'Designing Global Communities', as referenced in Wenger et al., 2000.

At the start of this section I identified that one of the defining characteristics of this group was that they were 'contextual pioneers'. Let us revisit what contextual means for this group. It was Lesslie Newbigin who proposed, in the words of James Bielo (2011), that 'Christians are missionaries and that successful mission work in the West meant learning the language and culture of the local mission field, wherever that might be and however familiar it might seem.' This is subtly, but importantly, different from Wenger et al. (2000) when they propose that these 'global' CoPs need to account for the various differences that differentiate national cultures and norms. Here, Wenger et al. are proposing that the nurture and practice of the CoP – its structures, forms and process – need to be culturally sensitive, whereas Newbigin proposed that the nature of the grounded practice itself needs to be culturally appropriate. In the context of this CoP of contextual pioneers, this means that the practice of each base community will be shaped and formed by the context if finds itself in. So, whereas the practice, or work, that shapes and informs the 'global community' of Wenger et al. will be common at both the global and local level, the practice, or work, of each of the 'base communities' in this community will be distinctly different.

This is not to say these different base communities within the core community have nothing in common, as they are, after all, working within a wider cultural context. However, there are fields of interest that underlie the practice of these base communities. Areas such as new monasticism, the Mind, Body, Spirit community, nature-centred spirituality and those working on new-build estates. These are represented by the shaded colours added to the figure below, because each of these, in some way, 'colours' and informs the practice of the base communities and the conversation of the prime community.

Figure 3: System of practice (2)

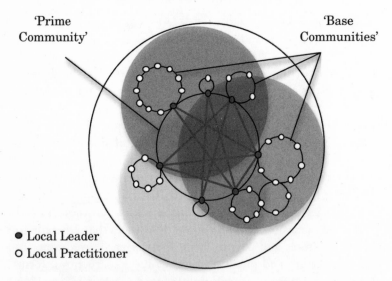

Source: adapted from R. McDermott and J. Jackson, 'Designing Global Communities', as referenced in Wenger et al., 2000.

The challenge of reification

This two-dimensional aspect to this CoP presents a challenge as to how the CoP of contextual pioneers understands itself and engages in its work. Wenger (1998) proposed that to engage in activity and give that activity any meaning, people must engage in a process of 'participation' and 'reification', as two sides to the same activity. These 'reified' things form an almost unrecognized social contract between different parties that not only facilitates common activity, but provide a basis for talking about and under-taking 'what it is we do'. Every day, each of us participates in

Figure 4: The process of reification

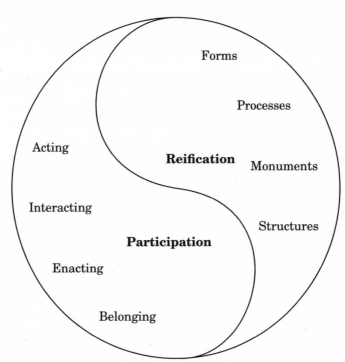

Source: adapted from Wenger, 1998, p. 63.

reified activities. At church we participate in worship through a set of reified processes, which we term liturgy. The liturgy for any and all churches is subtly but importantly different, whether you participate in a hymn sandwich, or a more charismatic expression of a lengthy time of corporate singing, followed by different activities on a platform. If you are the kind of person to go away on retreat you participate in the lives of other communities you visit, such as the island communities of Iona, the Taizé Community near Cluny in France, or the Lee Abbey Community in Devon. In each of these you participate in different reified activities, which have been determined as valuable by the communities that now inhabit and practise them. In short, it is impossible to participate in any corporate activity without some form of reification.

It is not that these reified things are never questioned, never change or sit as immutable. Quite the contrary: in order for them to have meaning they must be constantly negotiated, lest they become a fetish,[1] and thus counterproductive in our effort to work together.

Reification is a problem for this group at both the base community and prime community levels. If we explore the problem of reification at the base community level first then the problem is, in the words of Sage (an interviewee):

We're not doing the replacement or transfer of ideas but we are incarnating into the community, whom we recognize as our host, and as the host community we learn through them, then we find what the story of God is in and through them, to then co-operate, collaborate and animate that.

The model, or process, outlined by Sage is in contrast to models like Alpha, which is propagated by a central organization with a 'how to' guide and a tight set of rules to enable any participating church to get a course up and going quickly. Its popularity has been huge, but you would be hard pushed to call it a local and contextual missional response. However, its strength is that it provides a clearly outlined (reified) process, which enables almost anyone to pick it up and run with it.

This presents a challenge for contextual mission at the base community, because, in the words of Sage,

> if they [an individual] were a learner who likes to learn through more concrete terms 'tell me how to do it', they are not going to stay the distance very long. To be a pioneer you need to be able to learn empirically and learn as you go. If you are the kind of person who wants to be told what to do and how to do it, you are in the wrong place.

This then begins to make the process of reification a long and difficult journey for base communities.

Another challenge to contextual reification is that, in the words of Elvis Costello, '... there is no such thing as an original sin'. Everyone comes with previous experiences, which are loaded with expectation. This was picked up by Alex:

> To say we have a blank piece of paper for some is an exciting thing. When I first started [the community Alex recently left] I started with a blank piece of paper. Here I am working with the memory of what the congregation used to be ... the blank piece of paper carries with it a number of expectations.

This is not surprising because, as Wenger identified, a CoP is after all 'a system of relationships between people, activities and the world; developing with time and *in relation to other tangential and overlapping communities of practice*' (Lave and Wenger, 1991; emphasis mine). This would mean that people naturally take learned practice from one context into another, much of it unconscious and unconsciously. This exact process was taken a stage further by Sage who said,

> When you start to try and look at something that's beyond the normative life of what we mean by the word 'church' ... you realize you might well have been in quite a toxic environment. In my experience, depending on the environment you might have been in, you might spend between one, three or five years

'detoxing' from that experience. Others might detox like [snaps fingers] that. It's dependent on so much stuff.

The 'detoxing' Sage talks about here referred not just to the learned, *or reified*, habits, behaviours, processes of 'church', but also to the difficult experiences and inevitable disappointments of 'community' that people had faced.

So the processes of reification are a challenge to the development of this CoP of contextual pioneers, at both the base (local) and prime (larger) levels. But they are critical if Thomas Binder's (1996) assertion is true, when he states that the process of reification is critical to the formation of community.

Everly (an interviewee) summed this up nicely, when she said, 'The pioneers I see doing the best contextual stuff are too early to have developed in that process [reification] ... while others have developed this to the detriment of contextual mission.' She went on to say that 'Those who are sent out from a strong base like [a community known to her] don't experience the tension because, in that context, someone has decided what church looks like.' The process of both 'deciding what church looks like' and the process of reification are deeply problematic and ambiguous processes for this community of contextual pioneers; processes that are not to be constructed too quickly.

If my assertions above are correct, then surely this only amplifies the challenges of reification at the prime community level. This CoP might have a large degree of unity around the context and problem they are working within, but where does their 'common practice' go beyond there? Fundamentally, reification at the prime level is problematic because of the need of this CoP to act from within context. If each of the base communities were undertaking the same core activity, for example Alpha courses, then the reified processes for the core would be easier to discern, shape and participate in, because at least at the level of the base community 'they are all engaged in the same thing'. However, for this CoP, what is happening at the level of base community is different, informed and shaped by the context of the base community.

Deep learning, empirical learning

The processes and enactment of reification and participation are acts of what Lave (1991) termed a 'complex knowledgeable skill', but she presents a challenge to the ways we understand, learn and participate in this. 'In this late period of capitalism, widespread deep knowledgeability appears to be in short supply, especially in those settings that make the most self-conscious and vociferous demands for complex knowledgeable skill' (Lave, 1991, p. 65). In this practice at the level of the base community, Sage talks of how their community faced resistance to the journey of learning this complex knowledgeable skill:

> My perception was that one of the things that a consumer culture has done is that it has loosened what we might under- stand by responsibility and engagement. It has, in my view, been the same in the domain of church, so when people come with a very consumer mindset, a very individualized mindset, and neither of those make a recipe for a community ... So we said, OK let's lead from amongst ourselves and according to gift, and we'll rotate how that occurs and let's take a period of time and we'll explore who we are through an empirical journey.

This path of following an empirical journey is not uncommon to members of this community of contextual pioneers. In the life, practice and development of this CoP, as with community development, we need to acknowledge that the agency of change rests not just with its members but in participation in a journey of 'deep learning' to understand the work of pioneer ministers as a complex knowledgeable skill. This means they must learn a skill that demands so much more than simply repeating the per- formances of others. What resources people on that journey is the interchange of experiences, practices and performances of this complex skill, at both the base community and prime community levels.

But there is danger that communities that are so engaged in their own development, at the prime level (their own internal co-operation, collaboration and animation), become negligent of their local practice. An additional danger is that those whose primary place of practice is the core level begin to drive the learning curriculum of the whole community, and away from the empirical findings and experience of the base communities.

Creating a clearing in the landscape

As we explored earlier, Wenger et al. (2000) propose that CoPs develop through five stages: Potential, Coalescing, Maturing, Stewardship and Transformation. From this process of research I would propose that this particular CoP of contextual pioneers are in the middle of the second stage – coalescing. So, given the challenges outlined here, what could they do, or what could others do, to support this CoP through the stages of maturing, stewardship and transformation? From the points above I suggest four potential actions that would need particular attention.

- *Naming what they do.* Earlier we identified the ambiguity that exists around the term 'pioneer'. While this is almost an inevitability during the stages of potential and coalescing, we are now at the stage where the emerging CoP of contextual pioneers needs to name its particular charism or contribution; that is, what differentiates it.
- *Creating space for experiments in reification.* As we have seen, the process of reifying particular practices and processes is a complex and fraught occupation. Those who are doing this need a place to explore and discuss where and how those processes and practices have come about.
- *Negotiating tensions between 'Old Timers' and 'New Comers'.* Lave and Wenger (1991) discuss at length the tensions that exist between 'Old Timers' and 'New Comers'. This means the older groups work to preserve the practices and values they have invested in, over the radical younger generations' ideals and desire for change. This is a tension that will continue through the stages of potential, coalescing and maturity. Lave

and Wenger (1991) talk about the value that some Old Timers can add through legitimizing the questions and practices of the emerging New Comers. This is something this group already has experienced, but it is important not to undervalue these Old Timers.

- *Building mutuality.* Learning through this process will be key to the success of this CoP. There are ways in which this CoP is peculiar and particular, as it is operating within a complex and multifaceted environment. At the same time this CoP lacks the usual advantage of close proximity offered to most others. Proximity allows for close and consistent communication and negotiation. This CoP needs to find ways to build this mutuality despite its dispersed nature.

I would strongly argue this CoP already has among it some useful tools to enable growth through the stages of maturation, especially through the principles and ideas of new monasticism. New monasticism creates particular rules and patterns to protect and maintain particular practices. I suggest that this be used to facilitate this CoP through the difficult negotiations it will need to manage over the coming years, if it is to reach maturation and transformation in the way mission is conceived and implemented in the UK.

References

Bandura, A.,1977, *Social Learning Theory*, Englewood Cliffs, NJ: Prentice Hall.

Bielo, J. S., 2011, 'Purity, Danger and Redemption: Notes on Urban Missional Evangelicals', *American Ethnologist* 38.2, pp. 267–80.

Binder, T., 1996, 'Participation and Reification in Design of Artifacts: An Interview with Etienne Wenger', *AI & Society* 10. 1, pp. 101–6.

Boud, D. and H. Middleton, 2003, 'Learning from Others at Work: Communities of Practice and Informal Learning', *Journal of Workplace Learning* 15.5, pp. 194–202.

Engeström, Y., 1987, *Learning by Expanding: An Activity-theoretical Approach to Developmental Research*, Helsinki: Orienta-Konsultit Oy.

Hughes, J., N. Jewson and L. Unwin (eds), 2007, *Communities of Practice: Critical Perspectives*, Abingdon: Routledge.

Lave, J., 1991, 'Situating Learning in Communities of Practice', in L. B. Resnick, J. M. Levine and S. D. Teasley (eds), *Perspectives on Socially Shared Cognition*, Washington, DC: American Psychological Association.

Lave, J. and E. Wenger, 1991, *Situated Learning: Legitimate Peripheral Participation*, Cambridge: Cambridge University Press.

Marsick, V. J. and K. E. Watkins, 1990, *Informal and Incidental Learning in the Workplace*, London: Routledge.

Nicolini, D. and M. B. Meznar, 1995, 'The Social Construction of Organizational Learning: Conceptual and Practical Issues in the Field', *Human Relations* 48.7, pp. 727–47.

Steeples, C. and C. Jones, 2002, *Networked Learning: Perspectives and Issues*, London: Springer.

Wenger, E., 1998, *Communities of Practice: Learning, Meaning and Identity*, Cambridge: Cambridge University Press.

Wenger, E., R. McDermott and W. M. Snyder, 2000, *Cultivating Communities of Practice*, Boston: Harvard Business School Publishing.

Notes

1 I use the word fetish here in the sense that a fetish is something instilled with magical powers.

7

To Pluck Up and to Pull Down, to Build and to Plant

BETH KEITH

Fresh Expressions have contributed significantly to growth within the Church of England. Research on fresh expressions of church (hereafter fresh expressions) from the Church Growth Research Programme indicates that fresh expressions on average now make up 15 per cent of the dioceses' churches and 10 per cent of attendance (Church Army's Research Unit, 2013, p. 6). A typical fresh expression begins with 3–12 people and grows to 250 per cent of that initial team size (Church Army's Research Unit, 2013, p. 35), with 40 per cent of growth coming from those with no previous church background and 35 per cent of growth from those who had previously left church (Church Army's Research Unit, 2013, p. 6). Over the last few years I have travelled around the country to listen to those who have started some of these fresh expressions. While many of the stories shared have been encouraging, I have also heard leaders talking about the opposition they have experienced as they develop new forms of church. I have heard people pointing the finger, blaming certain theologies or church traditions and making grand statements about who or where the problem is. But it is much more complex than that. As a church we find ourselves in a clash between trusted institutional systems and innovative models of practice and theology. These differences are worked out in our church communities, involving individuals and congregations, each with their own, and their collective, experiences and understandings of what it means to be church.

To add to the complexity, these pioneering modes of ministry are developing here in the UK in a context of church decline.
The decline in attendance alongside the decline of power and
influence the Church exerts over British society has been labelled
as the shift towards a post-Christendom society. A number of
writers, in describing this as the Church moving into exile, have
alluded to the writings in Jeremiah, and specifically Jeremiah's
call to pluck up and to pull down, to build and to plant, as the
necessary pattern for the reimagination of the Church (Riddell,
1998, p. 40; Jamieson, 2004, pp. 10–12). However, evidence
from those involved in starting fresh expressions suggests that
while a reimagination of church may be necessary, questioning
and dismantling current forms of church can be divisive, pitting
old against new. Church history gives a mixed picture of how
positive the relationship between traditional and emerging forms
of church can be. Yet it is in this symbiotic mixed economy that
fresh expressions have been formed. Is a relationship of tension
and misunderstanding between established and emerging forms
inevitable, or can the Church find ways to recognize the same
Spirit at work in the other?

In response to this issue, this chapter begins by looking at
Jeremiah's call, to ask what if anything we can learn from this
prophetic mandate for today's context. To pluck up and pull
down, to build and to plant offers a vision of God at work in the
experiences of loss, defeat and possibility. It is a two-stage process
that challenges us to engage with loss as a route towards new life.
The call develops within the book of Jeremiah through dialectic
narrative as the people of God practise their faith in new contexts.
It suggests that re-theologizing is a vital part of living faithfully in
new times and places. But above all it is a prophetic call turning
despair into hope. As in Jeremiah's experience, it can be hard for
faith communities to acknowledge loss, which can easily lead to
denial or blame. The Church's struggle with failure may in part be
because it has neglected Scriptures such as the Jeremiah call that
speak of failure and loss alongside renewal and rebirth. To pluck
up and to pull down, to build and to plant offers a vision of hope
that, even in loss, God is at work birthing new communities of

faith. Qualitative evidence from a study of pioneers' experiences gives evidence of this, revealing a common journey of discontinuity and possibility that leaders engage with as they develop fresh expressions. This confirms the linkage between Jeremiah's call and the current context of ministry. Further engagement with this theological narrative, and in particular with the prophetic nature of this vision, can offer support and clarity to those engaging in ministry today, offering a vision of how life carries on and how newness can be embraced.

Jeremiah's call

Research on Jeremiah undertaken during much of the nineteenth and twentieth centuries focused on a search for the historical prophet. The historical critical methods employed amassed a wealth of understanding about multiple sources and later redactors. This revealed a text compiled out of many different perspectives, lacking overall coherence, and making any search for agreement through this method unworkable. This impasse exposed the limitations of this type of enquiry and saw the emergence of new modes of biblical analysis. Postmodern and faith-based voices influenced the shift away from a preoccupation with authorship and focused instead on the impact of the narrative. This move revealed that it is more fruitful to read Jeremiah as a narrative about exile, rather than the story of the prophet Jeremiah.

Running contemporary with this shift in Jeremiah studies, the term post-Christendom has been coined, in connection with which exile has become a key metaphor. However, it does not necessarily follow that the exile/restoration image can simply be transported into the present context, as exile refers to a specific time in Israel's history. The Jeremiah call – to pluck up and pull down, to build and to plant – sets out a vision of discontinuity and possibility. The use of these terms draws on the exile narrative but focuses specifically on the theological shape behind the call. As such, the use of the terms discontinuity and possibility do not exclude the overarching exile/restoration context, but rather focus on narrative aspects present within the call and draw attention to its theological function.

There is some debate over the nature of the call, which has been understood as Jeremiah's personal experience, a liturgical report of the prophet's ordination service or as an editorial addition to the text. However this is understood, its placing in the book is upfront and programmatic. The repeated inclusions throughout the book bring shape and further reinforce this as a key message of the Jeremiah text, making the call the viewpoint from which to read the book.

Jeremiah 1.10 is constructed from six infinitives, set out in pairs:

to pluck up (*lintosh*) and to pull down (*lintots*),
to destroy (*leha'abid*) and to overthrow (*laharos*),
to build (*libnot*) and to plant (*lintoa*).

These infinitives mark the call motif as a narrative of discontinuity and possibility. The use of *lintosh*, *lintots*, *libnot*, *lintoa* suggests that this call is particularly not about *trans*plantation. This verb to transplant (*štl*), to uproot a plant from one location and plant elsewhere, is used in Jeremiah 17.8; however, not in connection with the call verbs. In addition it is possible that the use of these similar-sounding verbs creates a wordplay as seen elsewhere in the book (Jer. 1.11–12; see Brueggemann, 1998, p. 27), further emphasizing that the two-part process is not a simple transplanting of the same entity. Moreover, 'to destroy and to overthrow' is not echoed throughout the book to the same extent as the other terms (Brueggemann and Miller, 2006, p. 24), suggesting the third and fourth verbs may well be later insertions (McKane, 1986, p. 10). If so, it appears that later editors saw the need to reinforce the first stage, the discontinuity phase, perhaps as an antidote to the human compulsion to move on too quickly to the building and planting phase. Together these suggest that the call is best understood as a two-stage narrative of discontinuity and future possibility. It is as much about endings as it is about beginnings, as the reader is invited 'to reckon with the reality of the discontinuity in the historical process out of which God can work a powerful newness, utterly inexplicable' (Brueggemann, 1998, p. 26).

The call motif is then applied and re-theologized as repeated references to the call appear throughout the book. These repetitions act as reminders, making sense of God's actions in pre-exilic, exilic and post-exilic contexts (Table 1). These alternative applications shift the focus away from the prophet's call and towards the theological function of the text as a narrative of discontinuity and possibility. The reworking of the call speaks as a warning in pre-exilic Israel, as an encouragement to embrace exile and as a proclamation of God's ability to create new communities in difficult times. It serves to remind the people of God that they are participants in God's work, and encourages an embrace of the painful two stage process, by which the community of faith is uprooted and grows again, seemingly from nothing.

The continuity of God's sovereignty or God's presence with his people is evident in all six call reminders. This both endorses the two-stage process of discontinuity and possibility and enables the people of God to find faith and hope in exile (Jer. 12.14–17; 18.7–9). This may be pastoral consolation for a displaced people, but is presented as God allying himself with and creating a new community among those rejected (Brueggemann, 1998, p. 218). The call is then used to reference the future restored Israel, marking a clear differentiation between the former and future planting (Jer. 31.5) and so maintaining the notion of discontinuity rather than transplantation (Figure 1). The call motif is used to mark the two-stage process (Jer. 31.28; 32.41) and it offers a vision of how life carries on, how newness can be embraced even when all that was known has been destroyed.

Table 1: Aspects of discontinuity, possibility and continuity across the call reminders

Call reminders	Discontinuity	Possibility	Continuity
12.14–17	Babylonians are God's instruments of judgement, bringing exile.	Future restoration for those in exile.	God's sovereignty.
18.7–9	Warnings of destruction can be averted.	Promises of restoration can be reconsidered.	God's sovereignty.
24.6–7	'Good figs' from Judah sent into exile.	'Good figs' will return.	God's presence with his people in exile.
31.27–28	God watched over the destruction and exile.	God will watch over the planting and building.	God's presence and sovereignty.
42.10		Future planting for those who stay in Judah.	God's presence and grief.
45.4	Disaster for all.		God's presence with Baruch, and sovereignty.

Figure 1: Discontinuity and possibility in the book of Jeremiah

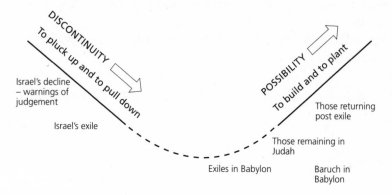

The function of the call

It is generally accepted that the book of Jeremiah developed as a dialectic narrative in which the prophet's words were edited and reworked. Developments within Jeremiah studies during the last 30 years have emphasized the process and impact of this developing text. McKane, Carroll and Childs, though disagreeing significantly, set up the case for the Jeremiah text as dialectic narrative, showing how texts were shaped, recast and re-theologized keeping the text alive within subsequent faith communities and in different contexts. The call reminders, applied to different situations, are an example of this ongoing reapplication. Walter Brueggemann (2003, pp. 7–14) uses a process of imaginative remembering; here the process of traditioning occurs as texts were told and retold for subsequent generations. The text embodies the interplay between revelation, redaction and re-theologizing in different eras. This legitimates the edited text and enables dialogue beyond the completed text and into the ongoing life of the Church (Figure 2).

This move towards narrative shifts the emphasis away from the prophet, while preserving the words of the prophet as belonging to the exilic communities and later as narrative within the canon. If the book is read as dialectic narrative the call may then serve as a powerful narrative for the Church. It provides the Church with a narrative about discontinuity and possibility. Moreover, it questions how the conversation continues, how the text to pluck up and to pull down, to build and to plant acts as prophetic voice for the current context.

Figure 2: The dialectic narrative between the call and later communities

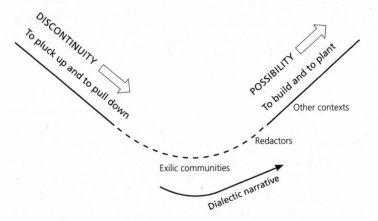

The emphasis placed on the call in Jeremiah 1 and subsequent call reminders throughout the book confirm that the call was understood by later communities as prophetic word. The call acted as evidence of God's continuing sovereignty and presence with his people. It was a voice of hope through difficult times, enabling the exilic communities to theologize their experiences and engage in faith. Clements, in examining the role of narrative within the exilic faith community, shows how Jeremiah's prophecies were edited and applied using firmly established features of Deuteronomistic theology. The writing down of prophecy and the subsequent editing process shows how the theological narrative developed serving the theological and literary needs of the redactors (Clements, 1996, p. 214). Within the narrative of discontinuity and possibility, the prophetic then acts as the driver, turning disheartening discontinuity into hopeful possibility.

In reworking the original text the editors construct a narrative available to speak beyond the historical demands of the text. The narrative is then able to speak to others in crisis, beyond the historical prophet and the exilic communities, and so find its contemporary theological significance. Imaginative engagement with the text allows the prophetic text to act as an agent of change, penetrating despair so that new futures can be believed in and embraced. The process of prophetic imagination and the move towards narrative provide the means by which prophetic literature can open up to become prophetic narrative for alternative contexts. These approaches enable the text to be understood and reworked in today's context, allowing the prophetic voice to speak again.

Figure 3: The prophetic turn

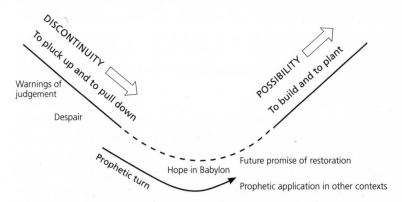

The three elements of discontinuity and possibility, dialectic narrative and the prophetic turn go some way to explain the function of the call within the book of Jeremiah and its continuing theological influence beyond. To pluck up and to pull down, to build and to plant represent the message of the book and offer a vision of God at work in the experiences of loss creating hopeful possibility. Furthermore, the call engages the Church today, prophetically driving the turn from discontinuity to future possibility and challenging the Church to imagine the text in the current situation. Openness to the prophetic nature of the call is challenging. However, in accepting a narrative of discontinuity and loss, space may well open up for a narrative of faith, hope and possibility. We read it not as the call of the historical Jeremiah but as a prophetic call to the ecclesial community to engage with a God who is not held to permanence and may well move through discontinuity and loss as a route to possibility and new life.

The Jeremiah call for today

Jeremiah invites us to imagine the world we live in today through the lens of discontinuity and possibility, dialectic narrative and prophetic turn. But how possible is that? Brueggemann and Miller suggest the text can offer interpretations for our society, which lacks 'an adequate script for truth telling about the abyss, the loss, and the possibility' (2006, p. 27). However they use Jeremiah to critique secular society where the text clearly also critiques religious practices within Israel (Jer. 5.30–31; 6.13–14). Consequently it would be questionable for the Church to use Jeremiah to critique society without first responding to the prophetic voice itself. Acknowledging such a script for truth-telling about loss and decline will raise challenges. As in Jeremiah's experience, it can be hard for faith communities to acknowledge loss. The dissonance between faith and reality can lead to denial, saying 'Peace, peace' when there is no peace (Jer. 6.14) or to a culture of blame. Steven Croft, speaking into the debate about church decline, warns against a fatalistic approach blaming others or ourselves, neither of which leads to growth (Croft, 2009, pp. 2–7). Accepting scripts such as the Jeremiah call, which speak of failure and loss alongside renewal and rebirth, could help the Church to live in hope within the current climate of decline.

The shape of the call from discontinuity to possibility incorporates a two-stage process, a downward dismantling phase followed by an upward phase of new growth, whereby the community of faith dies and is reborn, rather than transplants from one location to another. Churches showing a break with or dismantling of their previous church practice, followed by the growth of new things, may be evidence of the move from discontinuity to possibility. Decline across the Church of England is indisputable; however, the effects and experiences of decline vary greatly across the country.[1] Some pioneers are being brought into dying congregations, or placed in areas where questions over which churches to shut are live issues. Where decline is acute, the Church is confronted with the challenge of managing decline alongside investing in opportunities for new growth.

The Jeremiah text developed as people in different cultural contexts re-theologized the call to pluck up and to pull down, to build and to plant. The exile provided the conditions in which the people of Israel were forced to practise their faith within different contexts, and so a dialectic narrative developed. This process of re-theologizing was driven by the experience of exile, but enabled them to find hope and faith as they learnt how to sing the Lord's song in a strange land. This dialectic process between text and experience is perhaps analogous to the re-theologizing that occurs in the dialogue between faith and culture present throughout the life of the Church. Epochs of Christianity have mirrored epochs of culture, with new forms of faith developing alongside cultural developments (Bosch, 1991, p. 183) as theology and praxis is contextualized within the host culture.

Historical events and a greater awareness of culture have revealed the theological imperative for contextualization taking seriously human experience, social location, particular cultures and social change within cultures (Bevans, 2002, pp. 10–15). Contextualization and other related terms, such as incarnational mission and inculturation, have entered wide usage within the Church during the last 20 to 30 years, confirming the importance of a dialectic narrative within Christianity and providing a theological framework for dialectic practice in mission and ministry.

New forms of Christian community often begin in the places of changing culture (Romano, 1994, p. 135) where this type of dialogue happens first. Andrew Walls argues from evidence of mission movements, that this dialectic narrative not only enabled the birth of Christianity in different contexts, but also resulted in a fuller understanding of Christ: 'It is as though Christ himself actually grows through the work of mission' (Walls, 1996, p. xvii). It is this dialectic narrative, engaged in by pioneers and cross-cultural missionaries, that enabled the emergence of contextual forms of practice, which in turn brought renewal to the Church.

It is possible to see how a dialectic narrative between gospel and culture drives the growth of new forms of contextualized church. This is evident across the epochs of Christianity, often occurring through sodal movements such as monastic orders and missionary societies. Through this dialectic narrative, these movements have been significant contributors to the re-expression of Christianity in new ways and in new locations, engaging with new possibilities during times of discontinuity. Those developing fresh expressions from contextual mission engage in this process today.

Within the narrative of discontinuity and possibility the prophetic turn acts as the driver turning disheartening discontinuity into hopeful possibility. The presence of this prophetic turn is crucial to a church in decline. However painful it may be for faith communities to engage with a script for loss, the prophetic offers hope and future possibility. Evidence of such a prophetic turn today could include prophetic critique and visionary language driving the reimagination of the Church.

Experiences of pioneers

For the purpose of this research, data from a qualitative study of pioneers' experiences was analysed for evidence of discontinuity and possibility, dialectic narrative and prophetic turn. Between 2008 and 2010 a qualitative research project was conducted looking into the experiences of pioneers starting fresh expressions. Focus groups were carried out across England with practitioners working in a variety of contexts. These included pioneers working in cities, towns and rural areas, developing fresh expressions with a diverse range of people, from a variety of social and economic backgrounds. During the focus groups, participants were simply asked briefly to explain to the group what it was they were doing, and what challenges and opportunities they were finding in their ministry. Whenever an issue was raised it was because it was a live issue for the pioneer and not in response to a framed set of questions. The data generated from these responses was then sifted for evidence of the Jeremiah themes.

The criteria for practitioners chosen for this included their proven ability to start a fresh expression. Participants could be lay or ordained, paid or voluntary and were from a range of denominations; however, the majority of participants were Anglican and in paid ministry. The initial stage of research is summarized in the Experiences of Pioneers report. This outlines lessons learnt, highlights good practice and areas for future development. The report can be downloaded at www.freshexpressions.org.uk/pioneerministry.

The next stage of the research involved a more thorough examination of the pioneers' responses as data from the focus groups was analysed for evidence of the three themes found in the Jeremiah call: discontinuity and possibility, a dialectic narrative and the prophetic turn. This qualitative research involved 26 pioneers in 3 focus groups. The findings have since been tested against a further focus group of 11 pioneers, which confirmed the results. This provided evidence of a common journey that pioneers travel as they develop new forms of church comparable to the concept of discontinuity and possibility found in the Jeremiah call.

Out of the 26 participants involved in the study, 19 expressed the need for more distance away from existing church practice. This break could be in terms of practices, beliefs or structures. Understandably the pioneers each vocalized their own experiences differently. For example, one pioneer emphasized dismantling structures as the catalyst to change, whereas another emphasized belief changes. However, running through these differences was clear evidence of pioneers questioning existing practice and seeking a break or level of discontinuity from existing structures.

As pioneers engaged with the mission context, new experiences conflicted with existing ideas and beliefs. Pioneers began to ask awkward questions as they tried to balance what they were now encountering with their previously held beliefs about mission and church. Figure 4 depicts this here as a downward journey of questioning and dismantling, towards a breaking down of practices, beliefs and structures. The pioneers described how new growth followed, often developing from a deepened awareness of contextual and missional practice, experimentation in belief and practice, and modified understandings of church. It can be tempting to jump to this phase, to focus on the growth, but however unnerving this first phase is for both pioneers and for churches they were planting from, it was this dismantling that appeared to create the space necessary for a deeper engagement with context and, in time, the development of new contextual Christian communities.

Figure 4: Discontinuity and possibility in the experiences of pioneers

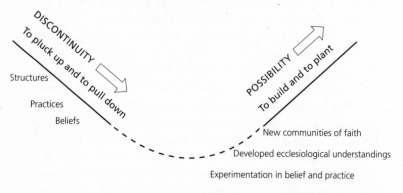

During this time of questioning and dismantling, pioneers sought out new structures, new practices and new beliefs that were appropriate to their journey. These new beliefs and practices were new to them but not novel. In fact this process pushed their understanding of mission and churchmanship to draw on the resources and practices of the wider Church – for example, drawing on monastic traditions and learning from cross-cultural mission. This process of drawing on other traditions was a creative response as pioneers tried to make sense of the Christian faith within their mission context. Other practices were not simply transplanted in; rather, pioneers grounded in their context sought out other traditions, re-theologized and creatively developed and shaped them within their own context. Eighteen out of the 26 participants provided evidence of this type of dialogue with their context, suggesting a link between pioneer ministry and dialectic narrative; however, their level of dialogical engagement varied quite significantly.

There appeared to be considerable differences in the experiences of pioneers connected to organizations such as Church Army, CMS, The Order of Mission and Venture FX,[2] organizations which could be referred to as sodal. These pioneers appeared more positive about the wider Church, were more engaged in their context, and more conversant about mission and its ecclesiological implications. Given the apparent differences, a closer analysis tracking differences in pioneers' experiences based on church context was undertaken. Before turning to this, some further information on sodal forms of church may be useful.

Modal and sodal forms of church

Current research on sodal forms of Christianity suggests that during times of decline, new possibilities often develop through 'second order' forms of faith, as new movements go ahead and beyond the decline to see new expressions of faith realized. Notable voices in this research include Romano's study of Roman Catholic founders and Winter's theory on sodalities. Other accounts are found in Murray (2004, pp. 319–39) and Whitworth (2008, pp. 59–93). Sodal structures, such as monastic or missionary movements, have repeatedly renewed modal forms of church, such as congregational or diocesan structures. In the early Church the modal synagogue and then diocesan structure grew through Paul's missionary sodality. Then during the Roman Empire and through the medieval period monastic orders renewed diocesan structures. Sodalities were then recovered in the

Protestant churches in the nineteenth century through the voluntary missionary societies. The recent emergence of new forms of monasticism provides evidence of this movement in the current context of decline.

These sodal structures retain an element of self-determination from the modal church, which enables them to act as frontier movements, often springing up in places of social change and developing fruitful models of praxis within that culture. The self-determination present in sodal structures allows a discontinuity of practice from previously established forms of faith and so creates possibilities for new forms of church to develop. The presence of self-determination within such a variety of sodal forms, including the New Testament church, medieval Roman Catholic monastic orders and Protestant nineteenth-century missionary societies, confirms the continuing importance of discontinuity as routes towards new growth within the Church.

In this study, pioneers were designated modal, sodal or mixed deployment status to evaluate the apparent differences in the data.

- Modally placed pioneers (12 out of the 26) were those developing fresh expressions within existing church structures. For example, a vicar or pioneer curate developing multiple congregations from a parish.
- Sodally placed pioneers (6 out of the 26) were those working outside existing church structures, developing new ways of being church within specific communities or contexts and connected to a sodal organization such as Church Army, CMS or The Order of Mission.

Sodal and modal pioneers were easy to spot. However, there was a whole group of pioneers who were somewhere in between.

- Pioneers with a mixed context (8 out of the 26) referred to individuals who were either trained or supported by sodal organizations but working in modal structures, or those trained and supported by modal structures but licensed to start fresh expressions outside of existing structures.

As the pioneers in the focus groups described the challenges to their ministry, 11 out of the 12 pioneers placed modally said their biggest challenges related to a lack of discontinuity from existing church structures and practice. This was slightly reduced in the mixed group where six out of the eight talked about a lack of discontinuity as the primary challenge. They appeared to begin the dismantling phase and then came up against immovable structures and became distracted by or locked into a narrative of antagonism with the existing church. They tried to question and dismantle; they tried to engage with this journey but were stopped here, and were restricted from engaging with this stage of discontinuity.

While most of the pioneers spoke really positively about the concept of mixed economy, that new forms of church could develop alongside more established congregations, in reality many pioneers were finding it really difficult and were frustrated that 'maintenance' issues reduced their ability to pioneer. Most had expected that they would spend a reasonable amount of time negotiating and educating the existing church community about mission. That this would become the primary challenge was a real surprise.

In contrast, none of the six sodally placed pioneers saw the existing church as an obstacle to mission; they were positive about the wider Church and happy with the level of connection they felt to it. Being sodally placed gave them a level of discontinuity with current forms of church that enabled them to journey down through the dismantling phase. In some cases they described in detail how their phase of discontinuity developed and had been resolved, enabling new Christian community to form.

When describing what it was they were pioneering, surprisingly, half of the modally placed pioneers made no mention at all of anyone outside of the church and no mention of contextual mission. These pioneers appeared to begin the dismantling phase, but struggled to achieve the discontinuity they sought. Some became antagonistic towards the Church, some distracted and some despondent about their ministry. This dramatically reduced their engagement with the context. More of the mixed group talked about contextual mission, with three-quarters describing the context or the community they were reaching.

In contrast, all of the sodally placed pioneers talked about context and mission; they were also significantly more conversant about the mission engaged in than other pioneers. They readily described their contextual practice, their experimentation with belief and practice, and how their understandings of church were being shaped and modified through their ministry. Unlike modally and mixed-placed pioneers they appeared to have evolved language appropriate for the task. This may have occurred through the training and support given by the sodal organization they were linked to. In some cases the organization acted as mediator or broker with a diocese to enable new structures to develop that were appropriate to the context and mission needs.

Figure 5: Evidence of the Jeremiah call in the experiences of current pioneers

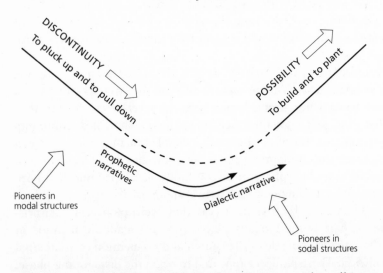

From these results it is possible to plot pioneers on the call image (Figure 5). Rather than just starting something new, pioneers appear to follow a common journey, which includes an initial stage of dismantling. This creates a level of discontinuity from previously held beliefs and practices and questions existing structures. Where access to discontinuity is restricted, as is often the case with those in modal contexts, pioneers become locked into a narrative of antagonism and become distracted from the mission task. In contrast, pioneers connected to sodal organizations have more freedom to work outside of existing church structures, and are released to work among non-churchgoers and those beyond the fringe of the existing Church. The placement of pioneers, whether in modal or sodal structures, drastically affects their relationship with the Church, their ability to engage with the mission context and in turn their ability to develop contextual forms of church.

It would be easy here to conclude that sodal structures provide the means for contextual mission, reaching out to those beyond the existing Church, and allow the distance needed from current church practice to enable contextual mission and church to develop. However, those sodally placed, developing new communities of faith away from existing churches, can become isolated and lack the resources that being connected to a mature church provides. Resources, long-term sustainability and developing leadership teams can be more difficult to manage when fresh expressions are developed with less connection to the wider Church. The placement of pioneers away from established church congregations can also remove those with evangelistic gifts from the wider body and inadvertently encourage a dichotomy between mission and ministry. Arguably, contextualization occurred post exile because the faith community was forced to practise its faith in new contexts. The cultural divide between church and society today suggests our new contexts are just outside the doors of our churches. Jeremiah's call challenges us to embrace our exile to move beyond the management of decline, or the urges simply to transplant, and to ask where God is calling us to plant.

A fruitful symbiotic relationship within the mixed economy, which allowed more freedom for leaders of fresh expressions within modal church structures and more connection and flow of resources between sodal and modal forms of church, could be a way forward. During the course of the research it became clear that some dioceses were developing their modal structures to enable pioneers to work more contextually. There was also evidence of parish churches acting as minsters, resourcing mission and sending out pioneers to work contextually. In this research these pioneers have been designated as mixed-placed pioneers. However, as these structures were still in the development stage it was unclear how these new structures would affect change in the long term.

Time for a prophetic turn?

While the presence of a prophetic turn is crucial to a church in decline, turning disheartening discontinuity into hopeful possibility, there was little evidence of prophetic narratives within the data. Possible evidence was found in seven participants, including the use of visionary language, prophetic critique and the prophetic role in the reimagination and renewal of the Church. This gives some evidence of the prophetic role of pioneers in renewing the Church. However, this is heavily outweighed by the responses of other pioneers in the study.

It is possible that the lack of clear evidence for a prophetic turn suggests that this element of the Jeremiah call is not currently relevant to pioneer ministry. However, in retrospect, I wonder whether prophetic narratives would have been more evident if pioneers had been asked other questions. Pioneers were asked to share about their ministry, their challenges and encouragements. In talking about their ministry pioneers were able to talk about a dialectic narrative, describing the context. In talking about challenges, issues of discontinuity were raised and encouragements appeared to cross both these themes. A couple of pioneers talked about the importance of vision while noting the lack of calling and vision language within the Church. They associated this lack of visionary language with difficulties in enabling church members to engage in mission. Perhaps asking questions about calling and vision may have helped, and certainly more research in this area would be valuable. In addition, given the historical evidence of resistance to the prophetic role of pioneers within the Church, it is perhaps worth questioning whether this dynamic is happening today and contributing to the pattern we see emerging in ministry.

At times, pioneers of new movements have been accepted as prophetic signs to the Church, such as Francis of Assisi; other plausible candidates being Anthony, Benedict and Booth. However, there are many others who were at the time deemed heretics and exiled, or executed, and who since are remembered as key figures within the faith, for example Athanasius, Wycliffe and Hus. The Jeremiah text is clear in questioning the ability of the recognized religious leaders to determine true and false prophecy (Jer. 5.30–31) and this tension is evidenced throughout the Church's historical treatment of pioneers. The histories of many religious foundations show that a new charism often generates confusion and provokes a negative response. 'However occasionally there is a shared experience of recognition where the one testifies to the presence of the same Spirit in the other' (Romano, 1994, p. 121). Pioneers have a prophetic role as individuals with the creative talents to lead people out of their cultural confusion in times of discontinuity and towards a renewed sense of meaning (Arbuckle, 1990, p. 66). The Spirit 'sets them on fire for a specific and unique prophetic task ... keeping them moving on ahead of the Church' (Romano, 1994, p. 61). The prophetic role of pioneers, seen in their critique of the established church, understandably continues as an area of antagonism throughout the Church's history. The relationship between pioneers and institutions has at best been volatile and at times destructive. However, this prophetic ministry in part depends on the institutional church recognizing and endorsing it. The Church has a profound role in discerning the same Spirit at work and encouraging the prophetic call of founders and pioneers.

Throughout the life of the Church, sodal movements such as monastic movements and missionary societies have grown up, some remaining connected to the established church tradition in which they developed and others establishing new traditions and denominations. Sodalities have arguably been most effective in expressing the gospel in new contexts when given the freedom to develop new practices yet in symbiotic relationship with modal forms. Church history gives a mixed picture of how possible a symbiotic relationship between established and emerging can be. However, it is in this very symbiosis that fresh expressions have been formed. To encourage this we need to hear again the prophetic call that God is at work in our decline and new growth, and though the journey may be painful there is a path of hope that others trod before us.

Conclusion

The Jeremiah call to pluck up and to pull down, to build and to plant is useful for imagining the role of pioneer ministry within the Church. The call represents a narrative of discontinuity and possibility. It is a two-stage process engaging in loss as a route towards rebirth. It offers a vision of God at work in the experiences of loss, creating future possibilities. It encourages a dialogue between Scripture and experience, re-theologizing faith within new contexts. It suggests that living faithfully today requires the Church to engage with the new contexts in which we find ourselves and to look for signs of God's presence. It invites us to build and to plant, to trust even where decline has left us feeling lost. The Jeremiah call acts as a prophetic turn, moving through discontinuity, to offer hope, inviting us to reimagine the prophet's words today, to ask what do we plant here, what do we build next? The ability of both pioneers and the wider Church to recognize the same Spirit at work and encourage the prophetic turn to new growth will affect the extent to which these fresh expressions of church will thrive, remain connected and in turn renew traditional church.

References

Arbuckle, G. A., 1990, *Earthing the Gospel*, Maryknoll, NY: Orbis Books.

Bevans, S. B., 2002, *Models of Contextual Theology*, rev. edn, Maryknoll, NY: Orbis Books.

Bosch, D. J., 1991, *Transforming Mission: Paradigm Shifts in Theology of Mission*, Maryknoll, NY: Orbis Books.

Brueggemann, W., 1998, *Exile and Homecoming: A Commentary on Jeremiah*, Grand Rapids, MI: Eerdmans.

Brueggemann, W., 2003, *An Introduction to the Old Testament: The Canon and Christian Imagination*, Louisville, KY: Westminster John Knox Press.

Brueggemann, W. and P. D. Miller, 2006, *Like Fire in the Bones: Listening for the Prophetic Word in Jeremiah*, Philadelphia, PA: Fortress Press.

Carroll, R. P., 1981, *From Chaos to Covenant*, London: SCM Press.

Carroll, R. P., 1984, 'Prophecy, Dissonance and Jeremiah', in L. G. Perdue (ed.), *A Prophet to the Nations: Essays in Jeremiah Studies*, Winona Lake, IN: Eisenbrauns.

Carroll, R. P., 1989, *Jeremiah*, Sheffield: JSOT Press.

Carroll, R. P., 1999, 'The Book of J: Intertextuality and Ideological Criticism', in P. Diamond and L. Stulman (eds), *Troubling Jeremiah*, Sheffield: Sheffield Academic Press, pp. 220–43.

Childs, B. S., 1985, *Old Testament Theology in a Canonical Context*, London: SCM Press.

Church Army's Research Unit, 2013, *An Analysis of Fresh Expressions and Church Plants Begun in the Period 1992–2012*, www.churchgrowthresearch.org.uk/UserFiles/File/Reports/churchgrowthresearch_fresh expressions.pdf.

Church Growth Research Programme, 2014, *From Anecdote to Evidence: Findings from the Church Growth Research Programme 2011–2013*, London: Church Commissioners for England.

Clements, R. E., 1996, *Old Testament Prophecy*, Louisville, KY: Westminster John Knox Press.

Croft, S., 2009, *Jesus People: What the Church Should Do Next*, London: Church House Publishing.

Jamieson, A., 2004, *Journeying in Faith*, London: SPCK.

Keith, B., 2010, *Experiences of Pioneers*, http://www.freshexpressions.org.uk/sites/default/files/freshexpressions-pioneers.pdf.

McKane, W., 1986, *A Critical and Exegetical Commentary on Jeremiah*, 2 vols, Edinburgh: T. & T. Clark.

Murray, S., 2004, *Post-Christendom*, Carlisle: Paternoster Press.

Riddell, M., 1998, *Threshold of the Future*, London: SPCK.

Romano, A., 1994, *The Charism of the Founders*, Slough: St Pauls Press.

Walls, A. F., 1996, *The Missionary Movement in Christian History*, Mary-knoll, NY: Orbis Books.

Whitworth, P., 2008, *Prepare for Exile: A New Spirituality and Mission for the Church*, London: SPCK.

Winter, R. D., 1974, 'The Two Structures of God's Redemptive Mission', *Missiology: An International Review* 2.1, pp. 121–39.

Notes

1 Factors associated with decline are discussed in Church Growth Research Programme, 2014.

2 Church Army is a predominantly Anglican society of evangelists, founded in 1882, to enable people to come to living faith in Jesus Christ. Church Army trains, equips and deploys evangelists to develop appropriate and relevant forms of Christian community for pioneering situations. The Church Mission Society (CMS), founded in 1799, now exists as a community of people in mission. CMS is committed to evangelistic mission, working to see our world transformed by the love of Jesus, through making disciples, resourcing leaders and transforming communities. Founded in 2003, The Order of Mission (TOM), is a dispersed community of leaders engaged in mission across the world. It is a group of people who see their primary vocation as missionaries, have taken lifelong vows of simplicity, purity and accountability and live by a rule of life. Venture FX is a scheme set up by the Methodist Church in 2008 to reach younger people with no Christian heritage. Venture FX pioneers are called to be at the edges, inviting people to be disciples of Jesus and to live out that discipleship in radical and relevant community with others, through the core values of innovation, imagination and incarnation.

8

Conflicts in the Church: Some Mythological Reflections[1]

GERALD A. ARBUCKLE

Human beings originally began philosophy, as they do now, because of wonder ... This is why the myth-lover is also a philosopher in his way, since myth is composed of wonders. (Aristotle, 982b)

The purpose of this chapter is simply to focus on some conflicts in the contemporary Church from a cultural anthropological perspective. Rarely have anthropologists turned their intrusive gaze on the cultural realities of the Church. Today I dare to do so. Anthropology, as Raymond Firth said, 'is an inquisitive, challenging, uncomfortable discipline, questioning established positions ... peering into underlying interests, if not destroying fictions and empty phrases ... at least exposing them' (Firth, 1981, p. 200). Let us see if I can live up to Firth's description.

I begin by defining what I mean by myth and narrative. I will then focus on one function of myth and narrative, namely their ability to legitimize the way people act. This will be illustrated with examples from what is happening within our contemporary Church. Finally, I will seek to explain why binary oppositions within myths evoke particular, ideological conflicts within the Church.

First, let me define this slippery word culture. Only those people who assume that the Church is a pure spirit can claim that it does not form a culture and cultures. It is no misty entity (de Lubac, 1956, p. 114). Inaccurate perceptions of and defective attitudes to culture, and therefore myth analysis, have led, and continue to lead, to bad theology, as well as faulty pastoral policies and practices (Arbuckle, 2011, pp. xix–xxiv). Culture is a pattern of meanings encased in a network of symbols, myths, narratives and rituals, created by individuals and subdivisions, as they struggle to respond to the competitive pressures of power and limited resources in a rapidly globalizing and fragmenting world. Culture instructs its adherents about what is considered to be the correct, orderly way to feel, think and behave (Arbuckle, 2011 p. 17). Note the emphasis on order and feeling. Culture is 90 per cent feeling!

The key word I wish to concentrate on is *myth*. Father Louis Luzbetak was right: 'The study of myth … is as difficult as it is important' (Luzbetak, 1988, p. 266). The knowledge of local mythology can 'provide contact points for the transmission of the Christian message [and] … myths can help locate points of conflict between the Gospel and traditional ways of thinking and behaving.'[2] There is very little philosophical reflection on the importance of myths simply because philosophers rarely take myths seriously.[3] Likewise contemporary theologians and historians, despite the volumes they have written, seem hesitant to ponder the importance of myths in analysing Vatican II documents and their impact on our contemporary ecclesiastical cultures.

Myths

Myths, according to anthropologist Malinowski, are charters for social organization; that is, they describe why things are the way they are, and why people should continue to act in the same way. Myths are value-impregnated beliefs or stories. They are the glue that binds people together at the deepest level of their group life. They are stories that people live by and for. They claim to reveal in an imaginative and symbolic way fundamental truths about the world and human life (Arbuckle, 1990, pp. 26–43, and Arbuckle, 2011, pp. 19–42). They are efforts to explain what usually is beyond empirical observation, and to some degree outside human experience. This is why Aristotle says myths are composed of wonders. And wonders can never be fully described. Or, as that master of mythology, John Ronald Tolkien, warned us, 'The significance of myth is not easily to be pinned on paper by analytical reasoning ...; unless [we] are careful ... [we] will kill what [we] are studying by vivisection' (Duriez, 2012, p. 174).

In brief, myths tell those who believe them what reality is and what it should be (Lincoln, 1989, p. 24). The fact is that no matter how seriously we seek to deepen our grasp of the meaning of myths, they will remain somewhat emotively ambiguous and mysterious, because they attempt to articulate what cannot be fully articulated. As Paul Ricoeur writes, myths contain a surplus of meaning; that is, myths have an inexhaustible supply of possible meanings (Ricoeur, 1976). Myths are not falsehoods, but truths that are imaginative insights, more profound than scientific and logical analyses to those who accept them.

Myths can evoke deep emotional responses and a sense of mystery or wonder, as Aristotle writes, simply because they develop out of the very depths of human experience. The emotional quality of myths is especially evident in what I call 'residual myths'. A residual myth is one with little or no daily impact on a group's life, but at times it can surface to become a powerful operative myth. They lurk in the culture unconscious, always waiting to re-emerge. Slobodan Milosevic, the Serb leader, manipulated Serbian public opinion in his incendiary speech of 28 June 1989, by invoking a residual myth of humiliation when he recalled the defeat of Serbs by Muslims in 1389. Similarly, the myths of the pre-Vatican II church still lurk deep in the collective unconscious of the Church's culture, and are forever rising to the surface. For this reason we speak of myths as reservoirs of memory.

Myths and history

Luzbetak writes that 'a myth in the technical sense is like a parable, play, novel or poem; even when not historical, scientific or within the realm of human experience, it can nevertheless be a veritable treasurehouse of truth' (Luzbetak, 1988, p. 266). However, myth and history do not necessarily contradict each other, because each relates to facts from its own standpoint; history observes facts from the 'outer physical side, myth from the inner spiritual side' (Kelsey, 1974, p. 4). Myths are moral commentaries on history. The example of Abraham Lincoln, tramping several miles through snow to return a few coins overcharged to a customer in his store, may or may not be historically true, but it conveys critically important values to the American people down through the ages. However, myths can twist historical facts, as we will see.

Narratives

Myth and narrative are two sides of the one coin (see Figure 1). Myths make our lives intelligible in the *past*, but the retelling of these stories in light of *present* needs is what we call narratives. In the process, the myths are enlarged, altered, or even discarded, though it is always assumed that the myths remain unchanged. The myths legitimize the authenticity of the narratives, even though they may conflict with historical facts (Arbuckle, 2011, p. 72).

Figure 1: Myths and narratives

Myths	Narratives
stories that make sense of the past	stories that apply myths to present context

The aim of myths and their contemporary application through narratives is to legitimize, as Malinowski asserts, actions. The following are examples of the ways in which narratives create new identities and in the process foundational myths are changed or revitalized.

Examples of narrative changes

Narratives of refounding

Refounding is the process whereby people relive the founding mythology of a group, and are so inspired by the experience that they imaginatively, and creatively, search for thoroughly new ways to relate to the contemporary world. Refounding goes to the roots of problems, renewal only to the symptoms. As Paul Ricoeur writes, a refounding narrative can encourage people to 'try new ideas, new values, new ways of being-in-the-world' (Ricoeur, 1970, p. 134) and consequently achieve radically new identities.

For example, the narratives of the Second Vatican Council called for a refounding of the Church, a radical cultural shift in values and behaviour, not merely a superficial renewal. The Council evoked a 'mythical earthquake', a movement 'from commands to invitations, from laws to ideals, from definition to mystery, from threats to persuasion, from coercion to conscience, from monologue to dialogue, from ruling to serving, from with-drawal to integrated' (O'Malley 2008, p. 307). Sure, the Council remained faithful to the authentic tradition of the Church, but this must not hide or downplay the fact that it evoked dramatic mythic and behavioural ruptures – ruptures that called for the refounding of the Church itself, not merely superficial adjust-ments of existing structures. As an anthropologist looking at the Council documents, I cannot stress enough the radical nature of the cultural breaks with the past. Certainly there is continuity, but to deny the enormity of these cultural ruptures is to deny the radical call to return to the founding mythology of the Church.[4]

What narratives now predominate in the Church? Let me high-light, as an anthropologist, several narratives that do not take this call to return to the founding mythology of the Church seriously. Though I identify different narratives, in practice they often over-lap (Arbuckle, 2013, pp. 9–30).

Narratives of cultural romanticism

Narratives of cultural romanticism idealize a cultural past. For example, sometimes it is said that the Church is not a democracy – it has never been and will never be one, and so Rome can justifiably ignore the values of participative or consultative leadership. There has been what is called a myth drift. Not only is this contrary to the spirit of Vatican II, but it ignores the original practice of the Church for a significant period of history. For example, historian Leonard Swidler concludes that as late as the beginning of the twentieth century fewer than half of the world's bishops were directly chosen by the pope (Swidler, 1986, p. 310).

Narratives of fundamentalism

Political and/or religious fundamentalism is apt to occur in almost every society or organization as a reaction to cultural chaos. People yearn for simplistic, clear-cut identities in the midst of this confusion. There are no grey areas of uncertainty, only absolute answers. People sense that history has gone awry and their task is to restore it to 'normality', as defined by themselves (Arbuckle, 2004, pp. 195–214).

Within the Catholic Church fundamentalism is present in different forms, in reaction to the dramatic theological and cultural changes introduced by Vatican II. The residual mythology of the pre-Council church resurfaces in narrative form. Sects like Catholics United for the Faith (CUF) have formed to defend the Church against what they call the 'evils of secular humanism', 'the loss of orthodoxy' or the 'liberalizing excesses that Vatican II inspired'. Catholic fundamentalists are highly selective in what pertains to the Church's identity, insisting on accidentals, not the substance of issues, and readily ignore papal teaching on social justice. As in all orthodoxy crazes, respect for truth and human rights can sadly suffer.[5]

Narratives of disconnection

In narratives of disconnection leaders proclaim that narrative policies of their institutions are true to their founding myths, but in fact this is not the case (Arbuckle, 1993, pp. 72–92).

For example, in 2000 John Paul II wrote that, in the conclusions of Vatican II, 'we find a sure compass by which to take our bearings'. That is, he insisted that the fundamental mythological theological shifts such as collegiality would be adhered to (John Paul II, 2001, p. 75). However, narratives emanating from Roman congregations since then have commonly contradicted this statement.[6] In 2001 Rome issued a document, *Liturgiam Authenticam*, without consultation with the episcopal chairman of the International Commission on English in the Liturgy (ICEL), reaffirming a ban on gender-inclusive language (see *The Tablet*, 12 May 2001, pp. 704–5). The document's narrative asserts that Rome has the right to intervene in liturgical matters, but this contradicts the Council's mythology. John Allen writes: 'The document strikes at the heart of Vatican II ecclesiology by centralizing power in the curia and by insisting that local cultures adopt an essentially Roman style or worship' (Allen, 2001, p. 13).

Narratives of acculturation

Narratives of acculturation are the conscious or unconscious absorption of the values and customs of another culture. For example, patriarchy is a social system in which the male gender role acts as the primary authority and power figure at the heart of all social relations. Integral to patriarchy is the assumption that men must rule and maintain female subordination. Within the Church, the insistence that exclusive or patriarchal language still be used in the liturgy is a narrative that denies the findings of contemporary scriptural research, facts of history and the insights of contemporary social movements for gender equality (Arbuckle, 2004, pp. 39–43, 69–72).

In pre-Pauline and Pauline Christian communities, women appear to have acted in almost identical ways to men (Abrahamsen,

1993, p. 816). As Maureen Fiedler records, women preached the gospel, went on missionary journeys, and filled some leadership functions in early Christian communities (Fiedler, 1998, pp. 121–2). All this was to change with the Peace of Constantine (AD 313), when persecutions against Christians ceased. From then on the Church's leadership embraced the patriarchal values and structures of contemporary Roman culture. Even some early fathers of the Church in their theologizing about the role of women in the Church often uncritically absorbed the contemporary cultural views about the gender superiority of men.[7]

Narratives that silence mourning

Narratives of mourning are processes whereby losses are formally and publicly acknowledged and allowed to slip into the past (Arbuckle, 1991, pp. 25–41). Then the future is able to be slowly, and more or less confidently embraced with all its uncertainties, fears and hopes. In both Old and New Testaments we see many examples of people who, once they begin to recount the story of their grief, are able to discover new hope, new visions of society, new identities.

The public mourning of grief can, however, be silenced. Tyrannical governments particularly fear the public display of grief at funerals of their victims, for it is there that the narratives of sadness can energize people to further resist tyranny (Brueggemann, 1987, pp. 72–91). Yet unarticulated grief remains like a powder-keg waiting to be ignited into all kinds of individual and community-destroying behaviour. Ovid, the first-century Roman poet, well described the reality of unnamed grief: 'Suppressed grief suffocates' (Ovid, Book V, eleg. 1, line 63).

Today the Church is overloaded with unarticulated grief. This is a consequence of repeated losses. Here are some of the issues that have caused, and continue to cause, so much unresolved grief: the departure of people in their thousands from the Church; the closure of parishes often without consultation; sexual abuse scandals; questionable liturgical changes; the failure of Rome and bishops to consult; witch-hunting of theologians; lack of due process in ecclesiastical trials;[8] discouragement of responsible dissent, even their public excommunication;[9] the controversial criticism of the Leadership Conference of Women Religious (LCWR) by the Vatican. Restorationists discourage or prevent narratives of grieving. Instead they are reviving the narratives of the pre-Council church in order to block people from creating narratives that would vibrantly relate the Council's theology to contemporary pastoral issues.

Polarities in myths

Controversial anthropologist Claude Levi-Strauss makes two positive contributions to our understanding of myths: their often inherent, complementary polarities and the ability of myths to reconcile these polarities. However, these myths very rarely spell out precisely *how* the reconciliation is to take place (Leach, 1970, pp. 54–82). Therefore, because people cannot live in uncertainties they gravitate to one pole or the other, often in an ideologically rigid manner. These insights throw more light on the continuity/ discontinuity debate regarding the documents of Vatican II.

In the mythology of democracy there are two complementary poles: the rights of the individual and the rights of the common good. The third quality, 'fraternity', is the balance between these two mythological poles. What 'fraternity' means in practice will depend on which polar opposite is emphasized. For Americans, fraternity means that the rights of the individual are to be respected, even though the common good may suffer.[10] Since the rights of the individual take precedence, the individual retains, for example, the unqualified right to own guns despite the clear, tragic consequences to the community.[11] Not surprisingly, therefore, interest groups such as the National Rifle Association are able to wield considerable unrestrained economic and political power. Even the medical profession constitutes a powerful lobby, through its professional associations and major insurance corporations. Any attempt by governments to redress the imbalance in favour of the common good is met with strong emotional opposition. Hence, healthcare reform also, which respects the needs of the common good, has been so difficult to achieve in the United States (Arbuckle, 2000, pp. 65–76, and Arbuckle, 2013a, pp. 93–4).

The documents of Vatican II are filled with ambiguities and tensions, resulting from the reintroduction of the polar opposites of key myths within the original creation mythology. Gone are the many certainties of the pre-conciliar apologetics, constructed on the assumption that complementary theological opposites did not exist. Here are some of the mythic ambiguities contained in the documents (see Arbuckle, 1993, pp. 39–43):[12]

> The Church is universal, *but* it is to be incarnated within local churches to reflect their diversities of culture.

> The Church is an institution under the leadership of the bishops who are committed to maintain order and unity, *but* it is also the People of God who, as pilgrims, are not concerned about rank.

> The pope has full, supreme, and universal power over the Church, *but* the bishops collegially govern their dioceses with authority that is proper to them.

These polar opposites are concretized in two often emotionally opposing theologies: the neo-Augustinian and the neo-Thomist. Mythologically, however, though the theologies are opposed to each other, 'neither one can exclude its opposite' (McCool, 1989, p. 216). Nowhere in the documents does the Council spell out precisely *how* these polar opposites are to be balanced in real life. In fact it simply could not do so. Rather, it rightly challenged all members of the Church to struggle to develop a living balance between the opposites through charity, ongoing mutual respect and dialogue. When this does not happen, however, people over-identify with one pole or the other.

Ultimately, this balance is achievable over time only if all sides are able to interiorize the vision of the Church as Christ's mystical body given us by St Paul: 'Now Christ's body is yourselves, each of you with a part to play in the whole' (1 Cor. 12.27 NJB).

Conclusion

Let me conclude with a summary and a sign of hope.

Symbols, myths and rituals are not replaced as quickly or as easily as buildings or landscapes, or mass-produced as neatly as automobiles or toothbrushes. The uprooting of the inner framework of cultures, even when there is conscious and intellectual assent to what is happening, destroys a people's stable sense of belonging. They are bound to experience lengthy periods of loss and confusion. The establishment of appropriate structures and power systems, based on the revitalized founding mythology, is a long and often tortuous process. It demands patience, the ability to live in a fair degree of ambiguity until these structures are firmly and confidently in place.

But culture gives people a vital sense of belonging. When uncertainty rears its frightening head, the residual status quo of culture resurfaces. People fall back on their tried-and-true ways of feeling and acting in order to weather the storm evoked by the fear of cultural change. As one experienced observer said, 'Culture can eat strategy for lunch!' (Clark, 2011, p. 133). Leaders skilled in cultural change are needed to lead people sensitively through mythic changes. If leaders fail, their followers are left in more confusion. Residual power structures re-emerge stronger than ever. Often there is a short period of concessions to change by those now in power, then a growing rigidity and insistence on widespread conformity and uniformity builds frustration to breaking point. Such is the case for some countries following the revolutionary movements of the Arab Spring, Egypt for example.

This theory helps to explain some significant conflicts that have followed Vatican II. The Council fathers did not foresee that cultures, especially a deeply embedded, long-standing, highly centralized and authoritarian culture of the pre-conciliar Church, do not change smoothly simply because a document says they should (Arbuckle, 1993, pp. 36–66, and Arbuckle, 2013, pp. 34–67). Many Council fathers and their successors were ill-equipped to lead cultural changes. Consequently, the residual mythology of the pre-conciliar Church rapidly resurfaced. This is especially evident in the restorationist behaviour of the Roman Curia. The pendulum has swung firmly in favour of the first parts of the polar opposites that I have described (Mannion, 2007, pp. 43–74).

At the same time thousands upon thousands of lay people, priests and members of religious congregations took the Council's documents with intense seriousness. The mythic beliefs became deeply embedded in their lives. The residual mythology of the pre-conciliar Church no longer made theological and pastoral sense to them. They have watched with ever-deepening sadness, even despair, the poverty of hierarchical leadership that became all too common in recent decades. Hence, the conflicts I have described.

Yet, something remarkable has occurred to give us hope. The residual founding mythology of the Church itself, not the pre-conciliar mythology, has dramatically resurfaced. Pope Francis, from the moment of his election, adopted a new style of leadership based on the founding mythology of the Church itself: 'unlike his predecessor, no mitre with gold and jewels, no ermine-trimmed cape, no made-to-measure red shoes and headwear, no magnificent throne'. And he 'deliberately abstains from solemn gestures and high-flown rhetoric and speaks the language of the people'.[13] To quote Elton John: 'Francis is a miracle of humility in an era of vanity ... This pope seems to want to bring the Church back to the ancient values of Christ and at the same time [bring it into] the 21st century.'[14]

I believe we can speak of Francis as a 'gospel comedian'. All good comedians, such as King Lear's Fool and, in the early days of the movies, Charlie Chaplin (and even Chaplin's somewhat infamous comedian contemporary Fatty Arbuckle), have one thing in common. Chaplin refused to be crushed by the pomposity and arrogance of government officials. In fact, such figures were reduced to objects of fun and even pity (Hyers, 1991, pp. 64–5).

True comedians are able to touch the hearts of their audiences at a profoundly deep level. We just feel they understand. They are liminal people, projecting in their behaviour society's fundamental incongruities such as hope and despair, order and disorder. Yet they are able at the same time to transcend these incongruities. They deliberately create disorder in the midst of order to give the appearance of incongruity. They call us into this incongruous situation to experience its tensions and then invite us to identify the resolution of these tensions. The social status quo is not set in concrete (Arbuckle, 2008, pp. 52–5).

Anthropologist Mary Douglas speaks of comedians as 'ritual purifiers'. She even proposes that 'perhaps the joker should be classed as a kind of minor mystic' (Douglas, 1966, p. 108) because comedians invite their audiences to critique orderly structures and status in society in search of values and truths about life. Good comedians mock on behalf of humanity the behaviour of those who unduly assert authority, who overly insist on rules and obedience to traditions. They do not just condemn the world of status, wealth, power and violence, but in some way provide us with a feeling of hope. Like biblical prophets, they hold out irrepressible hope that life is not necessarily preordained towards defeat, collapse and tragedy, that fate is conquerable.

Such is the role and attraction of Francis, a gospel comedian! Peter Berger asserts that humour is a revelation of the transcendence, a cautious call to redemption, and for this reason 'the actions of a clown take on a sacramental dignity' (Berger, 1969, p. 114). This is what St Paul is referring to when he describes to the fractious Corinthians his own role as a clown of Christ, without social status and power: 'We are fools for the sake of Christ, but you are so wise ... We are weak, but you are strong! You are honoured, we are dishonoured ... We have become the scum of the earth, the garbage of the world – right up to his moment' (1 Cor. 4.10, 13).

Pope Adrian VI declared in 1523 that 'We know well that even in this Holy See ... abominable things have happened ... We intend to use all diligence to reform the Roman Curia' (Accattoli, 1998, p. 7). A similar challenge now faces Francis. He must translate his symbolic gestures into wider structurally supported action at key levels of the Church. An anthropologist cannot minimize the enormity of the challenges and risks. We need to be ever mindful of the anthropological axiom: when strategies hit cultures, cultures win! We cannot underestimate the built-in cultural resistances to reform within the Church. Restorationism, with its roots firmly in pre-Vatican II mythology, is very likely to go underground and remain a powerful residual mythology just waiting for the chance to resurface once more with powerful force as it did after Vatican II.[15] My hope for Francis, therefore, is this: that he have insight into the ways in which culture can aid or hinder the fulfilment of the Church's mission, and that he possesses the intervention skills to make desired changes happen in the structures of the Church (Schein, 1987, p. 320).

References

Abrahamsen, V., 1993, 'Women,' Oxford Companion to the Bible, ed. B. M. Metzger and M. D. Coogan, New York: Oxford University Press.

Accattoli, L., 1998, When a Pope Asks for Forgiveness, New York: Alba House.

Allen, J. L., 2001, 'New Document Replaces 35 Years of Liturgy Work', National Catholic Reporter, 25 May.

Arbuckle, G. A., 1990, Earthing the Gospel: An Inculturation Handbook for Pastoral Workers, Maryknoll, NY: Orbis Books.

Arbuckle G. A., 1991, Change, Grief, and Renewal in the Church: A Spirituality for a New Era, Westminster, MD: Christian Classics.

Arbuckle, G. A., 1993, Refounding the Church: Dissent for Leadership, Maryknoll, NY: Orbis Books.

Arbuckle, G. A., 2000, Healthcare Ministry: Refounding the Mission in Tumultuous Times, Collegeville, MN: Liturgical Press.

Arbuckle, G. A., 2004, Violence, Society, and the Church: A Cultural Approach, Collegeville, MN: Liturgical Press.

Arbuckle, G. A., 2008, Laughing with God: Humor, Culture, and Transformation, Collegeville, MN: Liturgical Press.

Arbuckle, G. A., 2011, Culture, Inculturation, and Theologians: A Postmodern Critique, Collegeville, MN: Liturgical Press.

Arbuckle, G. A., 2013, Catholic Identity or Identities? Refounding Ministries in Chaotic Times, Collegeville, MN: Liturgical Press.

Arbuckle, G. A., 2013a, *Humanizing Healthcare Ministries*, Philadelphia, PA: Jessica Kingsley.

Aristotle, 1995, *Metaphysics*, 982b, *Selected Writings*, trans. T. Irwin and G. Fine, Indianapolis, IN: Hackett.

Berger, P., 1969, *A Rumour of Angels: Modern Society and the Rediscovery of the Supernatural*, Harmondsworth: Penguin Books.

Brueggemann, W., 1987, *Hope within History*, Atlanta, CA: John Knox Press.

Clark, R., 2011, cited by R. Ashkenas, S. Francis and R. Heinick, 'The Merger Dividend', *Harvard Business Review*, 89.8/9 (July–August).

de Lubac, H., 1956, *The Splendour of the Church*, London: Sheed & Ward.

Douglas, M., 1966, *Purity and Danger: An Analysis of Concepts of Pollution and Taboo*, Harmondsworth: Penguin Books.

Duriez, C., 2012, *J. R. R. Tolkien: The Making of a Legend*, Oxford: Lion Hudson.

Fiedler, M., 1998, 'Gender Equality: Theory and Practice', in M. Fiedler and L. Rabben (eds), *Rome Has Spoken*, New York: Crossroad.

Firth, R., 1981, 'Engagement and Detachment: Reflections on Applying Social Anthropology to Social Action', *Human Organization* 40.

Hyers, C., 1991, *The Comic Vision and the Christian Faith: A Celebration of Life and Laughter*, New York: Pilgrim Press.

John Paul II, 2001, Apostolic Letter, *At the Beginning of the New Millennium*, Sydney: St Paul's Publications.

Kelsey, M., 1974, *Myth, History and Faith: The Demythologizing of Christianity*, New York: Paulist Press.

Leach, E., 1970, *Levi-Strauss*, London: Fontana.

Lincoln, B., 1989, *Discourse and the Construction of Society: Comparative Studies of Myth, Ritual, and Classification*, Oxford: Oxford University Press.

Luzbetak, L. J., 1988, *The Church and Cultures: New Perspectives in Missiological Anthropology*, Maryknoll, NY: Orbis Books.

O'Malley, J. W., 2008, *What Happened at the Council?*, Cambridge, MA: Belknap/Harvard University Press.

Mannion, G., 2007, *Ecclesiology and Postmodernity: Questions for the Church*, Collegeville, MN: Liturgical Press.

McCool, G., 1989, *From Unity to Pluralism: The Internal Evolution of Thomism*, New York: Fordham University Press.

Ovid, *Tristia*, Book V.

Ricoeur, P., 1970, 'The Function of Fiction in Shaping Reality', *Man and World* 12.2.

Ricoeur, P., 1976, *Interpretation Theory: Discourse and the Surplus of Meaning*, Fort Worth, TX: Texas Christian University Press.

Schein, E. H., 1987, *Organizational Culture and Leadership*, San Francisco, CA: Jossey-Bass.

Swidler, L., 1986, 'Democracy, Dissent, and Dialogue', in Hans Kung and Leonard Swidler (eds), *The Church in Anguish*, San Francisco, CA: Harper & Row.

Notes

1 A version of the chapter was originally presented at the Catholic Theological Union, Chicago, 9 October 2013.

2 Luzbetak, 1988, p. 284. Luzbetak cites in agreement the assertions of Jacob Loewen. See Jacob A. Loewen, 'Myth as an Aid to Missions', *Practical Anthropology* 16, pp. 185–92.

3 See Kevin Schilbrack, 'Introduction: On the Use of Philosophy in the Study of Myths', in K. Schilbrack (ed.), *Thinking through Myths: Philosophical Perspectives*, London: Routledge, 2002, pp. 1–17.

4 'It is hard from [the standpoints of sociology and of history] not to stress the discontinuity, the experience of an event that broke with routine.' Joseph A. Komonchak, 'Novelty in Continuity: Pope Benedict's Interpretation of Vatican II', www.americamagazine.org/issue/684/article/novelty-continuity (accessed 14 January 2013).

5 See Arbuckle, 1993, pp. 51–4.

6 Bishop Fellay, Superior General of the traditionalist Society of St Pius X, reportedly stated that accepting the Council's teaching is no longer 'a prerequisite for the canonical solution' of the status of the society. At www.cathnews.com/article.aspx?aeid=31699 (accessed 8 June 2012).

7 For example, Tertullian in the third century declared that women are dangerous to men: 'You are the devil's gateway ... you are the deserter of the divine law.' Quoted by Fiedler and Rabben, 1998, p. 114. Because women, according to the culture of the time, were considered in some way impure, they had to be excluded from direct involvement in liturgies. The Synod of Laodicea in the fourth century declared, 'Women are not allowed to approach the altar' (Fiedler and Rabben, 1998, p. 115). The Synod of Paris in 829 told women not to press around the altar or touch the sacred vessels (Fiedler and Rabben, 1998, p. 116).

8 For example, the dismissal of Bishop Bill Morris of the Toowoomba diocese, Australia, 2011. He has never been told the names of his accusers nor what he was formally accused of; nor has he seen the official Vatican visitor's report. See Michael Kelly, 'Rites and Wrongs', *The Tablet* (21 January 2012), pp. 4–5.

9 For example, the excommunication by Bishop Thomas Olmsted of Phoenix, USA, of Sr Margaret McBride in 2010 for having made, according to reputable moralists, a justified decision to save the life of a pregnant

mother. She was accused of permitting abortion. See T. Roberts, *The Emerging Catholic Church: A Community's Search for Itself*, Maryknoll, NY: Orbis Books, 2011, pp. 151–3.

10 See Bruce Kapferer, *Legends of People: Myths of State*, Washington, DC: Smithsonian Institution Press, 1988, pp. 121–208; Les Carlyon, *Gallipoli*, Sydney: Macmillan, 2001, pp. 122–4. In the United States historically the tension between Federalists and Republicans, so evident in the time of President Thomas Jefferson, is an example of mythological polarities. See Jon Meacham, *Thomas Jefferson: The Art of Power*, New York: Random House, 2012, pp. 239–41; also, the tension between the states and federal government reflects the built-in tension within the Constitution.

11 The shutdown of the American government in October 2013 is an example of the inherent tendency to polarization within the administrative system. The leading article in *The Economist* (5 October 2013) states: 'America needs to tackle polarization. The problem is especially acute in the House ...' (p. 11).

12 See Arbuckle, 1993, pp. 39–43.

13 Hans Küng, 'The Paradox of Pope Francis', reported in www.ncronline.org/print/news/Vatican/paradox-pope-francis (accessed 28 May 2013).

14 http://blog.wenn.com/all-news/elton-john-praises-pope-francis/ (accessed 19 July 2013).

15 Pope Francis is firmly against restorationism: 'If the Christian is a restorationist, a legalist, if he (*sic*) wants everything clear and safe, then he will find nothing ... Those who today always look for disciplinarian solutions, those who long for an exaggerated doctrinal "security", those who stubbornly try to recover a past that no longer exists – they have a static and inward-directed view of things.' See www.americamagazine.org/pope-interview (accessed 1 October 2013), p. 11.

9

Located and Rooted: Contextual Theology and Pioneer Ministry

SIMON SUTCLIFFE

'All theology is contextual!'

That is often the claim of those who want to either relegate contextual theology as a lesser discipline or make a claim for its dominance in the arena of Christian thinking. Behind the argument for those who want to deny (or at least reduce the influence of) contextual theology as an academic discipline is a socio-historic claim that is, in essence, true. The argument suggests that all theologies are deeply informed by the culture, thought forms and existential questions of their time. So without doubt a particular theologian or ecumenical council is a product of its social and cultural milieu – how could it not be? So, the argument goes, all we need to do is study theology as a normal academic discipline (often known as systematic or doctrinal theology) and not worry about creating another genre of theological discourse that could be called contextual theology. The problem with such an understanding is that it denies the possibility that new, different models and methods for doing theology might be possible. In other words, a theological discourse that relies on a theologian drawing upon the past to understand the present is unlikely to exploit the possibilities of discovering the present in order to reassess the past. So it is necessary for a theological discipline to develop a way of doing theology that takes seriously that which is present and local and place it into an intentional dialogue with the tradition of the Church.

There are those, of course, who want to make a case for the discipline of contextual theology to dominate all theological discourse as the only legitimate form of theology. Again, there is merit to such an understanding. How are we to speak to a new generation of the things of God if we cannot find a way of relating our current situation to the ancient and yet dominant language of the Church that we call theology? But if we offer a new theological understanding (or language) without the ability to translate or interpret, we deny ourselves the opportunity to communicate with those whose dominant language is theology as expressed in the tradition of the Church. In other words, contextual theologians can isolate their work to such an extent that they cease to be seen as part of the community that is the Body of Christ.

As such this chapter is severely limited – it is neither in the remit of this book nor the scope of this chapter to begin to outline the various models and methods of contextual theology. It is impossible here to offer a 'how to' of contextual theology. What I hope to do is to make a case as to why pioneer ministers ought to be attentive to contextual theology, as a discipline, and why they should be the ones who are leading the charge to create innovative, imaginative and deeply profound articulations of God, faith, church and the human condition.

My proposal for this chapter is very modest – I simply want to explore two questions that appear obvious but, I believe, have been given relatively little exposure in the literature generated out of the Mission-Shaped Church movement. I want to ask:

- Why is theology important to a pioneer?
- Why is context important to a pioneer?

It is in the asking of these questions that we begin to determine the importance of contextual theology for those engaged in pioneering ministry; and in discovering the importance of contextual theology it is my hope that those who select, train and deploy pioneer ministers will recognize the significance of academia in the formation of those called to such a ministry.

Theology as language and memory: to be rooted

So why might theology be important to pioneer ministry? At first sight this may seem either a ridiculous question or an insulting one. I am not suggesting that pioneer ministers do not know or do theology, nor am I suggesting that pioneer training courses are deficient (although there is always room for more theology!). It is clear, though, from listening and working with other pioneers that our natural instinct is as practitioners. The joy of belonging to a community of practice like Venture FX is that I spend time with creative people who can both imagine new possibilities and work them into existence. Most of the pioneers I know have been 'hanging around' on the edge of church or ecclesia just waiting for an opportunity to 'get on'. They are doers, activists, highly motivated practitioners. A pioneer will pioneer whether the Church affirms them or not – it's in their blood.

So sometimes it can seem counter-intuitive to a pioneer to engage in theological enquiry that is not directly related to the job at hand. However, Daniel Migliore writes: 'Questionable indeed is the theology whose theory is no longer linked to transforming praxis. But the criticism is one sided. If theory without praxis is empty, praxis without theory is blind' (Migliore, 1991, p. 8). To be a theologian is a primary task of the pioneer. It is the reading, doing and expressing theology that forms part of the raw material for the creative and imaginative processes with which they are called to engage. Theology offers a richness to the visible and practical products of pioneer ministry.

I suspect most of what I have said is not new. But it does reiterate the need for a pioneer to spend time with some of the classic authors of our narrative; with Tertullian, Augustine, Aquinas, Teresa of Avila, Karl Barth, Paul Tillich, Sarah Coakley ... the list goes on. It is in their memory that the inherited church has found its shape and form.

It is only right, after suggesting that a pioneer's primary task is theology, to express more concretely what I mean by *theology*. I understand theology as the language and memory of the Church that has developed over thousands of years and in which I now participate. So just as a child learns language through the listening and participating in a particular cultural setting, so I, as a theologian and a pioneer, have learnt how to speak of the things of God by being present with the architects and innovators of Christian thought. It is what it means to be a Christian, to be rooted in that memory and narrative to such an extent that it begins to shape my thought and practice. But I am not simply a passive member of this tradition. Just as a child grows up to use language in their own way (just try and read a 15-year-old's text conversation), so I have to begin to take what is inherited and shape it for a new purpose in order that a future generation can participate and develop this vocabulary and memory we call theology, or, as Tom Greggs expresses it, 'Theology at its best should reflect upon the past tradition to lead the tradition into the future, and remind the Church of its future orientated direction' (Greggs, 2006, p. 30).

I am not suggesting that theology is a set of doctrinal standards or a mechanical methodology for thinking about God. Instead I am speaking of a dynamic process of memory and language that is constantly in flux, that draws deep from the past and reaches far into the future. As a pioneer theologian I am obliged to enter into that slipstream of consciousness and begin to shape it for my locality and for future theologians.

As with all memory traditions, there are those groundbreaking moments: granny's eightieth birthday party, the time my dad fell off my push bike, my first kiss, the first time I held my child. In the same way, theological memory is punctuated with kairos: the exile, the incarnation, the edict of Milan, Luther's 95 theses. These all mould my understanding of what it means to be a Christian – whether I know it or not! Equally language has developed that becomes commonplace to my community. In West Yorkshire where I grew up we went *chomping* for wood near bonfire night and my mother would *fettle* things; where I now live in North Staffordshire I am cold because I am *nesh*. Likewise theology uses words that are rarely, if ever, used by other communities, such as resurrection, sanctification, incarnation, ecclesia. Some of the words we do share with other communities take on new or different meaning, such as hope, pray, God and so on.

So as a pioneer I am a theologian – I cannot escape it. I am fashioned by the language and memory of an ancient narrative that gives form to my ministry today. I work with the stories, ideas and thought processes that I have inherited and begin to shape them for a new age. Perhaps that is the prophetic edge to pioneering, or at least, as Walter Brueggemann understands it:

> the prophet is called to be a child of the tradition, one who has taken it seriously in the shaping of his or her own field of perception and system of language, who is so at home in that memory that the points of contact and incongruity with the situation of the church in culture can be discerned and articulated with proper urgency. (Brueggemann, 2001, p. 2)

Context: to be located

It is easier to justify the importance of context for the pioneer. It is the context that forms the canvas on which the pioneer unleashes their imagination. This canvas is not blank; it is made up of the colours and textures of history and people groups. It is the weft and warp of society and forms the local and particular fabric that the pioneer is working with and, just as a pioneer is rooted in a particular memory, so they are situated in a particular location. I have written elsewhere (Whitehead et al., 2013, p. 141) about how to read a particular context, but for now I want to explore more fully what a valuable resource context is for pioneer ministry.

First, context is at the heart of the ethos of the Mission-Shaped Church movement. It was the Mission-Shaped Church report that gave birth to the vocabulary of *pioneer* and *fresh expression*. And on the Fresh Expression website it reads:

> A fresh expression is a form of church for our changing culture, established primarily for the benefit of people who are not yet members of any church. It will come into being through principles of listening, service, incarnational mission and making disciples. It will have the potential to become a mature expres-

sion of church shaped by the gospel and the enduring marks of the church and for its cultural context. (Fresh Expressions, n.d.)

Note how context is the heart, the centre, of any pioneer venture. The statement begins by highlighting that it *forms church for our changing culture* and ends with a church that is *for its cultural context*. In other words, at the heart of fresh expressions is the forming of ecclesia that begins by reading the culture and ends by being for its culture. So a pioneer is called to learn and articulate the narrative of a community and they will know when they are doing that well because their articulation will resonate with those around.

There is at least one more reason why context is important to the pioneer and it is to do with the business of incarnation. This deep mystery has gained great popularity over the last few years in the missional conversation and I wonder, as is often the case with popularity, if it has lost some of its power. In the world of fresh expressions, 'incarnational' is often used as shorthand to describe a ministry that is centred at the heart of the community (as opposed to the church community). So whenever a pioneer is working with those who can be labelled as destitute, deprived or dysfunctional then we can call their ministry *incarnational*; as if somehow the less middle class the job the more like Jesus we become. That understanding is both outrageously offensive to the people the pioneer works with and it reduces incarnation to mere function. It becomes more about where I am and what I do. The incarnation is far more radical than that. It is in the *incarnation* where eternity breaks through to reality; where the transcendent becomes concrete; or, as the great hymn-writer Charles Wesley wrote:

Our God contracted to a span,
Incomprehensibly made Man.

So context becomes vital because this is the locality, the space, where eternity breaks through. It is only by knowing and discovering the space that we begin to notice where God is 'contracted to a span', made real, made known.

A story

In the early days of my Venture FX project I had a student minister work with me for a week. I decided to take her into a pub that had gained a reputation over the years for being rough. It was reported that drug dealers and prostitutes used the premises as an office. The first time I ever went in I wore shiny shoes and a donkey jacket and the whole place emptied within minutes. I soon realized that they thought I was plain-clothed police! On this occasion we went in and began to notice. We noticed the women at one side of the room who were dressed for a night out – which was odd since it was lunchtime. It was also odd that they were sitting with men who, with my blind-date hat on, I wouldn't put together. We noticed that around the bar were a number of men who all looked as though they had stayed a little too long. We noticed at the other end of the room there were four or five loud women who had clearly been shopping and were now enjoying a well-earned drink. We noticed that in front of us were a number of characters who did not seem to fit in the scene. There was an Indian woman sitting on her own with what looked like half a lager; a man sat on his own wearing a Day-Glo jacket and a knitted hat (nursing a pint); and a woman on her own wearing an ankle-length loose hand-knitted cardigan who clearly had Down's syndrome. As we drank and felt more and more awkward, the loud women who had been shopping came to ask the barman excitedly (whom they clearly knew) if they could sing karaoke. Within minutes microphones were handed out and the small TV above the bar that had been displaying the news now displayed the words for 'Sweet Caroline'. If the music did not deafen us, the screeching of the women did as they yelled their words and tried to get everyone in the pub (including me and the ordinand) to dance. We tried to get out of the limelight (which was difficult since we were standing in front of the TV) and stepped backwards. We then witnessed the frenzy of others trying to avoid dancing but show appreciation for the performance. The woman in the long yellow cardigan then stood up and tried to get the Indian woman to dance – she was having none of it! She then set to work on the man nursing his pint in the Day-Glo jacket and the bobble hat. At first he seemed to be ignoring her advances but it soon became clear that he could not hear her (which is not surprising considering the 'performance'), but the situation became more apparent as the woman walked over to him and thumped him in the arm. He looked up. And she began to sign to him, he signed back and we realized that this young man was deaf. After what looked like a heated debate he eventually, although reluctantly, stood up – and they began a stumbled ballroom dance in the smallest space left between the tables. All the noise and screeching was dampened and the frenetic activity seemed to slow down as the focus of attention for all in the pub rested on the most unlikely dance partners in the most unlikely setting. I leaned over and whispered in the ear of the ordinand, 'I think we might have just seen heaven.'

It was not my ministry that was incarnational. It was the moment I realized that heaven and earth had collided; where eternity broke into my reality and I was left in awe. Heaven without reality is eternity. Reality without eternity is actuality. Incarnation is where the two come together in an explosion of wonder and mystery. What is so remarkable about the Jesus event is that this explosion occurred in human form in a particular world and a particular context. It is this unfathomable event that hints at the possibility of discovering God in the moment, in our situation. It is only in the knowing of our context that we can truly get to grips with what it means to be incarnational. It is the context that offers the conditions for divine encounter and the parameters of the pioneer's ministry so that 'the gospel can become a genuine part of a people group without damaging the innate cultural frameworks that provide that people group with a sense of meaning and history' (Frost and Hirsch, 2006, p. 37).

Context is important because it is foundational in the Fresh Expressions ethos and it is space in which God's activity can be witnessed. Theology is important because it roots us in a memory and language that shapes and forms us as disciples of Jesus.

So what does it mean to bring context and theology together? Why is contextual theology so important to the pioneer?

Theology that is contextual

Two of the dominant voices of contextual theology in the last 30 years are Robert Schreiter (1985) and Stephen Bevans (2002). Both seemed to have a suspicion of western theological form and content. They recognized that theology could no longer be seen as one coherent strand of thought that was applicable and reasonable in every time and place. This breakdown (or erosion) of a monolithic theological framework came from a number of angles:

- a greater understanding of the diversities of cultures in the world
- a development in the 'new sciences'
- a development in liberation theologies, from women and black African Americans to the liberation theologies of the South
- a suspicion of the colonial baggage that came with the missionary activity.

Both went on to suggest a number of models (or methods) for doing contextual theology. Schreiter identified three approaches: *translation*, *adaptation* and *contextual*. Bevans originally offered five models but added a sixth in the 2002 edition of his work: *translation*, *anthropological*, *praxis*, *synthesis*, *transcendental* and *countercultural*. Each theologian offers their own bias throughout and it is clear that neither of them favour a model of theology that does not give primacy to context as a theological source and instead believes that 'contextual models are important and enduring in the long run' (Schreiter, 1985, p. 16). So a way of doing theology that begins with context and 'works out' is more preferable than a model that begins with Scripture or tradition and 'works in'. But even then this understanding seems too reductionist. Contextual theology is a constant dialogue between Scripture and tradition on the one hand and context and experience on the other. So, as Stephen Pattison notes, the student (or pioneer)

> should imagine herself as being involved in a three-way conversation between (a) her own ideas, beliefs, feelings perceptions, and assumptions, (b) the beliefs, assumptions and perceptions provided by the Christian tradition (including the Bible) and (c) the contemporary situation which is being examined. (Pattison, 2000, p. 139)

In a later book that Bevans co-authored with Katalina Tahaafe-Williams (Bevans and Tahaafe-Williams, 2012), he asks the question, 'What has contextual theology to offer the Church of the twenty-first century?' After offering a précis of the twenty-first-century Church and outlining his own definition of contextual theology, he suggests four reasons why he believes contextual theology is important and describes its possible trajectory in the future, as outlined below.

A new agenda

In many ways this is the purpose of this chapter. Bevans argues that the existential questions we face today are different to those of the past and, therefore, 'will develop not only new answers but also new ways of understanding the classic questions of God, of church, of creation and of the end of the world' (Bevans and Tahaafe-Williams, 2012, p. 13). It is for this reason that I am convinced that contextual theology is of the utmost importance to the pioneer. It is our responsibility to help the Church identify a new set of questions from our particular contexts.

A *new method*

Bevans and others have led the way in helping us develop models and methods of doing theology that take seriously contexts and experience, but more can and must be done. I am not surprised that many of the pioneering projects I have come across take the arts as their primary way of communicating with the world. In Ian Morgan Cron's brilliant novel about an American pastor who ends up on a pilgrimage around the sites of St Francis there is a moment when the pastor, Chase, is trying to convince his church to think more widely about the way in which they communicate the gospel: 'I do know this: Beauty can break a heart and make it think about something more spiritual than the mindless routine we go through day after day to get by' (Cron, 2006, p. 198).

For Bevans, contextual theology has widened the scope of the presentation of theology to be more than verbal discourse. It now can be articulated by artists, painters, sculptors, poets, actors, musicians – a whole range of creative arts that break through the mundane and point to a beauty and wonder that cannot always be relayed through words. Whenever I speak of articulating theology I am not simply speaking of words, I mean the whole of communicative acts. As I write, the Church is being asked to respond to the government's same-sex marriage bill. Would it not be amazing if our response was an art exhibition or a series of poems.

New *voices*

Bevans' third hope for contextual theology is a desire to introduce new voices to the theological forum. This is a significant feature of contextual theology – it places the role of the theologian within the community, not in corridors of academia. This in turn allows new, sometimes unexpected, voices to contribute to theological enquiry. It is my conviction that some of those new voices are pioneer ministers in the British context. A key role for permission-givers is to create the space for these new voices to be heard in ways that do not alienate the pioneer but also allow the wider Church to hear the theological discourse as it develops.

Pioneers are not passive in this process; they too must seek out opportunities to be heard and, if space is not created for them, they must carve it out for themselves.

A *new dialogue*

The final reason for Bevans of the importance of contextual theology is related to one of the limitations of contextual theology as it has been practised over the last couple of decades. A sizeable limitation of contextual theology is that it is contextual! It relates to specific and particular contexts, which means it might not always be transferable to other contexts (and since the contextual theologian is so located in a particular context they might not see a reason for it to be transferable). So, Bevans argues, the next stage of *our* contextual theology is for it to enter into dialogue with other contextual theologies – in the global context. In that way our theologies are tested in the wider Christian community by those who appreciate and understand our desire to take seriously experience and location.

Contextual theology for pioneer ministry: voices

I fully agree with Bevans, but I wonder how, as pioneers, we might get to the point of engaging with those voices from radically different contexts from our own. Perhaps we ought to begin by sharing with one another those narratives and themes we have unearthed in our locality that say something of God and humanity. There have been many books written that have come out of the Mission-Shaped Church movement. Most of them have either tried to define and justify the place of Fresh Expressions and pioneer ministry in the mixed economy of church or have been a 'how to' of mission. Rarely, if at all, have there been books that have asked pioneers to write about theological themes from their context. What does *salvation* look like in your context? In your community, what is an appropriate understanding of *sin*? What is the relationship between local people and *creation*? What are some of the key themes and narratives told in your community and how do they resonate with Christian themes? Where does Christian theology seem redundant in your community, and how might you begin to construct a Christian identity in that place? Perhaps if we begin to wrestle with these questions between us we might discover both the confidence and the necessity of engaging with those from vastly different situations; not just about the 'what?' and the 'how?' of mission and pioneering, but about the new vocabulary and narratives we have discovered that might inform new ways of thinking theologically.

If we begin to share our theological wonderings and meanderings we might begin to see themes of harmony and discord: to discover that we have stumbled across a much greater understanding of God than our narrow context affords; or the opposite – to recognize that we have made assumptions that others will not or cannot tolerate. If we go back to our understanding of theology as memory and language, this process of collaboration and dialogue will help us to discover new ways of expressing and remembering, as well as shaping the present moment that will become the memory of others. All of this is a way of testing out among ourselves God's revelation *in situ*. It is how we begin to shape the memory for the present and for those who will follow.

If there is a need for pioneers to *do* contextual theology as a community of practitioner theologians in order to shape the memory, then there is also another dialogue that needs to take place. This dialogue is primarily between the community of pioneers and the inherited church that sponsors them. For me, that is the Methodist Church of Britain. Here my concern is for those pioneers who are related, however uncomfortably, to the inherited church, and however distant, particularly for those who long to see the Church become all that it could be, and for those whose passion and love for the Church is so strong that they cannot sit idly by as it slowly dissolves into the world around it. I do not want to dwell on the causes or the nature of this dissolution but I do want to direct this towards those who live with a dissatisfaction with the Church and long for more.

This dialogue is encouraged in Chapter 3 of the 2012 report

on *Fresh Expressions in the Mission of the Church* (Anglican–Methodist Working Party, 2012). The Jerusalem/Antioch drama in Acts is played out to argue for a need for the centre and the periphery to communicate with one another. The centre (Jerusalem, inherited church) and the periphery (Antioch, fresh expressions) are to be in a dialogue. This, the report suggests, is a useful analogy for our current ecclesial situation: 'The centre has to be prepared to listen to the margins: but the margins also have to be prepared to come back to the centre to tell their story, and to tell it within the framework of the Christian Tradition' (Anglican–Methodist Working Party, 2012, p. 80).

It is this 'framework of the Christian Tradition' that I am referring to as *language and memory*.

Stefan Paas (2012) also makes a case for this conversation, but in terms of innovation (as in research and development). Paas argues that church planting should be taken seriously by the Church not because it will produce more Christians but because it allows for innovation. The key to this innovation is to allow some space between inherited church and the emerging community who will try new things, new ways of being. This innovation can then seep back towards the Church and the inherited takes on the new ideas as normative. In other words the Church is blessed when it carves out enough space for new entities because it is part of the process of reformation and transformation.

You can see this happening with worship, mission ideas, structural organization and even styles of leadership. Café church, rules or rhythms of life, flatbed (non-hierarchical) leadership are examples of ideas that began on 'the periphery' but are now practised more widely in the Church. I am excited at the flow of movement that relates to mission and ministry and the ways in which these new entities challenge orthopraxis. It was here that I feel Davison and Milbank (2010) failed to recognize the nature of communities of practice. They seemed to understand them as one homogenous and static unit, as if the Church (or even the Church of England) was one community of practice. The Church, however, is and has always been an organic synthesis of communities of practice that have evolved over the years. Fresh expressions and emerging Christian communities are just another episode in those shifting sands. Does that mean the Church will no longer be the same as it once was? Yes! Will it still be the Church? Yes! Will it still be denominational? Perhaps not? My point is that new forms of Christian community do bring about new practices (form) and those practices often bring about new theological understanding (content). There is, however, another challenge for this dialogue between fresh expressions and the inherited church – orthodoxy.

I am aware that I am now pushing the limits of contextual theology, but I do believe that the new agenda and the new voices that Bevans looks for will also bring about new ways of thinking and expressing theological thought. This is the way in which we shape the language and memory for a new generation. A theology that takes seriously experience, context, the local, and builds a theology in an intentional and serious relationship with it, will, I believe, find new understandings and new expressions of the language and memory we have inherited. Some of that new thinking will find its way into the inherited church, and soon it will cease to be new. I want to call this *disruptive theology*. In marketing and manufacturing a *disruptive innovation*, a phrase coined by Clayton Christensen in his book *The Innovator's Dilemma* (1997), is a new product that dominates the market to such an extent that other products are no longer viable. An example would be the CD, which just about removed records and tapes from the music industry, then MP3 and now cloud-based technologies. Each becomes such a dominant product in the marketplace that it does not matter how good or cheap you make the original product, it is no longer favoured by the consumer.

It is my hope that this dialogue brings about a disruptive theology. A way of thinking, articulating, expressing divine action and being and the human condition that is new to the inherited church, but will eventually seep back into it as normative understandings of the Christian faith. Any sense of challenging orthodoxy is rightly met with caution, but it is vital that pioneer theologians are able to challenge the assumptions of the dominant voices in our church traditions – not because we have an inbuilt capacity to rebel (although that is possible) but because of a growing awareness that things look different from our particular perspective. In many ways this already happens: it is thanks to contextual theologies that notions of divine gender have been challenged; that assumptions of western (white) Christologies have been shown to be deficient; and that there has been a resurgence in pneumatology from the southern hemisphere where *spirit* is a personal and communal reality.

Future directions: agendas

So what areas of theology might pioneer theologians contribute to in the wider theological debate? In many ways that depends on the existential questions that are thrown up in the context of the pioneer, since it is context that should drive the agenda. Nevertheless, there are some areas of theological discourse that need the urgent attention of new voices and agendas.

Ecclesiology is the most obvious area for a pioneering contribution, but, in honesty, we have done very little to contribute to that debate. We have shown that church can be *done* differently but we have yet to articulate a deeper understanding of the nature and role of church for the twenty-first century that transforms (or disrupts) dominant ecclesiology. In the most recent addition to the Mission-Shaped Church movement, *Fresh Expressions in the Mission of the Church* (Anglican–Methodist Working Party, 2012), it was made clear that *church*, from a Fresh Expressions' perspective, looks very similar to how church has looked for centuries. Despite the fact that it was clear new churches were doing lots of radically different things, a final list of points was identified that would help us to recognize a community as a church. Point 3 notes that 'the Gospel is proclaimed in ways that are appropriate to the lives of its members' (p. 181), yet made no 'culturally sensitive' concession for any other point in the list. So, for example, it suggests a mature (what does that really mean?) expression of church would have an authorized ministry. Authorized by whom? What does authority look like in your context? Who has it? How is it perceived? Is it welcomed?

Christology has always been and I hope always will be a source of contention in the Church, from the Arian controversy to the quest for the historical Jesus and more recent studies of the Christa born largely out of the work of feminist theologians (Slee, 2011). When we read such famous texts as *Christianity Rediscovered* (Donovan, 1982) we see clearly that Jesus is reframed anew for a new cultural context and, of course, that is rejected by others who see and experience Jesus differently. That will always be the joy of contextual theology – it will offer a richness and diversity to the Church's faith and expression. I wonder, however, if the Jesus that is being expressed and articulated in many pioneering projects has the same cultural expression that has been offered by Christians in Britain for the last century? How do we begin to speak of Jesus in a majority-Muslim community? Can we describe Jesus the same if we work predominantly with drug dealers? So what does Jesus look like when we take our perspective seriously? Or is Jesus always supracultural?

This is My Body by Richard Stott

Creation is, I suspect, one of the easiest theological themes to use when relating to those of no faith. The Forest Church movement and other garden churches intimate the possibilities. As I write, one of the biggest news stories is about the controversial process of fracking for shale gas and the subsequent protests and government promises. It seems our current global context is ready to hear newly articulated stories of creation, of sustainability, of humanity's role and purpose in a larger cosmos. The problem, and our lack of confidence, stems from the reliability of science in the face of ancient but fanciful stories of our beginning. How is creation understood in your context? What is the relationship between the people and the earth? Between people and animals? Does nature have some divine quality?

Pneumatology is, as I hinted at earlier, a dominant theological discourse in the two-thirds world (World Council of Churches, 2012) but receives little attention in the West. If we believe that the Church is shaped by Jesus through the Holy Spirit, then those of us who are looking at new expressions of church cannot afford to ignore the doctrine of the Spirit. What that looks like and how it is expressed and articulated in local communities is open to bountiful creativity. Is it possible to speak of divine energy? Of creative activity? Do we begin with a British fascination with ghosts? Do we want to offer a countercultural understanding of the supernatural? Is there evidence of God's activity in your context? And if so how do we name it?

Sin is a complex and powerful theme in Christian theology and one that cannot be ignored by contextual theologians. It is of particular interest to pioneer theologians who are looking at forming new, emerging Christian communities. Sin is closely related to other themes that might impinge on their work, such as salvation, forgiveness and liberation. What does wrongdoing look like in your context? Is there a disconnection between people and God, and if so how does it manifest itself? How does forgiveness and reconciliation operate here? Where are people oppressed, denied their full dignity, due to systems and structures that are unjust? How will you know when you see salvation here? How does this community mourn – and celebrate?

Conclusion ... or rather ... a beginning

If we understand theology as language and memory that shapes the character of church and Christian discipleship then it places upon all Christians a responsibility to pass on that tradition to others or else it ends in the present. Equally, if we recognize context as the space in which encounter and revelation occur then we have a responsibility to shape that tradition accordingly for a new era of practitioners and theologians. It is my belief that those engaged in pioneering ministries are best placed to both receive and reshape this inheritance and by the very nature of forming new, emerging Christian communities will have the privilege of handing on that which is formed. In order to do this, pioneers need to be *rooted* in the ancient Christian narrative and *located* in a particular place. This means, above all, two things: first, a pioneer needs to know, wrestle, work with and understand those key texts, authors and moments of our story; second, a pioneer needs to read and articulate their own unique and particular context. Only then can they begin to express a theology that is truly contextual.

There is, it seems, another task of the pioneer. This task relies on the pioneer keeping an eye on the horizon, the eschaton, to engage with the Church to see more clearly the divine activity in the present in order that the Body of Christ is equipped for the future. It is this process of reformation and transformation that enables the Church to speak afresh of those things that matter to us. In order to do that, pioneering will need to mature into a theologically literate and articulate discipline that can speak confidently in the great councils, synods and halls of institutional church. It is time to move on from the old conversations and to introduce a new agenda with new voices.

To be informed by our past, truly present in our communities and longing for an alternative future seems almost impossible. Thank God for her Spirit – for without it we have little chance of fulfilling the call God has placed upon us.

References

Anglican–Methodist Working Party, 2012, *Fresh Expressions in the Mission of the Church*, London: Church House Publishing.

Bevans, S. B., 2002, *Models of Contextual Theology*, Maryknoll, NY: Orbis Books.

Bevans, S. B. and K. Tahaafe-Williams, 2012. *Contextual Theology for the Twenty-First Century*, Cambridge: James Clarke.

Brueggemann, W., 2001, *The Prophetic Imagination*, 2nd edn, Minneapolis, MN: Fortress Press.

Christensen, C. M., 1997, *The Innovator's Dilemma: When New Technologies Cause Great Firms to Fail*, Cambridge, MA: Harvard Business School Press.

Cron, I. M., 2006, *Chasing Francis: A Novel*, Colorado Springs, CO: Navpress.

Davison, A. and A. Milbank, 2010, *For the Parish: A Critique of Fresh Expressions*, London: SCM Press.

Donovan, V. J., 1982, *Christianity Rediscovered: An Epistle from the Masai*, London: SCM Press.

Fresh Expressions, n.d., *Fresh Expressions*, online. Available at: http://www.freshexpressions.org.uk/about/whatis (accessed 29 January 2014).

Frost, M. and A. Hirsch, 2006, *The Shaping of Things to Come*, Peabody, MA: Hendrickson.

Greggs, T., 2006, 'Why Does the Church Need Academic Theology', *Epworth Review* 33.3, pp. 27–35.

Migliore, D. L., 1991, *Faith Seeking Understanding: An Introduction to Christian Theology*, Grand Rapids, MI: Eerdmans.

Paas, S., 2012, 'Church Renewal by Church Planting: The Significance of Church Planting for the Future of Christianity in Europe', *Theology Today*, 68.4, pp. 467–77.

Pattison, S., 2000, 'Some Straw for Bricks', in J. Woodward and S. Pattison (eds), *The Blackwell Reader in Pastoral and Practical Theology*, Oxford: Blackwell.

Schreiter, R. J., 1985, *Constructing Local Theologies*, London: SCM Press.

Slee, N., 2011, *Seeking the Risen Christa*, London: SPCK.

Stott, R., 2013, *This Is My Body*, http://iaskforwonder.com/.

Whitehead, J., S. Nash and S. Sutcliffe, 2013, *Facilitation Skills for Ministry*, London: SPCK.

World Council of Churches, 2012, 'Together Toward Life', *International Review of Mission* 101.1, pp. 1–242.

10

A Gospel that Overcomes Shame

ANDREA CAMPANALE

I am a pioneer in South West London who has been engaging in mission to spiritual seekers for nine years. I train and lead teams to go to Mind, Body, Spirit type fairs, as well as pagan festivals. In these environments, we offer words of encouragement and comfort and create opportunities for attendees to either receive or participate in prayer. I would describe these people as interested in spirituality but wary of organized religion in general and the Christian Church in particular. Yet they believe there is more to life than purely the material and the rational. They are longing for meaning to make sense of their spiritual experiences, as well as an eternal purpose that will help get them through everyday struggles with ill health, loneliness and bereavement. Christians often see these interactions as potentially hostile but the overwhelming majority of seekers I meet are warm, sensitive and curious. They have much to teach us about constantly being open to the possibility of divine encounters, especially through dreams, creativity and the natural world.

As I have engaged in my mission work and then had the privilege of discipling some amazing young women who have come to faith in Christ from a seeker background, I have observed that the concept of sin is largely irrelevant. However, the people to whom I minister often have chronic feelings of unworthiness and a massive fear of rejection because they believe themselves to be basically unacceptable in some fundamental yet indefinable sense. This has led me to reflect on whether spiritual seekers are unique in displaying what I have come to realize are symptoms of shame. I have also sought to understand what the hope is Christians have that can free people from these crippling notions of self-loathing. My conclusion is that this is not a problem unique to my area of mission. Rather, shame is endemic in western, post-industrialized societies and the Church has so far failed to communicate a gospel that liberates the shame enslaved. The good news is, I believe, Fresh Expressions, and this gives us an exciting opportunity to unmask this dis-ease and make our message of the power of Jesus to heal and redeem newly relevant and impactful for our time and culture.

My journey into shame

I first began to become aware of the issue of shame following a conversation at a Christmas fair in Surbiton YMCA with a young woman whom I will call Tanya. As we talked, I started to feel just how much God loved her and how beautiful she was in the eyes of the Divine. I began to share this with her, but my words just made her cry. Tanya told me how she believed herself to be ugly and could not even look at herself in the mirror. Now it was my turn to cry! It seemed so desperately sad that such a stunning woman could have that poor an image of herself. It got me wondering: how could she have been so deceived that the truth of who she was had been utterly distorted?

Shortly after this encounter I was introduced to the book *My Own Worst Enemy* by Janet Davis. She is a spiritual director who has observed that women seem to have an internal script that is constantly criticizing and undermining self-esteem such that they fail to fulfil their God-given potential (Davis, 2012, p. 17). In her writing she has taken the stories of women in the Bible to explore and dispel the destructive messages that oppress and hinder women from experiencing the love and freedom that will enable them to be all that God has destined them to become (Davis, 2012, p. 21). Through this and a TED talk by Brene Brown on the power of vulnerability,[1] I began to become aware of shame as the root of my own struggle with depression and fear of intimate relationships. I also started to appreciate how much of what

I have experienced of church has unintentionally reinforced and compounded my shame rather than brought the liberation and acceptance that Christ has secured for me (Watson, 2005).

However, this is not a problem unique to women. Men are just as likely to experience shame, yet the triggers and how it will manifest itself will be different. As I have engaged in mission and started a missional community of Christians from a seeker background together with others, like me, disenchanted with charismatic, evangelical churches, the problem of shame seems to raise its unwelcome head over and over again. Many of us are wounded so that we believe ourselves unworthy of love and incapable of enjoying mutually nurturing and sustaining relationships. We live in fear of exposure that will lead to rejection and isolation. Yet, 'God so loved the world that he gave his only Son, so that everyone who believes in him may not perish but may have eternal life' (John 3.16). It has led me to conclude that if the Church is to see the gospel make a significant impact in our world, we need to refocus away from the problem of sin and relief from guilt, to show how the good news of Christ can free us from shame. This in turn will help us find reconciliation within our own selves, in our communities and ultimately with God.

But what exactly is shame and how does it impact our lives? What does the Bible say about shame and what relevance might Christ's life and death have for this issue? What could be the implications for mission in our postmodern, western context and how might our liturgy and practice need to change in the light of these? I am particularly interested in finding ways to help people overcome their shame and imagine what church as 'communities of insecurity' that practise vulnerability (Morisy, 2009, p. 109) and 'shame resilience' (Brown, 2012, p. 157) might look like.

What is shame?

According to the *Compact Oxford English Dictionary*, shame is 'a feeling of distress or humiliation caused by consciousness of the guilt or folly of oneself or an associate … a state of disgrace, discredit or intense regret'. The root of the English word is found in the Indo-European word *kam/kem*, meaning to hide or cover (Watson, 2005, p. 5), and this is the reactive response for anyone experiencing shame. It is to hide one's failure and ugliness from the eyes of an 'other'. For Dave, a victim of sexual abuse in childhood, 'Shame was and is the sense that I am in some way fundamentally bad or wrong and that everyone knows that or will find it out eventually' (Watson, 2005, p. 3). Often the terms shame and guilt are combined or used interchangeably, but there is a difference. Guilt is experienced when we become aware of doing something that is morally wrong or has distressing consequences for ourselves or others. However, shame is the feeling that I am deeply flawed as a person and must not let anyone see. This is because when we fail to live up to the internalized ideal of ourselves, there is a loss of face or humiliation. It can be felt as defeat or exposure to ridicule and create a sense of inferiority or worthlessness. Shame means to be stripped naked. It is both personal and social. Fear and shame are intimately connected – the fear of being irreparably and permanently diminished in the eyes of one's family or peer group or even one's enemies (Nicholls, 2001, p. 234).

But can shame be a good thing in moderating antisocial or immoral behaviour? The former Chief Rabbi, Immanuel Jakobovits, wrote famously in *The Times* newspaper comparing shame to pain. When we feel pain we are forced to address the issue and seek the advice of a doctor. It therefore promotes good health.

> Shame does the same for moral health. Without shame, we would disport ourselves like the brutes. Only when Adam and Eve felt a sense of shame did they clothe themselves … today, shame is being systematically displaced by brazen vulgarity.

He argued that the ills of society are due to the fact that 'people co-habit without shame, abort without shame, divorce without shame, and have illegitimate children without shame' (Harper, 'The Family in Danger', p. 1). Yet shame is definitely not a useful mechanism for addressing morally unacceptable behaviour.

Research shows that while guilt is as powerful as shame, it has a positive influence, whereas shame is only destructive. This is because when you feel bad about something you have done, the resulting discomfort can motivate you to change your behaviour and/or make amends. However, shame corrodes the belief we have in ourselves that we can change and do better. Therefore, the idea that still pervades society of shame as a good means for keeping people in line is dangerous. Contrary to reducing levels of antisocial behaviour, high levels of shame are closely related to problems of addiction, violence, aggression, depression, eating disorders and bullying. There is no evidence to prove that shame is helpful for encouraging positive lifestyle choices, but much to demonstrate that it is the cause of many damaging behaviours that have seriously destructive consequences for families and society at large (Brown, 2012, pp. 72–3).

Based on hours of qualitative research during the last 12 years, Brene Brown has proved that shame has reached epidemic proportions in our wealthy, western societies (Brown, 2012, p. 22). It can be seen in the frightening levels of addiction and mental illness, as well as the spiralling incidents of scapegoating and blame in organizations where success is driven by performance-related targets and increased recourse to law. Brown attributes this phenomenon to a preoccupation with scarcity. She states:

> Scarcity thrives in a culture where everyone is hyperaware of lack. Everything from safety and love, to money and resources feel restricted or lacking. We spend inordinate amounts of time calculating how much we have, want and don't have, and how much everyone else has, needs and wants. What makes this constant assessing and self-comparing so self-defeating is that we are comparing our lives ... to unattainable, media-driven visions of perfection, or we're holding up our reality against our own fictional account of how great someone else has it. (Brown, 2012, p. 26)

Ann Morisy, who describes herself as a community theologian, has also highlighted this as a symptom of what she describes as our 'dystopian times'; that is, 'a world that has gone wrong' (Morisy, 2009, p. 3).

These commentators give one possible explanation for the rise in shame-induced behaviours. Steve Pattison, in his book *Shame: Theory, Therapy, Theology* (2000), comes up with an alternative. He suggests that in previous generations there were clear external constraints placed upon individuals by virtue of the role or place that they had in society. With this came prescribed expectations as to the appropriate behaviour that accompanied such a position and shame was conferred by the community upon those who transgressed these socially constructed boundaries of respectability. We have now moved to a situation where identity is no longer externally determined but dependent on our sense of self. There is a multiplicity of choices as to the persona we can adopt and, having been largely set adrift from the constraints of needing to belong to a static, geographically rooted community, we can keep reinventing ourselves to ensure our face fits. Thus the alienation and rejection that is experienced as the manifestation of shame is now internalized and arises out of the anxiety that the image we are presenting is inauthentic and will be found out.

> The present era perhaps deserves the description of being 'an age of shame' for ... if some modern sociological theorists are correct, we are living in the age of the self-conscious, reflective self. In this context, individuals conceive of themselves as being detached from traditional structures and relationships. When traditional roles, expectations and norms, together with the practices and rituals that support them, have fallen away, guilt associated with conforming to static, widely understood rules becomes less significant than the shame that accompanies uncertainty about the self in an ever-changing world. (Pattison, 2000, p. 142)

So, if these observers are correct and we have a massive problem with shame, what does the Bible say about this issue and how does the saving work of Jesus bring hope and relief?

Theology and shame

We are first introduced to the concept of shame in the Bible with the Genesis account of the fall. The initial consequence of Adam and Eve's disobedience in eating the forbidden fruit was that they became aware of their nakedness, were afraid and hid from the Lord (Gen. 3.7–8).

> They were ashamed, not because they had discovered their sexuality as Freud and others have suggested, but because they were totally exposed with nowhere to hide from the holiness of God (v. 10). Fear and shame were inseparably linked. Both were the consequences of a broken relationship with God and with each other. (Nicholls, 2001, p. 236)

The other result consistent with the experience of shame is that they look for a scapegoat, someone else to blame to avoid taking responsibility for their wrong choices (Pattison, 2000, p. 114). Yet God does not deal with them as the consequences of their actions deserve. 'In the act of clothing the nakedness (v. 21) God initiates healing and restoration, helping them to be who they are despite what they have done ... He shows that he still accepts them and loves them, that they are of value and worth caring for' (Watson, 2005, p. 18).

In an Old Testament context shame is closely aligned with defilement and the need for exclusion to avoid contamination that might introduce anarchy, disease and death into the community. 'To a greater extent than is often recognized, the problem of sin in Israel was the problem of purifying the nation of its pollution without permanently expelling the unclean person' (Green and Baker, 2000, p. 157). It also points to shame as the opposite of giving proper and rightful honour. This idea dominates the message of the prophets, especially Jeremiah. The shame his prophecy exposes is the people's abandonment of their exclusive loyalty to Yahweh. What injures the Lord most is that their rebellion is an expression of their rejection of the relationship he offers as Father or friend. To repent is to acknowledge the shame and disgrace their autonomy has wrought, and recovery is about reconciliation that restores and renews the bonds of kinship (Musk, 1996, pp. 164–5).

In the Gospels, Jesus' teaching and miracles usher in a new age where shame is dealt with by restored relationship in God through Christ. The woman healed of constant bleeding (Luke 8.43–48) is not only cured of physical symptoms but, by reaching out to touch her, Jesus takes on her uncleanness, pronounces her acceptable and gives back to her the hope of relationship despite years of exclusion and isolation (Watson, 2005, pp. 20–1). As this encounter illustrates, Jesus enters into our shame, taking it upon himself to remove it once and for all. He knew the social stigma of being conceived out of wedlock, belonged to the lower classes, identified with the poor, ate with outcasts, counted fishermen and tax-collectors as his closest friends (Green and Baker, 2000, p. 164).

This redemptive act is imaginatively foreshadowed in the parable of the two lost sons in Luke 15.11–32. It is a story all about shame! Here an old man embraces shame by running to greet his younger son who had effectively told his father to his face that he wished him dead and then squandered the wealth that had been carefully accumulated as an inheritance. Later the father accepts further shame by seeking out his elder son. The older brother has excluded himself from the household celebrations and further disgraces the old man by failing to attend the welcome-home party for his brother. Jesus is suggesting that this is the larger story of God and humanity. God is the loving father full of honour and integrity, dishonoured and shamed by his earthly children. Heaven's answer is for God to come in the Son to be wrongly dishonoured, to imbibe the shame and be tortured to death (Musk, 1996, p. 164).

Appropriating the gospel for shame-based cultures

Having established that there is a problem with shame in the context where I am engaged in mission and sought a biblical basis for understanding and overcoming shame, I want to turn to how we might communicate the gospel in a shame-based culture. Japan is one such example.

Norman Kraus was a missionary to Japan and sought to develop a more contextual theology for this culture (Green and Baker, 2000, p. 153). He quickly identified that the Japanese had a very different understanding of justice. This meant that an explanation for why Christ died that relied upon Jesus' taking our punishment for the offences we have committed, referred to as penal substitution, had no relevance for them. He observed: 'where shame is a major factor in psychological and cultural development, relationships and ideals will be more important and persuasive than law and punitive threats' (Green and Baker, 2000, p. 158). It is public exposure and exclusion that are the means of regulating behaviour, and these are effective sanctions because social relationships and interpersonal dependencies are of highest importance. However, this makes forgiveness nearly impossible as to confess one's wrongdoing is to condone it and compound one's shame. It then becomes impossible to ignore the transgression. Atonement can only be achieved by excluding oneself, which might bring moral resolution but does not provide for a way back in terms of reconciliation. 'Indeed, suicide, which is the ultimate act of self-exclusion, epitomizes the dilemma' (Green and Baker, 2000, p. 161).

For a fictional representation of how this dynamic plays out, I love the film *Les Misérables*. The story centres on Jean Valjean, who at the beginning of the movie is chained to a line of fellow prisoners, under the watchful eye of his gaoler, Javert. He is well acquainted with suffering and embittered by justice that punished him for stealing bread. The terms of his release make work impossible, so once freed he quickly becomes destitute. He takes shelter in the doorway of a church and unexpectedly the priest welcomes him in and treats him as an honoured guest. However, Jean steals the church's treasures and flees. The police drag him back, but the priest says he has gifted him the loot. Having no reason to reimprison him, Jean is freed. This demonstration of forgiveness and unconditional love causes him to let go of hate and adopt a new identity so he can show compassion and justice to others. Jean stays true to his vow, becomes a fair employer and mayor of the town. He rescues Cosette, an orphaned daughter of a woman who was unjustly dismissed. But Javert, now police chief, becomes suspicious as to his real identity. Years later, while saving a young revolutionary with whom Cosette has fallen in love, Jean comes face to face with his nemesis and has the opportunity to kill Javert and end the years of running. However, Jean shows him the forgiveness and unconditional love that he received and lets him go. Javert cannot stand this. Confronted with grace, his beliefs are shattered and he can no longer live with the shame. He hangs himself. Meanwhile, Cosette marries, but Jean cannot let her know the truth of his identity and, dying, seeks sanctuary in the convent. The newly-weds find him and declare their love and gratitude for the man he really is. Jean dies at peace with himself, with God and with those whom he loves.

This story is a wonderful enactment of shame as the gap between our real selves and the selves we construct to present to the world. In the same way that Jean had to hide who he really was and create a socially acceptable identity in order to exist in safety, many of us live in fear of having our real selves exposed to scrutiny. We struggle less with the guilt at having done something wrong than with the shame of feeling we are unworthy of love and with the fear that if we are really known we will be rejected and spurned.

In shame-based cultures, as well as the Christianity espoused by Javert, the law should not be transgressed and wrongdoing can only be overcome with punishment. There is no way out of the accompanying shame other than suicide. But it is Christ's sacrificial love that frees us. Faith in Jesus addresses our shame as completely as our guilt. Like the priest, God does not disclose our offences but offers forgiveness and the hope of a fresh start. There is no need to hide who we really are because the Divine sees and delights in the beauty of our uniqueness. In the same way that Jean is reconciled and his true personhood is brought together with his constructed self by love, so Christ's willingness to die a shameful death demonstrates both the extent of his love and the potential for harmony between the ideal he preached and the embodied reality. It is by experiencing grace in the midst of shame that we can find reconciliation within ourselves, restoring identity, discovering purpose and the potential for meaningful relationships.

Similarly, the life and death of Christ addresses the problem of shame in the Japanese culture. 'Kraus discovered that the cross provides liberation from shame through revealing God's love, through vicarious identification, through exposing false shame and through removing alienation' (Green and Baker, 2000, p. 163). Jesus identified and took on our shame to the point of crucifixion. Yet more than that, Jesus died falsely shamed in order to expose the powers that were abusing society's laws and customs to oppress and control (Col. 2.15). Thus the cross also brings freedom from the lie of 'inappropriate shaming' in Japanese culture. Finally, 'in exposing the misplaced shame and lovingly revealing the true failure in us all, Jesus, the "friend of sinners", removed the stigma and hostility that alienates us from each other and God' (Green and Baker, 2000, p. 167).

But what of this is relevant for confronting the issue of shame in our highly individualized western context? For postmoderns, relationships and ideals are also more important than law and the threat of punishment. They too have shame reinforced and exacerbated by confession and feel shame as a pollutant that can only be dealt with by self-exclusion. 'Healing from shame therefore requires opportunity for cleansing, for inclusion and social reincorporation and relational restoration' (Mann, 2005, p. 57).

Yet a major difference between the shame-based culture of Japan and what we experience in the UK is our relationship to the 'other'. In Japanese society shame is the appropriate response to having been diminished in the eyes of family, peers or the wider community. However, in our context shame puts the spotlight on the self. We do not need anyone else to feel ashamed. It occurs within, so while social setting and cultural expectations can cause shame, even perpetuate it, in its post-industrialized form there is no need for an audience to feel shame. We live with the uncomfortable belief that others see us the way we see ourselves and are acutely aware of all the flaws and inconsistencies that must not be revealed. It is an internalized version of the external scrutiny of which we imagine ourselves to be subject. In the same way that Adam and Eve ate of the fruit of the tree of good and evil and gained knowledge and insight, we enjoy self-knowledge, but it is knowledge without love (Higton, 2008, p. 266). What is craved is a trustworthy and meaningful story that makes sense of our real self so that it need no longer be hidden behind a constructed, idealized version of ourselves. However, we are acutely aware of our inability to live up to such a story. We experience constant fear of having our inauthenticity exposed. This will permanently derail the self-realization project society continually tells us is the purpose of our existence, making mutually sustaining and nurturing relationships impossible. 'The shamed person wants to live by the story of the ideal self, or find a coherent story rather than an incoherent one. The purpose of mission is to allow people to see how the gospel can bring about this desire' (Mann, 2005, p. 38).

Implications for mission and fresh expressions of church

In our sacred text and faith tradition we have a wealth of stories that can be used to help the shamed begin to integrate their real and ideal selves. This might be done in a way similar to Janet Davis as she applies the stories of significant women in the Bible to uncover shame (Davis, 2012), or like Nathan's confrontation of David with the sin of his adultery in 2 Samuel 12.1–25 (Nicholls, 2001, p. 239). Comfort can then be found in the knowledge of God's provision and the possibility of forgiveness for sin. We can also know hope. While we are unable to be all that we want in truth and authenticity, the Spirit who enabled Jesus to fully embody who he said he was to the point of dying to demonstrate it is available to empower us. Thus our stories in dialogue with his, can provide us with the opportunity to feel we are really loved despite our idiosyncrasies and failings. As we begin to experience this, we find there is a way to reconcile the ideal and the reality, and the distorted image of ourselves can be healed. Once able to trust in our God-given identity, we can find the courage to trust others, let them see who we truly are and take the hundreds of small risks of vulnerability that go into forming the meaningful and mutually sustaining relationships that make life worth living. In this way redemption from shame is achievable, for 'shame does not respond to punishment; rather it is love that banishes shame' (Green and Baker, 2000, p. 163).

However,

> at-one-ment for the chronically shamed is achieved only via a series of 'moments' that move them to a place where they can live without the distorted relating that has become so much part of the story they tell. Such moments need ... to be made available to the chronically shamed person through the creation of safe, non-intrusive, non-judgmental spaces and communities that allow [them] ... to hear meaningful and sufficient stories of atonement and so, via storytelling, symbolic action and ritual, come to find the ontological coherence ... that so tragically alludes them. (Mann, 2005, p. 58)

This is what I am trying to achieve with my own missional community. I have preached on the issue of shame and written a number of blogs on this topic. Currently, as a group, we have been sharing our own stories; members use art and ritual in our worship and we have taken inspiration from the Bible and written our own prayers, psalms and even a creed. I have intuitively been feeling my way, but with the help of the people I am in relationship with who are at various stages of recovery from shame, the reading I have done, as well as my own experience of addressing shame through therapy, I have become convinced that this issue is the most pressing for the Church to address. I also think that if fresh expressions are to be more than just a change of style, those that are seeking to build new ways of being church might do well intentionally to seek to become shame-resilient communities so that our faith becomes relevant again and the gospel is genuinely good news for those in desperate need. Many emerging churches do prioritize making space for participation, creativity and the reframing of ritual (Gibbs and Bolger, 2006, p. 176), but I think this has been an instinctive reaction to observing the culture and the disconnection with traditional forms of church rather than a thought-through response to a root cause of dis-ease in our society.

Towards a shame-free future

As I was conducting my research into the topic of shame, there was one quotation that leapt out of the page at me.

> I believe that our failure to understand how shame and guilt function in different cultures and their inter-relatedness is a major reason for the slowness of church growth, especially among people with a developed world-view and a deep self-understanding. (Nicholls, 2001, p. 235)

All I have read and experienced has confirmed the sense I had that this could be a key to making the gospel relevant and meaningful again among a significant constituency in the UK. What is exciting is that we have the resources necessary to communicate the saving and healing work of Christ afresh, together with Christians who are willing to take risks in the tradition while remaining attentive to the Holy Spirit's leading.

Yet currently much of what we say in church reinforces shame. Confession compounds shame and our liturgy assumes pride rather than a crippling sense of unworthiness and the desire to hide our true selves. I have therefore begun to write and use others' 'shame-free' liturgies in our worship. Here is an example of a Eucharistic Prayer that I have written. I hope it is relevant to the issue and does not induce shame in those who are reciting it.

Screen Eucharist

The Lord is here
Our TV dinner is served

Lift up your hearts
Shielded to hide the wounds and scars

Let us give thanks to the Lord our God
Because you have sufficiently engaged our interest for the time being

We sit before you, side by side, isolated and distant.
Hoping to be distracted, entertained, transported to an alternative existence.
We eat without tasting, we gather without noticing, locked in a conversation that takes place between our ears.

Yet the God-man Jesus invites us to dine with him tonight.
A table has been laid and he waits for us to take our place beside him.
A banquet has been prepared and our favourite dishes are set before us.

He wants to know us. He is curious about our thoughts, preferences and dreams.
For through him all experience of life, love and the created world was made possible.
We are a reflection of his goodness and embodied potential for newness.
We are so grateful that because he practised what he preached to the point of dying to maintain his authenticity, we don't have to live up to the expectations of our ideal self.
We can be free to reveal who we really are and find that we are worthy to be loved by God and those with whom we long to be in relationship.

Even death on a cross could not stop him fulfilling his purpose and he rose to a new life.
We thank you that this means we too can look forward to our pain and loss being transformed into faith and hope if we choose to trust him in vulnerability.
Jesus returned to heaven so he could advocate on our behalf but he sent us a helper, the Holy Spirit, who gives us divinely inspired visions and insights to encourage and direct us.

Because of all that has been done for us in Jesus Christ, we can
join with angels and all those who have gone before, praising
God and saying:

Holy, holy, holy Lord
God of provision and presence,
heaven and earth are full of your glory
Hosanna in the highest.

Blessed is the one who comes in the name of the Lord.
Hosanna in the highest.

May we live an integrated life where we are at one with
ourselves and actively looking to make the most of every
opportunity to partner with you in bringing peace, healing
and justice to the spheres where we have influence, as Christ
demonstrated for us.

Who in the same night that he was betrayed with a kiss,
took bread, gave thanks, broke it and shared it among his
friends, saying,
'Take, eat; this is my body which is given for you;
do this in remembrance of me.'
In the same way, after supper he took a cup and gave you
thanks:
he gave it to them, saying,
'Drink this, all of you;
this is my blood which marks a new relationship between
humanity and the divine,
it removes all fears, regrets and hurts you have inflicted on
yourselves and others, that has kept us from one another.
Do this, as often as you drink it,
in remembrance of me.'

Christ has died
Christ is risen
Christ will come again

So as we remember the freedom and healing Christ offers us, we look forward to a day when he will return and restore all creation to beauty and wholeness.

Until then turn us from the impassive screen to see your reflected glory in the eyes of those we keep at arm's length.

Help us risk intimacy and build community such that the value of relationship is displayed and we show how dreams of a better and fairer world become reality when we live and work together in unity, diversity and mutuality.

We invite your Holy Spirit so this bread might become your body which sustains us and the wine your blood that reconciles us.

Empower and motivate us with your love.

Give us the strength to bear our suffering and disappointment.

Keep us discontent with living vicariously through the shallow and distorted image of 'the good life' as portrayed by celebrities.

And we look forward to coming home, where we are safe and loved, honest and fulfilled.

For it is only through our loving Creator, redeeming Son and enabling Spirit we can be assured that one day our longing will cease and all we have desired and glimpsed will be known in full.

Amen.

This is just one attempt at shame-free liturgy and I think there is much to do in creating resources that take the problem of shame seriously and help facilitate reconciliation with God and one another while remaining faithful to the tradition.

Conclusion

In seeking to articulate a gospel that frees people to be their real selves and know love and forgiveness in community, I believe we have an opportunity to make Christianity freshly relevant in our postmodern context. Yet the challenge is to live in the reality of this and ensure our practices and devotions authentically reflect our desire to embrace vulnerability and promote shame resistance. It is still early days in working this out but my hope is that fresh expressions will not only make church more accessible, but create places where reconciliation within people as well as between them is possible and the transformation of wider society becomes a natural consequence.

References

Brown, B., 2012, *Daring Greatly*, New York: Gotham Books.

Davis, J., 2012, *My Own Worst Enemy*, Bloomington, IN: Bethany House Publishers.

Gibbs, E. and R. K. Bolger, 2006, *Emerging Churches*, London: SPCK.

Green, J. B. and M. D. Baker, 2000, *Recovering the Scandal of the Cross*, Downers Grove, IL: InterVarsity Press.

Harper, M., 'The Family in Danger', http://www.harperfoundation.com/files/The_Family_in_danger.pdf.

Higton, M., 2008, *Christian Doctrine*, London: SCM Press.

Mann, A., 2005, *Atonement for a 'Sin-less' Society*, Milton Keynes: Paternoster.

Morisy, A., 2009, *Bothered and Bewildered*, London: Continuum.

Musk, B., 1996, 'Honour and Shame', *Evangelical Review of Theology* 20.2, April.

Nicholls, B., 2001, 'The Role of Shame and Guilt in a Theology of Cross-Cultural Mission', *Evangelical Review of Theology* 25.3, July.

Pattison, S., 2000, *Shame: Theory, Therapy, Theology*, Cambridge: Cambridge University Press.

Thomas, B., 1994, 'The Gospel for Shame Cultures', *Evangelical Missions Quarterly* 30.3, July.

Watson, J., 2005, *Shame*, Cambridge: Grove Books.

Notes

1 http://www.ted.com/talks_brene _brown_ on_vulnerability.html.

Redefining Sin

EMMA NASH

About a mile from my home, beside a busy road, stands a small chapel. Its noticeboard is placed so as to be clearly visible to motorists queuing at the traffic lights. There are two bold coloured posters on the noticeboard at the time of writing, each bearing a verse from the Authorized Version. On the left, in yellow type on a green background, we read: 'Be sure your sin will find you out.' On the right, black on yellow, are the words: 'God be merciful to me a sinner' (Num. 32.23; Luke 18.13). Every time I pass the noticeboard I wonder what these verses from the Bible communicate to those who drive by. Clearly, those who attend the chapel believe that it is important for passers-by to know that they are sinners, and that they can ask for mercy from God. My question, however, is whether people living in twenty-first-century Britain see themselves as sinners in need of forgiveness. I wonder what the reaction of the average driver would be to the assertion that they are 'a sinner'?

John Finney's book *Finding Faith Today* (1992) summarizes the findings of research he undertook into the way in which people become Christians. The study involved over 500 participants who had made a profession of Christian faith within the past year, and included a mixture of questionnaires and interviews. One of the many interesting findings of this study was that many of the participants, who came from a range of Christian denominations, appeared to have no understanding of the Christian concepts of sin and forgiveness. When asked about their feelings of guilt during the period in which they professed faith, 61 per cent of respondents either had no sense of guilt or answered 'don't know'. Furthermore, when asked what aspect of the Christian faith was most appealing, just 21 per cent of respondents mentioned the cross and forgiveness. The respondents had all made a recent profession of faith that had been accepted as genuine within their various denominations, 'yet the great majority appeared not to have grasped what is often taken as one of the most basic requirements of becoming a Christian – a "conviction of sin"'. Finney concludes: 'we can see that the appeal of the Christian gospel is by no means confined to the message of sin and salvation *even to those who do become Christians*' (Finney, 2004, pp. 50, 90–1).

A more recent study conducted by the London Institute for Contemporary Christianity sought to discover the attitudes of non-churchgoers to Christianity and the Church. One of Nick Spencer's findings was that, while interviewees insisted that they were people with high moral standards, these standards were determined by the individual and not by a moral law imposed upon them. Colin Greene notes that the problem with Christian theology of sin and the cross today is that there is no longer a universally accepted basis of morality. Moral values are determined by the individual, resulting in a serious weakening of the concept of sin that makes us guilty before God. The message of Christ's atoning death thus 'fails to connect with contemporary self-awareness' (Greene, 1995, p. 228). If people do not accept that others have the right to impose a moral code upon them, then correct behaviour is a matter of personal opinion, and right and wrong are determined by the individual. The notion of one over-riding divine law that determines correct behaviour and a divine judge who is angered when his law is broken is quite alien to modern thinking.

In his book *Atonement for a 'Sinless' Society*, Alan Mann offers a compelling analysis of contemporary postmodern culture. He argues that we live in a society that has no sense of sin or guilt. We have little sense of the 'Other', he explains, both in terms of the person who lives next door and in terms of the divine Other, God. If there is no Other, there is no one to hurt except oneself. The concept of sin has no meaning because it implies an external arbiter who does not exist. All moral decisions are a matter of personal choice rather than of responsibilities to others. Mann quotes Walter Brueggemann, who argues that we have become 'a self-indulgent society in which the disciplines of neighbourliness, that is the attention to the other, have disappeared' (Mann, 2005, pp. 4–26). If Mann is even partly correct in his analysis, it is hard to see how the doctrine of sin as it has traditionally been expressed could be meaningful to the majority of our contemporaries. It is equally hard to see how a genuine sense of guilt for transgressing God's moral law could be felt by many.

All this is potentially quite a problem for evangelism as Christian conversion has usually been understood as requiring repentance towards God. In the Baptist tradition to which I belong, repentance is an essential precondition of baptism. The second article of the Baptist Union of Great Britain's Declaration of Principle declares:

> That Christian Baptism is the immersion in water into the Name of the Father, the Son, and the Holy Ghost, of those who have professed repentance towards God and faith in our Lord Jesus Christ who 'died for our sins according to the Scriptures; was buried, and rose again the third day.[1]

Repentance towards God and faith in Christ who 'died for our sins' is absolutely central to a Baptist understanding of Christian conversion. A personal conviction of sin and a desire to turn from it is required when a person makes a lifelong commitment to Jesus in baptism.

Evangelical theologian John Stott describes conversion to Christianity in this way: 'People begin to become troubled in their conscience and to see the need for repentance. The Holy Spirit begins to open their eyes and they begin to see in Jesus Christ the Saviour they need.' We are all guilty before God, Stott argues, whether we feel guilty or not. When we are troubled in our conscience, recognize our sin and turn away from it and towards God, we are converted and receive Christ's salvation (Stott, 1975, pp. 100–15). Richard V. Peace describes repentance as 'a turning around in one's thinking'. He notes that the New Testament word *epistrepho*, translated 'convert', indicates a turning around and going the opposite way. This conversion involves *metanoeo*, an inner decision to turn, and *pistis* (faith). He also considers the related word *metamelomai*, being sorry for a past failure. Conversion in the New Testament involves turning from one's wicked ways to God, and results in the forgiveness of sins (Peace, 1999, pp. 244, 346–51).

If people are not 'troubled in their conscience', however, if they do not recognize any 'wicked ways', can they be 'repentant' in the traditional sense? Many apparently do not think they have anything of which to repent. And if there is no repentance, can there be genuine conversion? And if there is no conversion, can there be salvation? If salvation depends upon repentance, it may be that those who do not think they are sinners cannot be saved. In a culture without sin and guilt, the Christian gospel fails to connect with how people see themselves, and the cross, the central mystery of the Christian faith, seems to lose its power. This is a real problem for Baptists in particular and evangelicals more broadly when it comes to the way conversion has traditionally been understood, and it is a real problem for atonement theology, particularly penal substitutionary atonement, which is predicated upon the extreme seriousness of sin and hence the terrible penalty required to free humanity from it.

Summary of my research

I decided to undertake my own research into the beliefs of people new to Christianity. Inspired by *Finding Faith Today*, I wanted to find out what individuals who had recently made a profession of Christian faith believed about what Jesus had saved them from. Finney's research was 20 years old; to what extent did people today see themselves as 'sinners' – whether or not they used this word – prior to their conversion? I interviewed 11 people who had made a profession of Christian faith in a Baptist church within the last 3 years. I wanted those I interviewed to have undergone conversion recently enough to be able to recall their thoughts and feelings as far as possible as they were, rather than overlaid with the teaching of the Church, having been reinterpreted with hindsight.

Participants covered a wide age range, the youngest being 18 years old and the eldest in her seventies, and there was a good gender balance: five men and six women. I asked them to tell me their story, trying to ascertain what being a Christian meant to them by listening to the way in which they told that story, and making every effort not to lead them to a particular response. Then I listened to the recordings of the interviews and tried to determine, first, to what extent interviewees saw themselves as sinners in need of forgiveness, and second, what had attracted them to Christianity if not forgiveness for their sins. What had they been 'saved' from, if not from sin? Baptists are broadly evangelical and thus emphasize conversion and making a personal decision based on an understanding of the content of the Christian faith. As such, one would expect participants who had come to faith in a Baptist church to have received clear teaching on Christ's atonement and on the necessity of repentance and of personal, intellectual faith. It would therefore be all the more interesting to see how many talked about guilt, sin and the cross in their stories of faith.

Two of the questions I asked were taken directly from Finney's 1992 study:

- During the period you have described, did you find any parts of the Christian message particularly appealing?
- During the period when you [use own phrase, e.g. 'became a Christian'[2]] which of the following describes how you felt:
  (a) I felt a general sense of guilt
  (b) I felt guilt or shame about something in particular
  (c) I had no sense of guilt or shame
  (d) Don't know. (Finney, 1992, pp. 90, 49)

I asked the question about guilt last as I was interested to see if people would speak about guilt and sin without being prompted to do so. Most of the participants, 8 out of 11 people, said that they had some sense of guilt:

I don't think a day goes past ... I will get flashbacks ... maybe not every day, but every couple of days ... and something will come back into my mind and I think, my goodness, did I really do that? And I'm disgusted with myself.[3]

One person had trouble understanding the question, but finally said:

I wouldn't say guilt, more accountability ... Yeah, cause guilt's a kind of useless emotion because it doesn't achieve anything, it just makes you feel bad. Whereas accountability, you've acknowledged that there's a problem, and now you need to hold yourself to account in order to make changes.

It is interesting to note that this person went on to say:

Not so much that God was holding me to account, more that if there were things that I was unhappy with and things that needed to change then ... at the end of the day, it's going to have to be me that is the only person that can be held accountable, and therefore it's me that has to make the changes.

This person clearly continued to reject the notion that he could be held to an external moral code. He was accountable, not to God, but to himself.

Three people said that they had no sense of guilt. One older man felt that he had led a sheltered life and therefore had less to feel guilty for than some:

When I look at the sort of things that a lot of people have been through, you know, especially through the '60s, drugs and all the stuff that went with it, and alcohol, you know, I mean ... Never been there and so, you know, I haven't got that feeling that maybe some people might have and have said they have.

While discussing the question about guilt with a much younger person, I asked whether sin and forgiveness had been an important part of her journey. She explained:

I think I've always grown up with the discipline of that but it's not ... that hasn't been the main point of ... that's one of the rules you need to follow in Christianity, but that's not why you become a Christian ... I'm not ... saying that the only thing about Christianity is the love aspect, like I definitely think you need all the discipline aspect, like the self-discipline aspects and God disciplining you ultimately, but no that wouldn't be something I would, sort of, say would be something to do with *becoming* a Christian as much.

This articulate young woman had been brought up in a Christian family and had always gone to church, but did not feel that sin and forgiveness was at the heart of the Christian faith.

Most, but not all – eight out of eleven – expressed feelings of guilt or shame. The question about guilt and shame came last, however, as I was interested to see if people would speak about guilt and forgiveness without being prompted. Of the eight who said they felt guilty when asked, four had not mentioned sin, guilt or forgiveness up to this point, and a fifth 'guilty' person made just a brief passing reference to sin before admitting feelings of guilt at the final question. This suggested to me that, while most of the people I interviewed had some sense of being 'sinners' and could talk about guilt and forgiveness when prompted, it was not a large part of most participants' faith journeys. Just three people made more than a passing reference to sin and guilt *before being prompted* and then expressed feelings of guilt when asked. The other eight either did not feel guilty or did not mention guilt and forgiveness (other than very briefly) until prompted to do so.

Perhaps more surprising, just three people mentioned the cross and Christ's atonement before the final question. Of the three people who mentioned the atonement unprompted, one made only a passing reference to 'the Easter story and what Jesus did for us' and later explained that she had no feelings of guilt or shame. Two participants spoke about the atonement in more depth. When asked what she was taught about what it meant to be a Christian, one person replied:

Obviously the story of Jesus being the one that's come and we're not going to be perfect but it's Jesus that can save us from that and get rid of all the things that we've done wrong … going to church for me after I'd learnt a little bit more about Jesus, it became much more real to me. Because there's the story and, you know, 'our sins on a cross', but then there's the power of 'someone was on a cross'. And it was after that being a Christian became real and that relationship became real.

This was the response that most clearly followed the traditional evangelical teaching on the cross of Christ, and this person had clearly felt a 'conviction of sin' and experienced the joy and freedom of forgiveness.

If just two people spoke of the atonement as meaningful for them, and just two more spoke of guilt before being prompted to do so,[4] what was it that attracted people to Christianity? What parts of the Christian message were particularly appealing? A number of different aspects of the Christian faith were mentioned. Several people spoke about the fact that God is always there, answering our prayers and helping us:

I suppose it's just that having someone there all the time. You're never alone, you're never without someone who cares about you.

Some mentioned specific incidents when they knew that God was with them:

I can remember this particular day an overwhelming sense that God was there and he was listening, and I kind of didn't have to worry – whatever happened, it was going to be OK.

When asked what he was taught about what it meant to be a Christian, one older man explained:

I think to me it's been more of a … sort of a growing experience about God's love, it's sort of built up.

He struggled to explain what in particular had appealed to him about Christianity:

> It's difficult to sort of say one particular thing, I think it just runs through everything. It's about looking to God and praying to him and sharing all the little things with him.

For some, then, being a Christian was principally about the experience of a relationship with a God who loved them and listened to their prayers. Others spoke of finding happiness or a better life. One participant who had led a troubled life before his conversion explained that he had felt that his life would be better if he became a Christian:

> ... knowing God probably gave you a better life as well ... that was the instant appeal ... And to be fair, look what God's provided me with now: lovely wife, nice home ... Two of us on not bad salaries ... So we're very fortunate people.

Three participants spoke about the truth of Christianity; they need not search for meaning any longer as they had found the truth. When asked about what appealed to him about Christianity, one participant talked about his positive experience of the Alpha course and then his realization that he believed it was all true. Another man talked about his search for meaning, for a belief system that 'felt right' for him. He enjoyed the freedom to ask questions he had found in the Christian Church.

Another participant described an experience subsequent to his conversion in which he felt God saying to him 'It's all true'. This had had an impact on his personal evangelism:

> I would not now and have not since said to anybody initially what a wonderful person Jesus is, what I've said now is 'It's true, and you can find it, and this is where to find it.'

A few people talked about ethics – living a good life, following the example set by Jesus. One participant explained that she had always had a strong sense of morality, wanting to live well and to teach her children right from wrong. Now she can see that these are Christian morals:

> [I]t was only [when I knew some Christians] that I started to realize that actually I had the same views and thoughts and morals as them, and it's just been a slow drip-feed journey, really, for me more than anything into thinking yeah, actually, this is the road I want to take ... I knew that I wanted to be able to teach my children right from wrong, I knew that I wanted my children to behave in a particular way and have respect for others, you know, and all those Christian morals and ethics, but without realizing that they were *Christian* morals and ethics.

Finally, several people spoke about the importance of learning about the faith, reading the Bible and allowing it to speak to you:

> I think it's ... sometimes quite, even now, a shock when you're sort of praying about something or something's bothering you and you read the Bible and it's, like, whoa! ... I'm just carrying on reading day to day and, you know ... it's speaking to me.

To what extent did the people I interviewed see themselves as sinners in need of forgiveness? Most admitted to feelings of guilt or shame. Not all those who felt guilty mentioned guilt or wrong-doing before being prompted by the final question, however. In addition, very few spoke about Christ's atonement until prompted. When asked what in particular they had found attractive about the Christian message, *no one* spoke about the forgiveness of sins or Christ's atoning death. Instead, people spoke of the comfort of knowing that God was always with them; of the better, happier life they could have with God; of the search for meaning and the truth they had found in Christianity; of the moral compass and good example provided by Jesus; of the learning and day-to-day help they found in the Bible. Although an understanding of sin and forgiveness was there, *it was not the central focus of people's experiences of becoming Christians.*

John A. T. Robinson tells the story of seeing a church notice-board displaying the message, 'Christ is the answer'. Apparently someone had scribbled next to these words, 'Yes, but what is the question?' (Fiddes, 1989, p. 5). Presentations of the Christian gospel have very often declared that Christ is the answer to the problem of human sin but, as we have seen, this is not necessarily a problem people perceive themselves to have. Three possible responses suggest themselves to me. First, I would argue that we need to change our understanding of sin and hence the way it is communicated in evangelism. Perhaps we have understood sin in terms that are too narrow. Perhaps a broader definition of sin would help people exploring Christian faith today to identify with the term and to see its relevance for them. Second, we need to embrace theories of Christ's atoning work on the cross that emphasize aspects of the human predicament other than personal sin and guilt. Perhaps there are other ways of presenting the atonement that answer the anxieties of our contemporaries better. Third, I have come to wonder whether an intellectual understanding of one's own sinfulness matters as much as evangelicals have traditionally said it does. Space does not allow me to develop all three of these responses here. I will therefore focus on the first, asking how sin should be defined in twenty-first-century Britain.

Redefining sin

'Sin' has too often been defined in terms of 'sins'. Paul Tillich argues that, in churches, we focus on 'sins' – individual transgressions of a moral law – whereas the apostle Paul wrote of the concept of 'sin', singular. The individual actions named sins, Tillich explains, are expressions of sin, a more profound problem (Tillich, 1957, pp. 52–3). Alan Mann likewise laments the reductionist approach to sin that has often been taken; the making of lists of sins in an attempt to quantify something that is about the quality of our relationships with God and others (Mann, 2005, pp. 18–19). He quotes Douglas John Hall:

No word in the Christian vocabulary is so badly understood both in the world and in the churches as the word sin. Christians have allowed this profoundly biblical conception, which refers to broken relationships, to be reduced to sins – moral misdemeanours and guilty 'thoughts, words and deeds', especially of the sexual variety, that could be listed and confessed and absolved. (Mann, 2005, p. 18)

According to Tillich, the essence of sin is estrangement: 'Man is estranged from the ground of his being, from other beings, and from himself' (Tillich, 1957, p. 51). He uses the traditional categories of 'unbelief', 'hubris' and 'concupiscence' to develop his point. Humankind has turned away from God – this is unbelief, literally 'un-love'. Each person has turned in upon herself and become her own god – 'hubris' or excessive pride. And 'concupiscence' or desire means that the self turned in upon itself seeks to draw the whole of reality into itself (Tillich, 1957, pp. 54–9). The cure for estrangement is loving reunion: 'Love as the striving for the reunion of the separated is the opposite of estrangement. In faith and love, sin is conquered because estrangement is overcome by reunion' (Tillich, 1957, p. 53).

Echoes of Tillich's estranged self turned inward can be found in Alan Mann's description of the chronically shamed person of today. Mann describes the postmodern self which lives painfully with the gap between the 'ideal self' – the person he or she would like to be – and the real self, which is seen as deficient. This self-judgement '[destroys] the very basis of mutual, intimate, undistorted relating' (Mann, 2005, p. 31). Mann argues that atonement – literally 'at-one-ment' – is exactly what the chronically shamed post-industrial self needs: reconciliation between the self, others and the divine Other:

What is needed is a fuller, more meaningful, more biblical account of the plight of humankind that speaks appropriately and often about the atonement as a restoration and reconciliation between relational beings, both human and divine, who too often live with an *absence* of mutual, intimate, undistorted relating. (Mann, 2005, p. 49)

Mann and Tillich reframe the problem of sin in a very helpful way: sin is not so much the presence of unacceptable behaviour but the absence of a relationship of love with God, with others and also with oneself. Several of the people I interviewed as part of my research spoke about their experience of entering into a relationship with God: 'You're never alone'; 'it's been ... sort of a growing experience about God's love'; 'it's about a relationship'. Perhaps people living in twenty-first-century Britain might be interested in the promise of a mutual, intimate relationship of a quality their other experiences of relating cannot attain. Perhaps this would connect better with contemporary angst than the concept of seeking forgiveness for behaviour that contravenes divine law. Mann argues that the chronically shamed self craves intimacy – although this is in order to satisfy its own needs, not for the benefit of another, and this selfishness destroys the possibility of genuine intimacy (Mann, 2005, p. 35). As they learn to relate to the divine Other, people today might really learn to love.

One important aspect of Alan Mann's work is the notion that people today suffer from shame more than guilt. A number of writers have recently argued for a renewed understanding of shame and how it differs from guilt because of the importance for atonement theology (Watson, 2005; Green and Baker, 2003, pp. 153ff.). Some have drawn on the work of C. Norman Kraus, who writes from the perspective of the Japanese 'honour/shame' culture. Kraus describes shame as being focused on the self, a sense of being bad in one's own being; whereas guilt focuses on the act, a knowledge that I have done something wrong. Guilt can be erased through an appropriate punishment, which justifies the guilty person. Shame cannot be removed in this way, however; it requires a restoration of relationship that brings the offender back into the community (Kraus, 1987, p. 204). It has been argued that the categorization of cultures into 'guilt cultures' and 'shame cultures' found in some missionary literature is arbitrary and not justified by the evidence (Hesselgrave, 1983, pp. 464–5). The description of shame found in Kraus's work is extremely useful, nevertheless, in broadening our understanding of what sin is and how it manifests itself. It provides a direct challenge to the claim of penal substitutionary atonement that we have been objectively justified under the law regardless of how we feel. If sin is considered in terms of shame, then what is most important is the restoration of a relationship. People in Britain today may not consider themselves guilty under the law but they may identify with the estrangement Tillich describes and with the sense of ontological badness described by Mann.

Tillich and Mann both articulate the human predicament in terms of self-centredness, and Tillich writes of the excessive pride or 'hubris' that results in the estranged self becoming its own god. Feminist theologians have asked whether these kinds of descriptions reflect an inappropriately gendered view of sin, however. In her famous article 'The Human Situation: A Feminine View', Valerie Saiving Goldstein argued that while the man's sin is self-assertion, the woman's sin is self-negation. She suggested that the 'feminine' sins might be thought of as, among others, triviality, distractibility, dependence on others, gossip, sentimentality and irrationality (Saiving Goldstein, 1960, p. 109). Mary Grey also makes reference to Goldstein, adding the sin of choosing victimhood. She argues that it is inappropriate to encourage most women to be less selfish as they are socialized to subordinate their own needs to others', and are wont to err too far that way (Grey, 1994, pp. 233–4). Serene Jones goes further: 'Too often sin as "the bad things we do" overshadows sin as "the damage done to us" and "the social relations that define us"' (Jones, 2000, p. 120).

Maybe in some cases it is inappropriate to try to convince people of their own sin without first acknowledging the sin of which they have been the victim. This approach owes much to liberation theologies, which have emphasized the importance of conscientization, making oppressed people aware of the oppression they are experiencing. Structures of injustice, whether they be unfair economic systems that consign many people to poverty or the conditioning of women to be passive and compliant, are named as sin. It is estimated that one in five adult women in the UK will experience some form of sexual violence during their lifetime, and many never report this violence to the police for fear of being blamed or disbelieved, or because of their shame about what has happened to them (see www.rapecrisis.org.uk). In recent times there have been numerous stories in the news about the historic abuse of male and female children by people in positions of trust in institutions that were supposed to be caring for them. There has also been extensive news coverage of Operation Yewtree, which arose from the Jimmy Savile scandal and which has resulted in many arrests. Telling a man or woman with this kind of disturbing incident in their past that they are a sinner may be completely inappropriate. It may also compound their misplaced feelings of shame; they may already feel that they are 'bad'. What is needed is a presentation of the gospel that liberates them from the sin done to them.

Liberation theologies offer another potential meeting point with contemporary 'sinless' culture in that they raise awareness of the structures of injustice in which we are all involved. In fact, despite their origins among poor communities in Latin America, I would argue that liberation theologies are particularly helpful in convicting an affluent society like twenty-first-century Britain of its sin. The Catholic theologian Albert Nolan, who writes from the context of post-apartheid South Africa, explains that unfair economic structures that make a few rich while keeping many poor are, in an important sense, sinful (Nolan, 2009, p. 157). The emergence of the Fairtrade movement has raised awareness of the way in which producers in the two-thirds world are forced to accept rock-bottom prices for their produce. Fairtrade food products are now readily available in most supermarkets, although they are more expensive than comparable brands. Some clothes on sale in the British high street are manufactured by garment workers in the two-thirds world who are forced to work in unsafe conditions.

The collapse of the Rana Plaza building in Dhaka, Bangladesh in April 2013 highlighted this issue as the British media reported that clothing for Bonmarché, Benetton and Primark were all being made in the building. The building's owner, Mohammed Sohel Rana, was arrested while trying to flee the country for suspected negligence leading to the deaths of over 1,000 people. Mr Rana was an obvious hate figure but it was interesting to note that the press quickly picked up on the way in which multinational clothing companies were implicated in the terrible yet completely avoidable tragedy. It was argued that, in their search for the best deal from their suppliers, companies such as Benetton and Primark shared responsibility in some way with the factory owner for the unsafe conditions that resulted in great profits for the multinationals as well as such grief and misery. Alongside Mohammed Sohel Rana and the clothing companies, shoppers on the British high street are also implicated in their search for the best bargain without giving thought to the way in which that great price was achieved. Perhaps we, too, sinned when we profited from the unsafe labour of others. Nolan argues that people who set up these kinds of economic systems, as well as those who profit from them, are guilty of sin:

> [A]ll those who knowingly and willingly built [unjust] structures by making the laws, designing the policies, fabricating the rationalizations for it, and promoting its false values would be guilty. But not only them. All those who reproduce the system daily by knowingly and willingly benefiting from its injustices and making excuses for their conformity to the demands and temptations of the unjust arrangements and relations are also guilty. (Nolan, 2009, p. 159)

If Christian evangelists defined sin in such a way as to include these kinds of structures of injustice, it would be hard for anyone living in contemporary Britain to say they had not sinned. If 'sin' rather than 'sins' were talked about; if sin suffered as well as sin perpetrated were acknowledged; if the sin of self-negation were emphasized as much as the sin of pride; if sinful economic and social structures were included in the definition – then perhaps the notion of sin would not seem so irrelevant to contemporary British society.

Conclusion

It could be argued that the 11 people I interviewed and the 500 people Finney surveyed back in 1992 came to Christian faith anyway, and hence Christian evangelism does not need to change. Despite the mismatch between the anthropology presented by Christians ('human beings are sinful') and people's self-understanding ('I am a good person'), people still become Christians. Some might wish to challenge the depth or reality of their conversion if it has apparently taken place without repentance, but the fact remains that Finney's 500 participants and my 11 had all had the sincerity of their conversion tested in some way by the local church who had prepared them for confirmation, baptism or the Catholic Rite of Christian Initiation of Adults (RCIA). If people are coming to genuine Christian faith despite this mismatch between their view of themselves and the Church's teaching on sin, what does it matter?

I would argue that it matters because these people are the exception rather than the rule. People are not coming to Christian faith in large numbers today and church attendance has dropped off dramatically in recent decades. According to the 2011 census, 41 per cent of the UK population do not consider themselves to be Christian.[5] A much larger percentage – between 80 and 94 per cent – do not attend church (Ashworth and Farthing, 2007, p. 6; English Church Census, 2005). The secularization thesis is contested, but I note that it seems a reasonable conclusion to draw from the above statistics that the Christian faith is failing to captivate a large number of people. As an evangelist I am inspired to ask whether there is anything I should be doing differently in order to connect better with this large number of people.

It seems clear to me that the Church's teaching on sin and the atonement needs to be improved. Rather than limiting our description of sin to 'guilty thoughts, words and deeds, especially of the sexual variety', we need to present sin as a profoundly relational dysfunction, an estrangement both within ourselves and between ourselves, our neighbours and our loving heavenly Father. Furthermore, our understanding of 'neighbour' needs to include those living on the other side of the world who are influenced by our consumer choices, as well as those living next door. This is a challenge for Christian apologists, for preachers from all traditions, for those who teach children in Sunday school and for those who prepare people of all ages for first communion, confirmation, baptism and the RCIA. If an adult with no church background is taught by an evangelist that she breaks God's law in small ways every day and must repent, she may well find the teaching incredible or offensive. If a child being brought up in a Christian community is taught that he must say sorry for the bad things he does each day, he may accept the teaching in childhood only to reject it in adulthood when he comes into contact with the view of morality held by the wider society in which he lives. In every situation where sin and repentance are described and explained, and particularly when the people being taught are very young or in the early stages of exploring Christianity, the broadest possible view of sin should be presented so as to connect with contemporary views of the human condition.

Whenever I am waiting at the traffic lights outside the chapel described above, I wonder what message or biblical text might connect better with members of our 'sinless' society as they drive past. What might be good alternatives to 'Be sure your sin will find you out' and 'God be merciful to me a sinner'? One possibility is found in Revelation 3. The risen Christ declares: 'Look! Here I stand at the door and knock. If you hear me calling and open the door, I will come in, and we will share a meal as friends' (Rev. 3.20 NLT). This verse is a direct invitation to relationship with Christ. In its original context, the risen Christ stands at the door of the church in Laodicea and asks to be let back in, but the text also speaks powerfully to those who have never experienced relationship with Christ. Sin in this text is the absence of Christ; he has been left standing outside. Sinners – those who do not have Christ in their lives – are invited to let him in so that they can 'share a meal as friends'. This is a beautiful and gentle picture of friendship with God. It does not require people to acknowledge wrong in their lives in the first instance; instead it invites them to spend time with a person and experience a friendship like no other.

References

Ashworth, J. and I. Farthing, 2007, *Churchgoing in the UK: A Research Report from Tearfund on Church Attendance in the UK*, Teddington: Tearfund.

Dye, T. W., 1976, 'Toward a Cross-Cultural Definition of Sin', *Missiology* 4.1, pp. 27–41.

Fiddes, P. S., 1989, *Past Event and Present Salvation: The Christian Idea of Atonement*, London: Darton, Longman & Todd.

Finney, J., 1992, *Finding Faith Today: How Does it Happen?*, Swindon: British and Foreign Bible Society.

Finney, J., 2004, *Emerging Evangelism*, London: Darton, Longman & Todd.

Gorringe, T. J., 2000, *Salvation*, Peterborough: Epworth Press.

Green, J. B. and M. D. Baker, 2003, *Recovering the Scandal of the Cross: Atonement in New Testament and Contemporary Contexts*, Carlisle: Paternoster Press.

Greene, C., 1995, 'Is the Message of the Cross Good News for the Twentieth Century?', in John Goldingay (ed.), *Atonement Today: A Symposium at St John's College, Nottingham*, London: SPCK.

Grey, M., 1994, 'Falling into Freedom: Searching for New Interpretations of Sin in a Secular Society', *Scottish Journal of Theology* 47.2 pp. 223–44.

Hesselgrave, D. J., 1983, 'Missionary Elenctics and Guilt and Shame', *Missiology* 11.4, pp. 461–83.

Jones, S., 2000, *Feminist Theory and Christian Theology: Cartographies of Grace*, Minneapolis, MN: Fortress Press.

Kraus, C. N., 1987, *Jesus Christ Our Lord: Christology from a Disciple's Perspective*, Scottdale, PA: Herald Press.

Mann, A., 2005, *Atonement for a 'Sinless' Society: Engaging with an Emerging Culture*, Milton Keynes: Paternoster Press.

Nolan, A., 2009, *Hope in an Age of Despair and Other Talks and Writings*, Maryknoll, NY: Orbis Books.

Peace, R. V., 1999, *Conversion in the New Testament: Paul and the Twelve*, Grand Rapids, MI: Eerdmans.

Peace, R. V., 2007, 'Conflicting Understandings of Christian Conversion: A Missiological Challenge', in J. J. Bonk et al. (eds), *Speaking About What We Have Seen and Heard: Evangelism in Global Perspective*, New Haven, CT: OMSC Publications.

Priest, R. J., 1993, 'Cultural Anthropology, Sin, and the Missionary', in D. A. Carson and J. D. Woodbridge (eds), *God and Culture: Essays in Honor of Carl F. H. Henry*, Grand Rapids, MI: Eerdmans/Carlisle: Paternoster Press.

Priest, R. J., 1994, 'Missionary Elenctics: Conscience and Culture', *Missiology: An International Review* 22.3, pp. 291–316.

Saiving Goldstein, V., 1960, 'The Human Situation: A Feminine View', *The Journal of Religion* 40.2, pp. 100–112.

Spencer, N., 2003, *Beyond Belief? Barriers and Bridges to Faith Today*, London: The London Institute for Contemporary Christianity.

Stott, J., 1975, *Christian Mission in the Modern World*, London: Falcon.

Tillich, P., 1957, *Systematic Theology*, vol. 2, London: James Nisbet & Co.

Watson, J., 2005, *Shame: Biblical Reflections and Pastoral Advice on Living with Shame*, Cambridge: Grove Books.

Wink, W., 1984, *Naming the Powers: The Language of Power in the New Testament*, Philadelphia: Fortress Press.

Websites

Census 2011, http://www.ons.gov.uk/ons/rel/census/2011-census/key-statistics-for-local-authorities-in-england-and-wales/rpt-religion.html.

English Church Census 2005, http://www.eauk.org/church/research-and-statistics/english-church-census.cfm.

www.baptist.org.uk.

www.rapecrisis.org.uk.

Notes

1 See http://www.baptist.org.uk/Groups/220595/Declaration_of_Principle.aspx.

2 I slightly amended this question to use the participant's own phrase to describe their experience of conversion.

3 When quoting participants, '...' usually indicates that part of the sentence has been edited out for the purposes of clarity. I have tried to convey the participant's line of thought without taxing the reader with 'like's, 'you know's and fragments that detract from rather than add to the plain meaning of the sentence. On occasion, '...' indicates several sentences that have been missed out for the sake of brevity.

4 Two people spoke of the atonement other than briefly before the final question. Three people spoke of guilt other than briefly before the final question. One of those who had spoken about the atonement also spoke of guilt. Therefore just four people spoke of guilt or the atonement more than briefly *and* felt guilty when asked.

5 Census 2011 statistics are available at www.ons.gov.uk.

The Upper Room

KIM HARTSHORNE

The seeds of what grew into the Upper Room Community were planted in 2000 when a housewife had a dream. This was shared with three other women who gathered weekly to pray for their small market town, in the south-west of the UK. In the dream, churches were collaborating to open a centre where people in need could come for practical support and care, help with debt, addiction, homework clubs, community and friendship offered alongside prayer and space to explore Christian spirituality. The women in the prayer group had varied denominational and social backgrounds, some working and others volunteering in the local Cyber Café and Home-Start scheme.

Fourteen years later, the Upper Room Community offers two drop-in sessions a week, a Sunday gathering for worship and Bible Study, a monthly communion service and lunch, a monthly Community meal, along with advocacy and support, prayer and friendship. Starter boxes are supplied to people moving into emergency accommodation from homelessness or domestic violence in partnership with a local housing association; Street Pastors and a local parish church Sunday school use the leased space in the town centre free of charge. The NHS mental health support team refer people into the Community who are recovering from suicide attempts.

This is the story of the journey from dream to reality; it is one of inconsistency, confusion and ordinariness, human frailty, love and transformation, intermingled with the mystical leading of the Holy Spirit. It has led us to places we never knew existed, to witness things we did not believe we would see, to know ourselves in Christ more deeply and to meet people who have changed us for ever.

Context

The town is small and outwardly affluent, on the edge of the Cotswolds, but is polarized socially and economically. It is home to members of the aristocracy and numerous wealthy individuals; the wealth management company St James' Place occupies a prominent location at the gateway to the town, juxtaposed by deprivation on several large housing estates. In early 2004 research by the Learning and Skills Council exposed very low levels of numeracy and literacy in the town, combined with low levels of attainment and aspiration, and lack of access to services and transport.[1] At around the same time, Social Services data revealed many local families to be under pressure, with high numbers of children being admitted to A&E and involved in road traffic accidents on one estate. The report's publication stirred a sense of injustice among the women and reminded them again of the dream. They began to pray with a renewed commitment, to study the Bible for God's heart for those who struggled, and to seek out contacts locally with experience in service provision.

At this time there were 11 Christian churches representing all the major denominations in the town but none engaged in local mission, outreach or community development. The churches mainly served the white middle classes and had an air of squeaky-clean morality that deterred anyone with the baggage of a complex past. It was hard to imagine where any of the families cited in the statistics would be welcomed and cared for.

The women attended various churches between them and so one of these churches was asked to give its blessing and guidance to the idea of a project among the marginalized. Approval was refused by the church's leaders, due in part to a belief that women were not allowed to lead, but also a 'believe/behave/belong' ecclesiology that did not approve the mixing of mission and community development. After much prayer, they decided to go ahead without the support of a church, and finance was raised by one of the team selling her house to enable the project to go ahead. The women found vocation in this risky obedience to the stirring of the Spirit, despite the lack of support from the Church. Their own life stories informed their conviction that redemption and acceptance by God through Christ could transform lives marked by shame, mistakes and rejection, and that this was news worth sharing.

In 2008, premises were leased for a prayer space in the centre of town and the Upper Room opened to offer welcome, belonging and an experimental non-church space. Two drop-in sessions a week run by volunteers were the starting point. The plan was to be accessible and lower the social barriers that made people feel they did not belong in church, developing friendships through which the gospel could be authentically shared and voices heard.

The founding story

The initial struggles engendered what Gerald Arbuckle describes as a 'founding' commitment to openness and equality (Arbuckle, 1993, p. 21). (Interestingly the latest research on Fresh Expressions shows the majority of new forms of church are led by unpaid lay women, so perhaps God did know what she was doing after all!) It was a simple beginning with no written plan, well-developed theology or paid leaders. The women simply saw from the Gospels that all Christian people were called to join in the active working towards justice and redemption of the eschatological kingdom and, in the disciples, that God could use ordinary people if they put themselves at his disposal. Charismatics who establish new forms of church have been lampooned by some opponents of missional ecclesiology, but the women were undeterred. Commitment to equality of access is modelled in the commitment to indigenous leadership by those who have come up through the Community, and in the worshipping life of the Upper Room where all can participate in the giving and receiving of the

Eucharist. The community have developed confidence in bringing what can be seen as a prophetic challenge in the message they first heard from John Wimber: 'Everybody gets to play!' (Wimber, 2008, p. 7).

From the outset, the team became aware that each person who came to the drop-in shaped and added something of their uniqueness to the whole. Over time they learned to lay down whatever agendas they may have started with and instead see God ahead of them at work in every situation. This commitment to *missio Dei* is the thread that has run through the history of the Community from the initial dream to the present: that God so *loves* the world (rather than being motivated by wrath or revenge), that he is already fully present and active in it. An incarnational mission model assumes God is not afraid of the world and does not expect his followers to sit on the sidelines of society lamenting its condition, but to see where he is present and join in his redemptive activity.

The commitment to following has required flexibility and responsiveness to learn from new people groups with differing needs, allowing community rhythm to take shape in response to what people need. This has meant learning about the effects of trauma, post-traumatic stress disorder and other conditions that people asking for help have presented with. At the Reformation, Martin Luther emphasized the Church as a group of individuals who hear and respond to the voice of Christ, rejecting Roman Catholicism's emphasis on the corporate body summarized in the Nicene Creed as 'one, holy and catholic'. This emphasis on the individual and their own response to God has remained an identifying feature of post-Reformation Protestant ecclesiology, locating holiness as personal and in the response of the individual believer. However, that perspective can lead to an increased focus on the life and morality of each believer, which can emphasize works rather than grace as the means of salvation. In a society where many people have no understanding of the faith and complex lives, they may be seen as 'profane' and to be kept separate by some churches. As a starting point for mission, this communicates either fear or moral superiority and lays a heavy emphasis on certain behaviours being necessary before welcome and belonging will be offered.

The deliberate combining of social action and development for individuals and communities with mission and faith-sharing grew out of a sense that the relationships in the Trinity could be reflected in relationships in the community and lead to healing and restoration. Friendship would allow the team to share their own stories of messy lives changed by God naturally, as opposed to making people the 'target' of evangelism. There was no formal programme or set of materials, no pressure around faith, only conversation offered alongside care. Faith was to be caught rather than taught in the early years. In recent years the ecumenical World Council of Churches (WCC) has acknowledged that the way in which mission is done must embody Christ along with the message, following years of western exporting of cultural practices around the world dressed up as the gospel (Bevans and Tahaafe-Williams (eds), 2011, pp. 112–13).

Sisters are doing it for themselves!

Only women gathered in the Upper Room drop-in sessions for the first year, drawn from social networks at work, school gates and mums' groups. It is interesting to reflect upon the differences in structures and working practices that evolved as women worked together. Meetings were scheduled around childcare and school hours; tasks assigned according to enthusiasm and willingness. There were no hierarchy, job titles or salaries for the first three years. The women prayed and confessed together and shared rituals for healing and forgiveness; they shared brokenness and faith in Christ as healer and restorer. One woman on the team survived domestic violence and then treatment for breast cancer during the early years of the project; others who came were experiencing marital problems and mental illness, and the company of women rallied around to provide emotional and practical support.

In the early years, the team of women was isolated in the wider Christian community and were refused membership of the local

'Churches Together' organization. The women felt they were cast as problematic. Rosemary Radford Ruether notes the challenge women bring when they 'ask critical questions about the role of religion in the sanctification of patriarchy ... and began to take the shaping of the symbolic universe of meaning into their own hands' (Ruether, 1986, p. 2). She identifies some churches that posit feminism as apostasy and it is fair to say this was the response the women met with.

Ruether identifies a need for a period of 'women-church', to act as

> communities of nurture to guide one through death to the old symbolic order of patriarchy, to re-birth into a new community of being and living ... deep symbols and symbolic actions to guide and interpret the actual experience of the journey from sexism to liberated humanity. (Ruether, 1986 p. 3)

Perhaps all the women needed the healing and space to reimagine their own identities that this early women-only phase brought.

It's raining men!

When a contingent of homeless men started coming to the drop-in, the dynamic suddenly and completely changed. Some of the women volunteers found this very difficult as the nurturing and peaceful atmosphere changed and some of the regular visitors stopped coming. Some of the men were addicted to alcohol; others experienced mental illness and could be volatile, so more robust guidelines and safe working practices had to be developed. Training and good practice were needed and wider networks were developed and training acquired to equip volunteers and trustees.

A male support worker was hired who had experienced mental illness himself and was on his way to recovery. Immediately, he hit it off with the men who were homeless, through his disarming honesty and black sense of humour. He was uncertain about the role, due to his self-identified weaknesses, but his openness about failure and struggle made a deep point of connection. The men came to the drop-in sessions to chat, drink tea and shelter from the weather, often falling asleep on the sofa after a cold night. Socks, boots and coats were requested and sleeping bags regularly supplied.

Over time these relationships became deeper and more open as the men shared some of the tragic past experiences that had led to their dereliction. Theological questions were aired as the men wondered where God had been in their past experiences, and they wrestled with shame about their own choices and actions. Helping people articulate their pain and grief about past hurts and suffering led to theological reflection that sent the team back to their Bibles and on to their knees, wondering if these people were in fact 'sinners' or more sinned against.

The traditional penal substitutionary atonement theory most of us had inherited from our evangelical backgrounds seemed suddenly to offer no help, with its angry God who seems so ready to take offence at others' misfortunes and bad choices. Bosch describes this as a narrowly defined salvation, a 'crisis theology' in which the person of Christ is narrowly and legally identified as the means of salvation. This is then separated from the work of Christ as more broadly containing the providential activities of God, oriented towards the well-being and transformation of society and individuals seen throughout the Old Testament model of care required by Torah (Bosch, 1991, p. 394).

At the Upper Room, the prayers prayed with the men were expressions of lament and pain, crying out for mercy and rescue in desperation for their circumstances to change. We began to read the Beatitudes in Matthew 5.1–12, the story of those invited unexpectedly to the wedding banquet in Matthew 22, the command to serve others practically elevated as serving Christ in Mathew 25. We found that Christ preached peace to those who were far off, as well as those who were near (Eph. 2.17) and that we could only love because he had first shown love to us (1 John 4.19). Yet this generosity of grace seemed at some point to have morphed into a doctrine of 'salvation by middle-class values' in church, and anyone questioning this dichotomy was neutralized with the label 'liberal'. All this deconstruction happened in snatches of conversation, fuelled by reading and prayer as theological under-pinnings shifted to illuminate the context. It occurs to me that we often have the theology we need, and the theology we had arrived with was perhaps not examined enough, not rigorous enough, to withstand the exposure and testing of this environment and the questions and issues that came with it.

During the course of a year, we ate meals with the men, lis-tened and talked with them and celebrated their birthdays with cards, cake, candles and singing. They very much liked to have a photograph of themselves, reinforcing their sense of personhood. After this period, they were each offered housing with various housing associations and all accepted, even though some had lived rough for many years. There was a sense that the normaliz-ing of interaction and friendship in the Community had enabled them successfully to negotiate their re-entry into residential life in society.

The men taught us much more than we offered them, and were very honest if they felt they were being patronized or pitied. They questioned our use of resources and money, and the way they shared food and took care of each person in the group was incredibly humbling. They shared their views on Scripture and God readily and included us in their community of friendship. Despite the obvious inequality in terms of possessions and owner-ship, relationships were quite open and based on an equality of personhood and interconnectedness. The men had no veneer to hide behind or resources to use to manipulate people's good opinion, and their stripped-back honesty allowed us the gift of seeing ourselves through their eyes. It was a process that enabled a deeper vulnerability and authenticity to emerge.

Contextual theology

Bevans describes contextual theology as a way of doing theology that takes into account or puts two realities into a mutually crit-ical dialogue. The first is the *experience of the past*, recorded in

Scripture and preserved and defended in church tradition. The second is the *experience of the present*, or a particular *context*; explaining that experience is central to understanding contextual theology (Bevans 2011, pp. 3–17). He describes the process as a dialogue between local context, experience and the events of our time, with Scripture and tradition that represents Christian understanding down the ages. This is a practice that includes a wider range of voices and experiences than traditional academic theology and in fact prizes highly the voices of experience.

The wisdom and learning received from the men who were homeless would be included and valued by this process and speak truths to the Church that it cannot otherwise see, offering perspectives that are not yet valued or heard. There is a sense that prophetic truth is found at the margins, as the challenges it speaks are not easily given space at the centre. As Stephen Bevans notes: 'A theology that is done out of poverty and vulnerability will be able to inspire and uphold the church' (Bevans and Tahaafe-Williams (eds), 2011, p. 12).

Walter Brueggemann speaks of how often we as Christians are double-minded, trying to resolve easily the tension between our desire to settle and trust the dominant world narrative as it presents itself to us, with the need for a prophetic perspective that 'names and makes palpable the crisis already pulsing among us'. He describes 'the work of truthfulness as the process through which persons "switch worlds"', and posits the ancient prophets as '*imaginers*; and those ... who follow in their wake are *imaginers* after them ... they challenge us to go beyond what is given and taken for granted and to go where we had not thought to go and where, in fact, we are most reluctant to go' (Brueggemann, 2012, p. 18).

The need to create church in a way that could incorporate the voices of the men and value their wisdom and story broke the team out of their churches and into a space beyond their imagination, where the receipt of all experience could be joyfully brought into dialogue with Scripture, tradition and context.

Rip it up and start again?

For the first few years the women running the drop-in sessions continued to worship in various local churches. At the same time, theological and ecclesiological struggling were taking place. None of the churches seemed to grasp what we were engaged in, in terms of trying not to impose a set of beliefs or a power structure where we were transmitting 'right' beliefs, but instead waiting to see where God was at work and allowing space to follow. Personnel changes in the team saw some people move on and others join, and a point arrived where the beginnings of a worshipping community formed around the Upper Room. This would enable an experiment to see what might meet the needs of our friends, some of whom did not read confidently or like being indoors for long, the majority having no experience of church or faith.

Deconstructing and reflecting upon our past church experiences led to a renewed commitment to the Church universal, and to authentic relationships, vulnerability and equally valuing all. Laurie Green's *Lets Do Theology* (2009) was hugely helpful at this stage and *lectio divina* using the Lectionary was adopted as a way forward that joined us to the wider body of the Church and maintained the importance of the Scriptures. We were struggling towards a way of valuing each person's experience, instinct and understanding and a simple structure where power was shared and not concentrated in the hands of one or two who 'knew all the answers'.

We have tried all kinds of things in the years since: responding to seasonal patterns with walks and social activities in summer and gatherings around Scripture in autumn and winter, 24/7 prayer stations, bringing poetry and music, times of silence and stillness, all trying to find a balance between the need to imbibe the wisdom of Scripture and relate it to our real lives, growing relationships and establishing habits of prayer, contemplation and action, balanced with managing the amount of preparation. This is a constant juggling act in a small group where some are not yet confident to take a lead.

Eat me

From the outset, eating and hospitality were important rituals for welcoming people in, and also a practical matter as many people were hungry. The team was initially unaware of the sacramental pattern in the act of eating together as no one had come from a background where this theology was articulated. The sense of a sacred pattern around eating together developed over time and began to shape community life. The book *Mealtime Habits of the Messiah* by Conrad Gempf (2005, pp. 132–5) became significant and deepened our understanding of the radical hospitality of Jesus. Over time, more of community life began to be structured around eating. This has grown to be the essence of discipleship and mutual transformation; disconnected and castigated individuals grow in friendship and trusting mutual relationships, and in this way we have grown into a community rather than simply remaining a project or offering events or services.

Eating together around a table has been redemptive for vulnerable people and families at risk of breakdown. It gives parents a place to rest briefly while their children are fed and entertained, and the strain of lone parenting can be carried by the Community for a while with space to speak about parenting struggles with other adults. Gathering on bank holidays and during school holidays is particularly important for this group, for whom the additional strain of unattainable 'perfect' family life is hard to bear. The Community take trips out to the seaside or zoo together in order to enable access to relaxed childhood experiences for families under strain. All these activities include food, even if only beachside picnics and tea, chips or ice cream. It is a big deal for people who often feel excluded or isolated to have trips and parties to talk about after the weekend or holiday season, especially the children.

In the rhythm of community life, meals take place around communion services and also in homes. The sharing of the gospel message takes place conversationally against a backdrop of talking, eating and praying together. Rather than seeing people as the object or target to be witnessed *at*, the Word is considered and pondered among friends and becomes a mutual conversation where doubts are aired and questions mulled over together.

Worship: praxis and inclusion

The sacramental life of the community grew through partnership with a local Anglican priest who was open to the needs of the community and helped shape worship appropriately. Initially we assumed liturgical worship might be inaccessible and that more experimental or alt worship should be tried, but it became clear that people who came were interested in accessing the liturgical tradition, but more simply and in a relational and accessible environment.

The developing relationship with the local priest over time led to closer ties with the Church of England and this became a natural home for the community. The advent of ecclesial experimentation via the *Mission-Shaped Church* report in 2004, supported by Rowan Williams, made space for us in the wider Church. This relationship between the traditional and the new models the genius of the idea of a 'mixed economy'. The kindness we have received has been a blessing to us all as the community has explored the depth of the tradition. People with no church background have been drawn to be baptized and confirmed at the Upper Room and found identity and belonging through the rituals. This has opened up communication and partnering with the inherited church, which benefits all.

In terms of communion, we keep an 'open table' where all present are invited to take bread and (non-alcoholic) wine and to participate in serving. The open access may be offensive to some who see it as a mark of approval for those who are in 'good standing' before God. For Anglicans this restriction is enshrined in canon law. For the Upper Room, however, the sacraments represent the outrageous free gift of grace, unearned in any way and therefore *always* undeserved. Apart from Christ, none of us can ever be in good standing before God. As Isaiah 64.6 reminds us, all our righteousness is like filthy rags before him.

The praxis model shows it is possible to act ourselves into a new way of thinking.[2] Experience has taught us that when people who are marginalized participate in the communion service in some way – by offering the cup of wine to others, acting out or reading the passage of Scripture with others – they are drawn into the action of the ritual, and taking bread and wine with others becomes transformative. Many find themselves stunned and changed by this participation, and encounter Christ through the breaking of bread in a vivid way. The welcome draws people irresistibly and cuts through privileged ownership by insiders or any hierarchy of worthiness. The act of communion is so powerful as to be able to change the whole world, one life at a time! It communicates the love of God more fully than hours of sermons or baptismal preparation, but has the same effect; many who join in ask to be baptized within a short timeframe.

If the Eucharist is a foretaste of the kingdom, then it needs to be accessible to those who will be gathered in from the highways and byways and given a seat at the eschatological banqueting table mentioned in Matthew 22, where the worthy and unworthy alike are gathered in. Those joining in may not be confident with complex liturgical words and practices but they do understand the powerful message being sent by God via an invitation to a meal with friends that is freely and joyfully given.

Many mission models emphasize the Eucharist as an essential part of ecclesial life and a catalyst for the outward sweep of service and mission, yet the Church remains precious around the opening out of this free gift it stewards. Yet Pete Ward says, 'communion recounts and makes present the gospel of Jesus Christ ... it encapsulates the Christian story in both word and action (Ward, 1993, p. 13). This embodying quality has been evidenced in the Community, with the bread and wine providing a powerful experiential means of communication to people who have little theological framework to establish conceptual meaning.

There should be a 'practical awareness of others ... that unites our act of worship with the service of God and the poor and makes the Lord's Supper a meal of true revolution' (Martelet, 1976, p. 183). Gustave Martelet suggests that one day political and social action could take the place of the eucharistic offering, stating:

> [S]uch a secularization of the mystery would be *spiritually* as serious (even though *socially* less shocking) as its profanation by injustice or the lack of care for the deprived of the world ... our participation in the Eucharist must entail in our lives action which truly transforms the inhuman conditions that are to be found in the world. (Martelet, 1976, p. 184)

The missional life of the community is offered up as an act of worship to the God who gathers us in for his love and transformation to flow.

Liturgy

Daniel Hardy emphasizes the need for all of the life experience of a congregation to be gathered up and 'visibly incorporated' in the liturgy and drama of the Eucharist, 'enacted as the common meaning of the people together before God', and that this knits a community together (Hardy, 2001, p. 255). As the life experience of many of the Upper Room Community is of abuse, trauma or mental illness, the liturgy needs to include lament and to express pain and shame in a way that Anglican worship rarely acknowledges, so some permission for alternatives has been negotiated with the Bishop. A young man writing prayers using the psalms to express pain, or a vulnerable woman agreeing to offer the cup of wine for the first time, are ways in which people can be drawn into participation in the authentic worshipping life of the Community. Often 'the Voice' version of the gospel passage is spoken aloud by everyone present.

Inculturation is the process whereby the good news of Jesus Christ is able to make sense in all its myriad cultural and social contexts, and yet it has not been fully successful 'because it has not truly encountered people in their everyday cultural reality and become embedded in their lives and experience'.[3] When the life experiences of the people who have been drawn in and come to faith are expressed in community liturgy, then inculturation has completed its cycle. However, the need to create relevant and usable worship can be time-consuming and shared material prepared by other ecclesial communities is not easy to access. The Church has not yet risen to the challenge of offering appropriate liturgy for this kind of community and the skills are not always present in small experimental groups to do this confidently.

The reception of new groups and demographics into the Church of England may make more visible the issues faced by these groups and over time may begin to bring a challenge in liturgical terms. A visit by Archbishop of Canterbury, Rowan Williams, to the Upper Room in 2013 was received by the community as evidence that people at the margins are being included and seen. The introduction of new forms of church was in part designed to reach new people groups who are usually absent from the life of the Church, and this is beginning to succeed according to recent research.[4]

However, there is a long way still to go. Many challenges are still to be articulated from the experiences of the marginalized, and how these are understood by a powerful organization with inflexible traditions. Inevitably, given the demographic profile and established nature of the power structure in the Church, most of the perspectives shaping our liturgies for worship come from a place of privilege. Male, white, middle class, housed, formally theologically educated, straight, clerical, economically powerful, middle aged, literate, Northern hemisphere: these cultural lenses will likely be represented in the Liturgical Commission, shaping the many, many words that are spoken daily in worship all over the world by Anglicans. Are these words usable with integrity in a worshipping community like the Upper Room, or do they express experiences and understandings of God that are unfamiliar or inaccessible to the people who come?

Gutiérrez implies that the solution to the power imbalance is that the Church needs to get out more, to engage

> beyond the boundaries of the Church. This is of prime importance. It implies openness to the world, gathering the questions

it poses, being attentive to its historical transformations ... the real questions of the modern world ... Instead of using only revelation and tradition as starting points, as classical theology has traditionally done, it must start with facts and questions derived from the world and its history. It is precisely this opening to the totality of human history that allows theology to fulfil its critical function vis-à-vis ecclesial praxis without narrowness. (Gutiérrez, 2001, p. 56)

He suggests theology must bring critical reflection to society and the Church rather than upholding any dominant position and 'thus fulfil a liberating function for humankind and the Christian community' (Gutiérrez, 2001, p. 56).

This speaks to the Church as only fulfilling its calling when it is engaged in society and committed to changing what oppresses and distorts human flourishing. Worship from this perspective is active and engaged in societal structures – 'the liturgy beyond the liturgy' described by the Orthodox tradition – with experience incorporated into liturgy and service inside the Church. The doctrine of God's ongoing providential presence at work in the world is based on the coming of God into human affairs in the incarnation (Bunting, 1996, p. 44).

This predisposes Christians to action in society as a way of participating along with God in the ongoing redemption of human life. The presence of an Anglican church in every parish is an outworking of that ecclesiology locally. The Anglo-Catholic slum priests of the Victorian era in particular modelled this understanding of praxis, becoming involved in the lives of the new industrialized classes and working for improvement to their living conditions and sanitation as a natural mingling of their expression of faith and worship. Revd Robert Dolling said, 'I speak out and fight about the drains because I believe in the Incarnation!'[5] Given the desperate state of our frayed social fabric here in the UK, this seems a heavenly opportunity for the Church to act itself again into a new way of thinking and return to the founding story of kingdom.

Vulnerability as a missional practice

David Bosch shows that in the Gospels Jesus 'turns to all people who have been pushed aside ... the call is an act of grace, a restoration of fellowship, the beginning of a new life ... the tradition tells of Jesus as the hope of the poor' (Bosch, 1991, p. 27). This relates the incarnation to the plan of God, 'inaugurating his eschatological reign ... among the poor, the lowly and the despised ... the wretched life of the poor is contrary to God's purposes and Jesus comes to put an end to their misery' (Bosch, 1991, pp. 27–8). He consistently challenged 'attitudes, practices and structures which tended arbitrarily to exclude certain categories of people from the ... community', acting as an agent of reconciliation who drew the marginalized into the reality of God's reign through feeding, healing and belonging (Bosch, 1991, p. 31).

Throughout its history, Israel waited for God to reinstate his kingdom and therefore their own status and power, but, in Christ, God's power came in a different form as a servant (Phil. 2.7) as he submitted himself to the limitation and paradox of the 'now and not yet' of God's reign. It is interesting that in this era some in the Church continue to call for the reinstatement of power and influence, not noticing this change in *modus operandi*.

The latest research into the effectiveness of fresh expressions of church across 11 dioceses of the Church of England identifies that the majority are led by new and unrecognized leaders, many women, whom the report labelled as 'lay lay' leaders – that is, the nobodies![6] These pioneers were simply getting on with establishing new forms of church and successfully reaching new people, unencumbered by the complications of serving establishment. This should not surprise anyone. Rowan Williams, referencing Thomas Merton, said 'The truth can only be spoken by a [person] nobody knows, because only an unknown person is there no obstruction to reality' (Williams, 2013, p. 17). Unpaid 'lay lay' people represent an ecclesial democratization that is restoring humanity and the Church through voluntary care and service. Collaboration between clergy and laity could build on this model together and maybe it would help the Church to get out more.

There is so much to be gained when we work together and honour one another's gifts and perspectives.

At present it feels as though the Church is still fighting valiantly to regain its influence in the public sphere but without being willing to radically rethink its structures, systems and methods. Research shows that younger people perceive the Church to be unjust and a 'toxic brand' for its treatment of gay people and women.[7] Perhaps it is time to let our expectation of power and control give way to more collaborations and experiments at the grass roots, run by the 'nobodies' who are in touch with local needs. They can adapt more flexibly to local contexts and are unencumbered by the heavy demand of old buildings, bureaucracy and unsustainable cost structures. Partnering together in clusters that include new and inherited churches would foster the sharing of ideas and encouragement and enable traditions and spiritual practices to be reframed for new generations. We need to be able to serve our communities in news ways from below, trusting God for our future.

Bosch says, 'we extrapolate the practices of Jesus to our own time and ... advocate ... serve those on the periphery, raise up the oppressed and broken to recover before God and people their full humanity' (Bosch, 1991, p. 34). This approach is much needed in our hurting society. Bevans describes the post-Cold War world as a place of exclusion that elicits angry and defensive reactions and suggests this could be countered by reconciliation that 'proclaims that in Christ and in his community, healing is possible' (Bevans, 2011, p. 391). This can only 'be made credible through a Christian community that is committed to giving itself over to the possibility, and to living it out in the authenticity of its life' (Bevans, 2011, p. 391).

This speaks of ministry that is slow, patient and powerless, allowing the pace of the journey to be set by the people who suffer. Bevans cites Eleanor Doidge's work with Native American Indians where she asks: 'Are there people today prepared to set down their tents and work to build honest relationships – for years in fact – where the truth can be told and trust can be re-established?' (Bevans, 2011, p. 391).

The long-term approach requires stability and can be costly; it is deeply relational, drawing the missionary into the pain and struggle that is seeking to be reconciled. Bevans says 'to be a prophet is almost inevitably to suffer' and cites Koyama's distinction between 'doing mission with a "crusading mind" and doing mission with a "crucified mind"' (Bevans, 2011, p. 361). This kind of mission is characterized as 'participation in the dialogical life and mission of the Trinity' (Bevans, 2011, p. 361). Prayer and contemplation are essential to the 'arduous work that takes place at any border crossing', and vulnerability comes with 'learning to acknowledge one's own wounds' (Bevans, 2011, p. 349).

The experience of the Upper Room echoes this as we have learned to journey slowly together with people who are marginalized and to acknowledge our own brokenness, weakness and struggle. We have experienced healing through the company of others and had our humanity restored through the gift of others' open hearts. We have experienced the stripping back of what we seek to hide behind and our own need for salvation and mercy. The violation of the safe space by others' pain and separation also has to be negotiated repeatedly, restoring relationships and owning the hurt we feel when problems occur. It is excruciating at times and painstaking, but also vivid and lively and leads to new life together as risks are taken and trust grows. Accepting weakness and following the lead given by those who come is crucial to even-handed relationships. John Caputo sees this in the character of God:

> My idea is to stop thinking about God as a massive ontological power line that provides power to the world, instead thinking of something that short circuits such power and provides a provocation to the world that is otherwise than power. (Caputo, 2006, p. 13)

Powerlessness, weakness, and how God inhabits these to bring transformation from below, are ongoing areas of exploration in many new forms of church, and also in parts of the established church now weakened (Wells and Coakley, 2008).

The metaphor of friendship is one that is appearing more frequently as a mission model for a postmodern world. Its inherent overtones of mutuality and equality mirror the self-giving, overflowing relationships of the Trinity. Steve Summers (2009, p. 157) explores the trinitarian basis of relationship and friendship as the basis for a contemporary ecclesiology of the Church. He emphasizes relationship over against Descartes' individualistic view that only the self can be known. Summers observes that the discovery of the true self can only take place through interrelationship, communication and socializing (Summers, 2009, p. 157). Summers does not seek to oversimplify community as an easy model, especially for people who are vulnerable or desperate, but suggests that the Holy Spirit provides the motivation and strength to create such a community for those who need it most: 'A grouping of persons in relationship may exist where care for the other is placed above care for oneself. This is precisely the sacrifice that … could make community a reality' (Summers, 2009, p. 161).

He describes the Eastern Orthodox doctrine of *theosis* as the basis of the participation in relationship or union with God and in the church community, describing the mutuality as one who loves and is loved, and this leads to the development of full personhood. Jesus called us friends (John 15.15), speaking to the restorative power of relationship with him in a world of isolation and separation. If this friendship could grow strong between the different traditions of the Church, as well as the older and newer forms, ecclesial life could flourish and bear witness to Jesus in its midst.

Conclusion

The Upper Room's impact after six years together can be characterized by lots of small steps taken together by people submitting to and learning to trust the initiative of the Holy Spirit and adding up to healing, restoration and transformed lives. For example, a reading tutor was found for an isolated mum who could not read, so she could help her children with their homework. She then asked for advocacy regarding her disabled child's education.

Six years on, she has two part-time jobs and has saved up and taken her family on holiday. She has a vibrant relationship with God. A young man who was referred by the mental-health team and who never left his flat now has friends, volunteers at other groups and was recently baptized. A woman estranged from her son revived her relationship with him and spends time with her grandchildren again, following prayer and sharing of her pain with others. People bring along a friend or neighbour who is in need. The trustees gathered a group to start a foodbank in the town following evidence that many people were struggling to manage. Collaboration and friendship between the parish and the new community has been a blessing to both groups. All of these shifts have emerged out of deepening mutual relationships.

The call has been to model radical Christian inclusion as a biblical response to a polarized town, sharing resources and friendship with people who have suffered disadvantage. Its effectiveness can be seen in its value to those who are drawn from the margins into the worshipping life of a supportive community, and in a dialogue with the wider Church that 'offer[s] the church a new look at itself' through the eyes of weakness and not of power (Bevans and Tahaafe-Williams (eds), 2011, p. 17).

References

Arbuckle, G., 1993, *Refounding the Church: Dissent for Leadership*, London: Geoffrey Chapman.

Bevans, S. and K. Tahaafe-Williams (eds), 2011, *Contextual Theology for the Twenty-First Century*, Eugene, OR: Wipf & Stock.

Bevans, S., 2011, *Prophetic Dialogue*, Maryknoll, NY: Orbis Books.

Bosch, D., 1991, *Transforming Mission*, Maryknoll, NY: Orbis Books.

Brueggemann, W., 2012, *The Practice of Prophetic Imagination*, Minneapolis, MN: Fortress Press.

Bunting, I., 1996, *Celebrating the Anglican Way*, Cambridge: Grove Books.

Caputo, J., 2006, *The Weakness of God*, Bloomington, IN: Indiana University Press.

Gempf, C., 2005, *Mealtime Habits of the Messiah*, Grand Rapids, MI: Zondervan.

Green, L., 2009, *Let's Do Theology*, London: Mowbray.

Gutiérrez, G., 2001 [1974], *A Theology of Liberation*, London: SCM Press.

Hardy, D., 2001, *Finding the Church*, London: SCM Press.

Martelet, G., 1976, *The Risen Christ and the Eucharistic World*, New York: Seabury Press.

Ruether, R. R., 1986, *Women-Church: Theology and Practice*, New York: Harper & Row.

Summers, S., 2009, *Friendship: Exploring Implications for the Church*, Edinburgh: T. & T. Clark.

Ward, P., 1993, *Mass Culture*, Oxford: Bible Reading Fellowship.

Wells, S. and S. Coakley (eds), 2008, *Praying for England*, London: Continuum.

Williams, R., 2013, *A Silent Action: Engagements with Thomas Merton*, London: SPCK.

Wimber, C., 2008, *Everybody Gets to Play*, Boise, ID: Ampelon.

Notes

1 Learning and Skills Council report, http://www.readingroom.lsc.gov.uk/.../gloucs-cofinancing-action-plan-2005-07.pdf (accessed 8 October 2013).

2 The praxis model is a tool of liberation that emerged from the Communist revolutions in the 1960s in South America and became enmeshed in Roman Catholic social doctrine. See Pierre Frey, Gustavo Gutiérrez or Leonardo Boff for further exploration.

3 A. Gittins, in the Foreword to G. Arbuckle, *Culture, Inculturation and Theologians*, Collegeville, MN: Liturgical Press, 2010, p. xii.

4 http://www.freshexpressions.org.uk/news/anglicanresearch (accessed 12 January 2014). Research carried out by the Church Army into new forms of church across 11 dioceses.

5 http://anglicanhistory.org/england/dolling/osborne/21.html (accessed 12 January 2014).

6 http://www.freshexpressions.org.uk/news/anglicanresearch.

7 http://www.churchtimes.co.uk/articles/2014/31-january/features/features/time-to-get-serious (accessed 31 January 2014).

Index

INDEX